Gold Fe...

This book is dedicated to my mother who possesses both a golden spirit and a heart of gold

Gold Fever

A complete guide to golden plants

Karen Platt

First published 2004 by Karen Platt.

British Library Cataloguing in Publication Date

Platt, Karen
ISBN: 0-9545764-1-1

35 Longfield Rd
Crookes
Sheffield
S10 1QW
England

Cover design:
AC Design, Sheffield
www.acdesign1.co.uk
alan@acdesign1.co.uk

Printed and bound in Singapore

Title Page: Acer platanoides 'Princeton Gold'
Page 2: Robinia pseudoacacia 'Frisia'
Page 3: Hypericum 'Summer Gold'
Below: Acer shirasawanum 'Aureum'

Front cover:
Top from left to right:
Hebe ochracea 'James Stirling'
Viburnum lantana 'Aureum'
Acer platanoides 'Princeton Gold'
Bottom from left to right:
Lavatera olbia 'Variegata'
Sambucus racemosa 'Sutherland Gold'
Hypericum 'Summer Gold'
Back cover:
Top from left to right:
Hydrangea 'Summer Light'
Hosta fortunei 'Aurea'
Dicentra spectabilis 'Goldheart'
Bottom from left to right:
Platycladus orientalis 'Morgan'
Cephalaria gigantea
Acorus gramineus 'Ogon'

www.karenplatt.co.uk
k@karenplatt.co.uk

www.seedsearch.demon.co.uk
k@seedsearch.demon.co.uk

CONTENTS

INTRODUCTION

Primarily known for my comprehensive work on 'black' plants, the results of ten years research into these plants is found in my book 'Black Magic and Purple Passion' second edition. In 2002 I founded The International Black Plant Society. Have I turned my back on black and become a golddigger?

The truth is that golden plants are a perfect companion to darks, so fit wonderfully into the scheme of things. This is black gold. The colours tie together, one enhancing the other, providing a superb contrast of the brightest and darkest tones.

I chose to concentrate mainly on foliage, as far more yellow-foliaged plants are unknown and overlooked than their floral counterparts. Newer yellow-foliaged plants are often sun tolerant. Gone is the chlorotic, burnt foliage of some of the older plants. Enter sunshine in the spotlight. A beacon in the shade, this is just the colour for light at the end of the tunnel.

New to this book are my hot partners and cool companions and a liberal sprinkling of golden glories. Companion planting is one of the most important aspects of gardening, so I have made it easier for you to select and grow plants together.

My research has once more been thoroughly executed on both sides of the Atlantic as well as the southern hemisphere and I bring to the reader a complete encyclopaedia of yellow foliaged plants plus favourite yellow flowers, variegated plants, spring and autumn colour and colour from canes.

Apart from my own horticultural knowledge and experience, I work with breeders, growers and collectors around the world to ensure my descriptions are correct and factual, and also to bring you the very latest in plants. My opinions are honestly expressed.

This book goes beyond descriptions, it explores the colour in depth and why we use it, where to use it and how to make good plant companion associations. Where possible I have captured plants on film too, at shows and gardens.

The yellow garden is not all daisies. In all, these 1350 descriptions of golden plants and over 275 photographs plus garden designs and inspirational ideas should have the garden dripping in gold!

Karen Platt
October 2003

Follow the sun...

Humulus lupulus 'Aureus', Rosa glauca

HOW TO USE THIS BOOK

The layout is almost self-explanatory. To begin, I explore the psychology and symbolism behind the colour yellow in all its shades and tints plus how to use it in the garden with ideas for special planting schemes from gold on gold to all the colours which work so well with the golden tones.

A comprehensive A-Z format of golden-leaved plants follows. This section concentrates on all-gold leaves, with one exception; if variegated plants are also found in the same genus, they are placed in this section alongside the all-yellow leaved varieties, so that you can, for example, take your pick of all *Acer,* and plants are not unnecessarily divided up into two sections. Here you will find full cultural advice on how to make your selections and most importantly, how to keep them happy.

Where only variegated plants are found, they are in their own section which follows on from the main A-Z. Following on from this, you will find favourite yellow flowers. Plants that have some other aspect which is yellow, such as golden canes or spines, are also in their own sections which follow on from the main A-Z. There is also a section on extremely rare, and very sought after palms and exotics which will make any avid plantsman dribble with excitement.
Plant names are believed to be correct, they are checked thoroughly, see more of this on my book of plant synonyms, Plant Names A-Z.
Most of the plants I have seen and described honestly, in one or two cases I rely upon a description from a very reliable source. Synonyms are given in italics in brackets, and the name of the person who found, introduced or bred the plant is also given where known, together with the year of introduction. Plant breeder's rights are also noted where known.

Companion plants, where included, follow each genus. There are suggestions for using gold on gold in Golden Glory, for using yellow mainly with blue in Cool Companions and for using it with orange, red and purple to black in Hot Partners.

Garden plans are given as jumping off points, hopefully to start your own imagination revving and get you experimenting with colour, foliage and texture. Remember, a garden is not built in a day!

Just one of the fabulous new golden plants, large-leaved Petasites 'Golden Palms'

Tolmeia 'Cool Gold'

Leucothoe axillaris 'Aurea'

Paxistima myrtifolia 'Aurea'

Aruncus dioica 'Aurea'

Astrantia 'Sunningdale Gold'

GOLD RUSH

Gold plants are coveted just as much as the precious metal itself

No matter what the shade or tint of yellow, the gold rush in these times, is more likely to be for a fabulous newly introduced golden plant. Newly bred golden-leaved plants have become more sun tolerant, and some can retain their colouring all season long. Forget the old chloritic looking plants associated with yellow. Think healthy, vibrant and glowing.

Goldfinger spreads its warmth in the garden like a touch of Midas. Display jewel foliage and flowers with abandon. Kiss goodbye to grey skies and let the sunshine in. New golden-leaved plants shimmer like never before to compete with the golden glory of yellow flowers.

Mecardonia 'Gold Flake'

SPORTING GOLD

Most gold plants are found as sports. Sports arise as a variation on a given plant. A dark green conifer for instance, can suddenly sport yellow growth. Sports can sometimes be unstable and revert. They are also known as mutants.

Chuck Pavlich, in the Pacific Northwest U.S. has found some wonderful gold-foliage sports hiking in the mountains. Some get lucky and find one or two, but Chuck has a goldmine of his own. His golden-eagle eye never misses the bright sparkle of a gold or variegated mutation. What Chuck has a knack of finding are attractive gold forms of natives. Apart from the plants included in the book, he also has a golden sport of *Rhododendron 'Rocket'*. The green forms of *Gaultheria* are something I can pass by unnoticed, even though they are pleasant enough in both berry and foliage. I would never walk by the golden ones from Chuck, both are highly ornamental and attractive. *G. procumbens 'Aurea'* has bright yellow foliage and oustanding, showy red fruits. Foliage remains gold year round in sun and can develop a pink blush in areas which receive plenty of sunshine. This creeping, rhizomatous shrub makes excellent ground cover. *G. x wisleyensis gold* form has yellow-green leaves with a red-pink blush on red stems and retains its gold colouring too.

Dan Heims of Terranova Nurseries, Oregon, U.S. is chief amongst breeders introducing golden plants, and the recent colour breakthrough in *Heuchera 'Amber Waves'* puts this plant at the top of anyone's list. *x Heucherella 'Sunspot'*, is a fabulous cross too with real sunshine foliage. Dan Heims has a wholesale catalogue full of interesting plants, including Tolmeia and Astrantia on the previous page.

In Detroit, U.S. I came across Ron Livingston who has golden hosta to knock your socks off, tremendous work here. Be prepared to swoon.

In England, another nurseryman with his eye very much on sports, is Martin Cragg-Barber who has spotted and introduced many golden-leaved and variegated sports such as *Rumex obtusifolius 'Golden My Foot'*. Martin runs Natural Selection Nursery and propagates plants in very small numbers.
In England, Peter Catt has been improving on some golden-leaved favourite shrubs such as *Spiraea*.

Tim Fuller of Plantsman's Preferences Nursery told me about *Ophiopogon 'Spring Gold'*, one of my favourite plants now in yellow! It does not form as dense clumps as the black form, and in 4-5 seasons Tim has still not seen any flowers. It has proved hardy in Norfolk, England.
Watch out for *Hesperis 'Frogswell Doris'* sweetly scented pink flowers over yellow foliage.

In Germany, there was a breeding breakthrough in 2002, spearheaded by Garry Grueber of Kientzler. *Mecardonia 'Gold Flake'* is an incredible cross which many people said could not be done.

Plant breeders and nurseries are going for gold

Gaultheria procumbens 'Aurea'

COLOUR BLOCKS

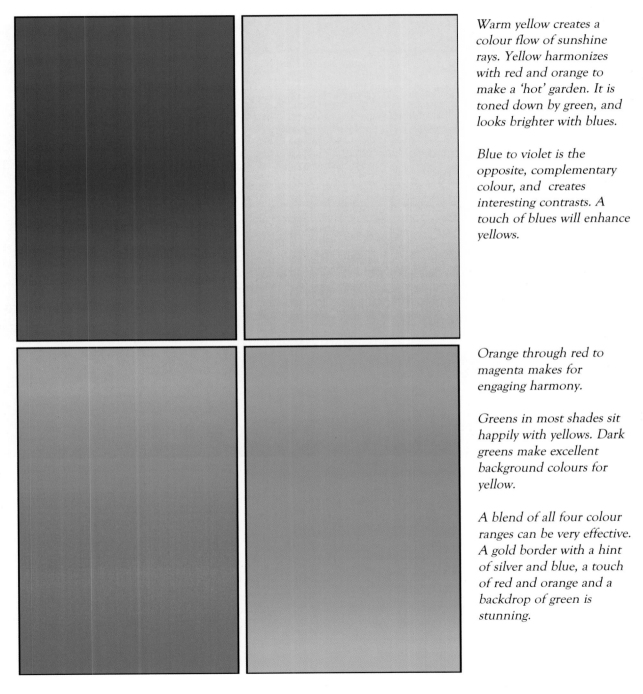

Warm yellow creates a colour flow of sunshine rays. Yellow harmonizes with red and orange to make a 'hot' garden. It is toned down by green, and looks brighter with blues.

Blue to violet is the opposite, complementary colour, and creates interesting contrasts. A touch of blues will enhance yellows.

Orange through red to magenta makes for engaging harmony.

Greens in most shades sit happily with yellows. Dark greens make excellent background colours for yellow.

A blend of all four colour ranges can be very effective. A gold border with a hint of silver and blue, a touch of red and orange and a backdrop of green is stunning.

11

Harmony reigns in the garden at Barnsdale

Golden *Humulus lupulus 'Aureus'* wraps itself
around a pergola working its way over to meet
Lonicera 'Graham Thomas'. At their feet *Solidago,
Anthemis* and *Achillea* shine like beacons amongst a
green oasis. Touches of blue in *Lavandula* and
Campanula, and in the fence and seat complete the
perfect harmony of this harmonious setting.

Colour harmony is colour flow, colour in a never-ending rhythm

Choosing colours that work together is supposed to be enhanced by using the colour wheel. Instead of using a colour wheel, I have devised colour blocks, gradations of tints of blues, yellows, reds and greens. To my eye, nature itself does the best job. Look for colour harmonies that please, and use those. Allow the colour to do the job, let it resonate. Pick up similar hues and tones around the border. Echo the central cone of a daisy, or the blue flower of a gold-leaved shrub. The muted chartreuse of *Alchemilla mollis* can be echoed as well as the gold in a variegated plant. Think about colour in broad terms, not narrow and one-toned. Explore the depths and you will become a better colourist.

Yellow is one of the three primary colours. It is a warm colour usually used in the creation of 'hot' gardens. Yellow harmonises with red and orange making a hot combination in the garden. Violet is the complementary colour, making an excellent contrast. Yellow reflects more light than any other colour and lends its brightness to others when planted in close proximity whilst in itself it glows brighter still. Yellow with blue intensifies each colour in turn. The way in which the eye perceives complementary colours placed together is known as simultaneous contrast and can be used to great advantage by the gardener. For instance, a yellow-leaved hosta in a sea of green foliage, makes the greens appear slightly more violet-blue. This is a great colour-enhancing trick of nature.

Luzula sylvatica 'Hohe Tatra' shines in the winter garden

Clear, unsaturated colour stands out from its surroundings, intense, lucid yellow leaps out and comes forward to meet the eye. Unsaturated colour tends to recede. This is the reason why one can successfully create a one-colour garden by using different tones of the one colour. A narrow range of pale colours creates a tranquil, quiet setting. Deep saturated colours are rich and sometimes gaudy, but they can make for a lively and exciting garden.

In plant combinations the tones are important too, yellow and green make a strong tonal contrast and sit happily together. Violet and yellow are complementary colours offering both bold colour contrast and strong tonal contrast. Variegated plants and golden foliage in shade provide interesting pattens where the eye cannot always detect the colours so well. A dark green hedge behind pale flowers has great tonal contrast.

William Robinson wrote in 1883 that "when we garden we are painting with living flowers." I would add that the paint never dries. The garden is an ongoing, life-long experiment. Moods change. Colours interact. Colour harmony is colour flow in never-ending rhythm.

LIGHT

From bright to soft, light illuminates in different ways

Light in gardens is ever changing, from the sun rising in the east to the time it sets. It hits plants at different angles thereby affecting their appearance. At sunrise and sunset, the sun is at its lowest, offering much desired low light in the garden. Hot flower colours such as yellow shine at this time of day.

Exploit this sun power by planting so that the golden garden catches early or late light. Midday light is almost white casting harsh shadows, but in shade blue and violet become vibrant and this can be used to good effect in a gold and blue scheme. Powerful, bold, saturated colours look best in hot climates, pale colours work better in cooler climates.

Light does not just change throughout the day, it alters according to season too.

The best light in England is in Cornwall. Fuchsia magellanica 'Aurea' amongst lush foliage at Trebah.

The soft, cool light of spring subdues plantings of bright colour, rendering bold yellow foliage fresh and clean, not gaudy and garish. Spring flowers and emerging foliage wear yellow as if nature is aware that at this time of year, this is the right colour to be. The soft spring light effect is continued in summer at the beginning and end of each day. However, midday sunlight at the height of summer is never a good time of day to walk around the garden. By autumn, light is again soft and flattering and the yellows of autumn foliage and bright yellow berries are once again in perfect harmony. At this time, light is often diffused by mists. In winter, long shadows create drama and we find structure and form are highlighted more than anything else. Dull, earth tones of winter and stark bark and trunk are highlighted by any splash of colour. Heathers and conifers are perfect for winter with their golden cloaks.

WHY IS IT YELLOW?

Carotenoids are nature's largest group of colouring components, usually hidden and masked by the presence of dominant chlorophyll (green pigment). Carotenoids absorb more blue light and appear yellow-orange. These natural pigments play an important part in photosynthesis. They absorb light in the 400-500nm region of the visible spectrum and are responsible for the characteristic red-orange-yellow pigments found in plants and animals. Yellow-leaved plants have a higher number of carotenoids which protect the plant tissue from becoming burnt. Many green-leaved plants undergo a dramatic colour change before the season ends. The surging sugar concentrations in autumn leaves and the decrease in production of chlorophyll results in the glorious autumn colours we love so much. Yellow leaves at this time are produced on plants with carotenoids but few anthocyanins. Yellow-orange carotenoid decreases too, but not nearly as rapidly as chlorophyll. Unlike chlorophyll, carotenoids do not need light to produce pigments because the pigments are already present in the plant. They are responsible for the colour found in carrots, daffodils, bananas and so on.

Xanthophylls are derived from carotenoids, differing in that they contain oxygen. Xanthophylls are responsible for yellow pigments.

Anthocyanins are the red pigments, these provide a natural sunscreen for plants dependent on the availability of carbohydrates within a plant. Anthocyanin colour can change with acidity, so pH is important here. Anthocyanin also requires light, and is formed within the leaf when chlorophyyl breaks down, which is why autumn colouring of plants is best on bright sunny days. Tannins are also present and are responsible for the brown tones, especially those on oak and elm.

BOTANICALLY SPEAKING

The specific epithet (the second word in a botanical name) gives an indication to the plant's characteristics. There are several words which relate to yellow, the most commonly used are *aureus* and *luteus*. Most refer to leaves, but *chrysanthus* especially refers to flowers.

aureus means yellow or gold and plants bearing this name are usually reliably of that colouring , although a few are more chartreuse. *aureovariegatus* means gold-green variegated and *aureomarginatus* gold margined green leaves.

chrysanthus means yellow-flowered.

flavescens means to turn yellow, *flavovirens* is yellowish-green, *flavus* is bright yellow whilst *fulvus* means tawny or reddish yellow.

galbinus is another epithet meaning yellowish-green, *giluus* means dull yellow.

helvolus is light yellowish brown and *helvus* is pale honey coloured.

icterinus means yellowed or jaundiced.

luridus means dirty yellow but yet another indication of yellow colouring is the specific epithet *lutescens* meaning pale yellow or yellowish, *luteolus* means yellowish too and *luteus* is a good indication of a yellow plant.

maculatus means blotched and spotted and so you will come across *aureomaculatus* for yellow spotted.

ochraceus means cream, *ochroleucus* yellowish white or buff.

pallescens means becoming pale and *pallidus* is a useful pointer towards paler plants, often cream.

stramineus means straw-coloured and *sulphureus* is an excellent, reliable indication of a sulphur coloured or pale yellow plant.

vitellinus is the epithet used to depict plants of egg-yolk yellow.

xanthinus is also used for yellow, *xanthospilus* for spotted yellow.

SYMBOLISM

Yellow is a colour with two sides to the coin. On one hand it is the symbol of happiness and warmth, joy and sunshine. On the other hand it is the symbol of deceit and cowardice.

Goethe in his book on chromatics separated colours into positives and negatives. The King of positives is yellow which he believed best represented brightness, cheerfulness and liveliness, offering a mild stimulus. Using the colour is said to lift the spirits and project optimism. Women used to wear yellow ribbons in their hair in the hope that their loved ones would return from war.

Yellow is used for warning signs because of its high visibility. Also for the flashing lights of ambulances and motorway maintenance vehicles. It is the colour we are advised to wear at night when walking in the dark to be visible to oncoming traffic.

It perks up a subdued colour scheme of greys and blues. It never goes unnoticed, being a real go getter and attention grabber. It can be very loud indeed. It represents sunlight, cheerfulness, youthfulness and sympathy. Radiant shades are usually perceived positively by consumers.

The colour children most often paint. The happy colour, associated with fond memories and childhood. It is also the unpleasant taunt of the shool yard 'yellow belly custard'.

We say of someone who is thoughtful and puts others first that they have a heart of gold. As good as gold and golden boy are expressions of goodness.

Yellow holds the promise of a brighter future, we look forward to the golden years. The best years of our life.

Gold suggests grandeur, the excesses of riches. Coveted, craved for and desired. Opulent and shining. The most precious of metals. We have to remember that all that glitters is not gold. Gold is the colour of the achiever. The ultimate award is a gold medal. It represents luxury, joy, royalty and the sun.

In China yellow is associated with the Emperors. A golden field of wheat and the harvest symbolise generosity and the goodness from the land. Yellow is perceived as a beneficial colour.

To the Japanese, gold is symbolic of the heavens and is used to decorate statues of Buddha and religious temples. Yellow interestingly has the same symbolism as the West.

In Asian colour symbolism, yellow means against evil or for the dead.

For the native American Indian, yellow symbolises overcoming challenges through unconditional love. However, to the Cherokees yellow symbolises trouble and strife.

Colour symbolism in chakras denote that yellow is associated with well-being, clarity, confidence and optimism.

For many cultures, yellow is the symbol of the East, where the sun rises.

In the language of stained glass establised by Dante, gold or yellow is the symbol of the sun, the goodness of God, of treasure and rewards in heaven. Gold is the colour of spiritual achievement, the reaping of harvest, the good life and the treasures of the earth.

Yellow is associated with both Taurus and Leo in astrological colour associations, both strong.

In Stars and Fate, Tahdet ja Khotalomme, the author, asserts that the sun colours belong to sun-ruled Leo types. Yellow is not for the faint-hearted.

In the Language of Flowers, yellow represents many things according to the given flower. For example yellow carnations represent disdain, whilst yellow Iris is for the flame of love, yellow roses mean you are all that is lovely and yellow jasmine is for grace and beauty. No yellow carnations please!

Silence is golden so they say

YELLOW IN ALL ITS HUES

"Suddenly entering the gold garden" wrote Jekyll, "even on the dullest day, will be like coming into sunshine."

A golden and red bed at Morrab Subtropical Gardens, Penzance, Cornwall

IS IT GOLD?

A ray of sunshine, a drop of gold

It sounds so much nicer than yellow which makes me think of custard, and the very few school dinners I had to suffer. Yellow, a colour associated with cowardice, something which has no place in the garden, or anywhere else for that matter. Yellow in all its shades from piercingly bright to mellow ochre and the jewel-like quality of amber are easy to use.

Yellow can be quite daring, bold and bright. Radiant like the sun. A drop of plutonium planted in the garden. Bright as in radioactive. A beacon of light with real oomph. Illumination! Being so obvious and noticeable can make it rather vulgar. Yet it is an encouraging colour, one that invites you to walk into the garden and draws you to its side. It has power, energy, warmth and vibrancy.

This colour range is perfect for drawing attention to a structure in the garden, such as an opening, entrance or archway. Draw the eye away from an eyesore by placing this colour strategically in another part of the garden. The favourite colour of bees who are attracted to yellow above all other colours.

Abutilon 'Canary Bird'

Capable of brightening the garden all day long. After a hard day's work you can bask in the glow from plants in the mellow sunshine of a summer's evening. However, yellow is not just about sunshine and summer, it breathes more than a fairy dusting of gold all year round and a ray of summer warmth into the depth of winter. The soft lighting of spring and autumn are particularly suitable to plantings in this colour range.

Yellow reflects sunlight, spreading rays of joy and light On a north facing wall or in shade it is the best ally to illuminate. In a small, dull garden, or just a bed or corner of the garden that is looking drab and dreary, try gold, I guarantee it will alter the space and your garden will feel fresh as though a spring breeze has blown away all the cobwebs. It offers a huge palette to work with in regard to both foliage and flower. Yellow is perfect for colour echo borders, where the eye dances from yellow flower to yellow leaf to yellow cane to yellow central cone to yellow bark. Yellow is used here in all its hues, deep or pale, vibrant or an echo of a saturated hue, solid, speckled or splashed. Use the variance of colour fade to advantage, flower or foliage which emerge saturated in spring, then fade to more subtle colouring or vice versa.

Thankfully, it can be subtle if you choose the right plants in delicate shades of this sunshine hue. However bright or pale, it always adds an airy quality to the garden. From deep, energetic sunshine hues to pale, calming mellows, this colour adds a sparkle, a glimmer, a dusting of gold.

Like gilt-edged stocks, these are safe, easy plants for the garden, ultimately desirable. They flow through the garden like molten gold.

Add the g-factor to your garden.

Allow me to introduce you to the goldmine of plants.

GOLD

The colour has more than a glimmer of hope about it. The most valuable metal. Symbol of ultimate wealth and riches. Fiery and warm, holding the sun's rays. For some the reason to carry on, for others the cause of all their sorrows. The promise of riches and wealth and fortune untold. The golden handshake at the end of life's work. A golden halo, a circle of light around the sun, shining its goodness for all to see.

Gold itself comes in shades of brassy to antique. It is a more romantic or perhaps dramatic way of looking at and describing yellow. Nearest to gold is perhaps the inflorescence of *Stipa gigantea*, fabulous against a dark background. Some conifers are representative of antique gold and *Hebe ochracea 'James Stirling'* which desperately wants to be a conifer, is in this hue. By gold, the gardener means yellow, usually of a brightish hue. Some insist on these plants being called yellow, others like to describe them as gold. If you look yellow up in the Oxford Concise Dictionary, it says yellow is the colour of gold. 24-carat gold is actually deep yellow with a hint of orange. Gold alloys, from 8 to 22 carats, can be obtained in a range of shades from greenish yellow, through pale to deep yellow as well as pink and red. All these shades are found in leaf.

Gold, a glass of fine Sauternes.

Pure gold, molten gold, solid gold, gold dust, a band of gold.

Golden leaves glow in low light, spreading warmth.

ACID YELLOW

Lightning bright

drops of citrus lemon

a squeeze of fresh lemon juice

What a shocker, just leaps out with citrus hues. Unadulterated bright lemon, these plants have more than a squeeze of lemon juice about their foliage and flowers. A superb colour to use in deep shade, where anything else would just be lost in the dark, this colour will still shine like a beacon. The beacon needs to be used wisely or it will blind and dazzle. Beware also, some plants will lose their yellow colouring in shade, turning lime or chartreuse. For others it is the perfect position and the right plant in the right place will lighten any dark corner. It is perhaps in this colour range that we find most plant misnomers, for plants named lemon are often a quieter shade than one would expect.

Lemon is also valuable for plants which can be featured in the sensory garden having the refreshing smell of lemon. *Thymus x citriodorus* (lemon thyme) and *Mellisa officinalis* (lemon balm) and *Aloysia triphylla* (lemon verbena) are three herbs with fruity, lemon notes. The former two also come in variegated green and gold varieties and there is an all-gold lemon balm. *Backhousia citriodora*, an Australian native known as lemon myrtle is said to have leaves which smell more like a lemon than a lemon itself.

MELLOW YELLOW

Soft and as sensuous as yellow can get

Mellow yellows blend well with pastels. This sympathetic, muted colouring mixes easily into other colour schemes and does not leap out. These are quiet, subdued yellows, they can sometimes look too wishy washy on foliage. These more delicate, mellower tones are my favourites for flowers within this colour range. Pale but not washed out. *Cephalaria gigantea*, its delicately coloured flowers waving on long stems is such a pleasure to use. *Potentilla recta 'Pallida'* is so subtle too echoing the colour of pale primroses. Often unassuming in their quiet, understated beauty. Pink sits better with primrose yellow than with stronger yellows.

Creams come in to play here too, with the faintest hint of lemon. Clotted creams, buttercream and vanilla ice-cream. Honey, butterscotch, caramel and brandy. Delicious and fun to use. Have I whet your appetite for these plants in shades that are almost edible? Don't dribble yet, wait until the plant A-Z.

This colouring also embraces straw, ochre, umber and sienna, these are warm hues like sunwashed walls in Morocco, Tunisia and Yemen or the terracotta of the Mediterranean. Pale yellows look wonderful against a terracotta coloured background and stand out against dark greens to blacks.

Turmeric, the yellow spice used to colour curry. What could be more perfect than saffron and turmeric, spice colours for an Indian summer garden blended with burnt orange, toffee-brown, honey and the delicate shades of apricot and peach along with the complicated notes of amber.
Amber has strong, warm tones, yet is easy to incorporate by the barrow load. As fresh as the best amber-coloured liquid that is Darjeeling tea. Quite a surprise colour in the garden. A rare jewel.

SUNSHINE YELLOW

Dazzlingly bright and visible

Bright, sometimes startlingly so, but ever cheerful. A carefree colour, glowing and vibrant. Yellow draws the eye and can be used effectively at the back of the border or in shade. Apart from blazing red, it is the most visible colour in the garden, which needs a little care in its use and siting. Think of grey skies, then the sky lifts and through the parting, dark clouds comes a ray of sunshine, this is the stunning effect of yellow in the garden. Less is more with this strong colouring, wield its power carefully. Saturated yellows are often too much in summer, too strong and dominant, especially in temperate climates. The egg-yolk yellow of most daisies can be overpowering and is easy to overdo. Remember to use different hues of this colour, especially when choosing many plants from one family. One of the most luminous small trees, and one of the most often planted is *Robinia pseudoacacia 'Frisia'*, a real dazzler!

A golden garden at Chelsea

YEAR ROUND SPARKLE

Retain the promise of spring throughout the year with golden plants

Fill your garden with the warmth of the sun's rays, a drop of sunshine or a flood of golden light. Create a sanctuary where you can bask in the imitation of sunshine reflected from the plants and where your senses will be lifted and your cares left at the beginning of the garden path. Golden foliage gives a sunny feel, even on fairly cloudy days to lift the spirits. Feeling blue? Plant gold. The happiest, brightest colour of the palette. Nothing is more alive. Gold is stimulating, it energises not only a dull border, but transmits its vibrancy to your senses. Gold is the colour to brighten the garden, adding a sparkle second to none. It shimmers and lights up dull corners, providing a great contrast, vibrant and glowing. It is the colour of spring, many early flowers are yellow, so cheering after the long winter. You do not, however, have to have all your egg-yolks in one bowl, yellow is not restricted to one season. Rather it is the colour of all seasons.

SPRING FLING

We are greeted with harbingers of spring early in the season which predominate in golden hues. Sunshine yellow Narcissus (daffodils) and Crocus break through the earth. It is like the sun coming up or the electricity coming back on after a power cut in the middle of winter. Bright yellow flowers of *Forsythia* bedeck a corner of many gardens. *Primula* shine forth in a myriad of welcoming, soft yellow hues, coy and bashful. Bright spring colour is not only part of the border, it spreads its golden cloak in the bog garden too, where *Caltha palustris* (kingcup) makes a vibrant glowing statement in spring, accompanied by the striking leaves of variegated iris, *Iris pallida*

'Variegata' and the deep tones of *Lysichiton americanus,* a perfect threesome by a pond's edge, superb with the unfurling leaves of *Hosta*. For yellow is not confined to flowers, glorious spring yellow foliage catches the eye and is more valued for its continuous glow, often long after flowers have ended their performance. *Valeriana phu 'Aurea'* unfolds its golden leaves which are amazingly bright in spring. *Laburnum* is one of the champions of the spring garden, often best displayed as a tunnel where one can fully appreciate its pendent blooms. Plant gold at its feet for the pot of gold at the end of the rainbow. Mats of golden yellow buttercups with dark foliage such as *Ranunculus 'Brazen Hussy'* will prove a great accent, creating dark carpets with drops of molten gold in its flowers.

Foliage emerges often in subdued, or greenish-yellow shades as if it has not summoned sufficient strength to be overpoweringly bright. *Carex elata 'Aurea'* might emerge greenish but still offers a different hue to the sunshine yellow of *Tulipa* and a contrast to the green of other leaves. The acid yellow bracts of *Euphorbia polychroma* make a wonderful colour echo. *Sambucus racemosa 'Sutherland Gold'* unfolds its well dissected foliage, all the deeper colour and larger-leaved for being pollarded.

In spring be dazzled by unfurling *Hosta*, watch those leaves uncurl, it is fascinating! Use these fantastic plants in a *Hosta* walk, under the dappled shade from trees or as edging to other herbaceous perennials. A bold planting, would include different leaf types and colours of green, blue and of course gold.

The golden garden awakens like no other, its brilliance is unsurpassed.

SUMMER SUNSHINE

The golden glow does not end with the glory of spring

However, yellow can get too bright in cooler climates, where it appears fine in warmer climates. Subdue the effect under English skies by choosing a less bright hue. Think of brilliant yellow in Australia and South Africa, it is found all over in native plants such as *Acacia* with their bright yellow flowers. Under the burning hot sun, it does not outshine its welcome. *Rosa 'Golden Showers'* is about the right tone for an English garden. Paler coloured yellow to chartreuse foliage will calm an overbright planting of intense yellow flowers.

Achillea spread their golden flat heads of flowers, whilst *Clematis* climb and scramble with the glorious yellow flowers of *C. 'Bill Mackenzie'*. Tall spires of *Verbascum* shine in yellow columns. Other great golden plants with spires of golden flowers are *Ligularia, Eremurus, Digitalis* and *Delphinium*. *Iris* and *Lilium* light up borders. *Hemerocallis* and *Crocosmia* are champions of the late summer garden, with golden flowered *Dahlia 'Moonfire'*. Golden *Berberis 'Bonanaza Gold'* and *Lonicera nitida 'Baggesen's Gold'* echo the flower colours.

Bright yellow is easier to cope with if you have a linking plant. *Alchemilla mollis* is an easy linker, its chartreuse-yellow flowers make an easy transition between green and yellow, even bold yellow. Other good linkers include *Euphorbia*, such as *E. 'Lambrook Gold'*, and *E. sikkimensis*.

GOLDEN AUTUMN GLORY

Many plants give their best coloured foliage effect in spring, some paling in the height of summer, reappearing with renewed vigour in autumn. Saturated yellows can blaze in low light. At this time of year, the daisy family is still going strong, *Chrysanthemum, Leucanthemum* (shasta daisy) *Helenium* (sneezeweed), *Helianthus* (sunflower), *Osteospermum* (African daisy), *Rudbeckia and Inula*. To use all in their strongest hues will obliterate even the sun. Many grasses look their finest in autumn with seedheads in full flow. The growing season ends with a blaze of yellow on the leaves of many a handsome tree and shrub. Best colour is found in the golden bronze of hickories, golden aspen and poplar, the light tan of beech, yellow of ash, birch and eastern redwood. Black maple turns glowing yellow, big-leaf maple yellow-brown whilst silver maple is dull yellow. Mellower then spring, but nevertheless glorious. More breathtaking for it knows its the final encore. *Ginkgo biloba* goes out in a blaze of sunshine-hued foliage.

Autumnal yellow is the echo of a breath of spring, the fading sun about to leave the stage until spring renews its strength, yellow takes the final bow and leaves the stage in a glorious blaze.

WINTER BRIGHT

Yet still, the winter garden has its beacons of light

Ever-golden grasses glow. Later in the season *Eranthis hyemalis* (winter aconites) are like drops of pure yellow amongst a ruffle of green leaves. The canes of *Cornus sericea 'Flaviramea';* such valuable plants, glow yellow in winter when cut back each spring. Conifers stand like sentinels, many showing fabulous golden colouring at this time of year. Winter heathers too take on winter hues of gold, making fine companions to conifers at this time of year when so few other plants work as hard to colour the garden. Conifers are valuable for their form and texture. They can creep and drape, make tiny mounds, small cones, taller conicals, loose or dense fastigiates or beautifully branched specimens.

Colourful summer conifer

In the conifer and heather bed at Bridgemere Nurseries, yellow stands out like a beacon.

The Regeneration Garden by Mark Ashmead at Hampton Court had great texture shown to perfection against a blue concrete background. Golden grasses in the foreground surround the dramatic water feature.

USING GOLD IN THE GARDEN

Subtle hues make excellent drifts, stronger hues make good exclamation marks. So if you are fond of dazzling sunshine or the quieter glow of evening, yellow is the colour to opt for. It is an adaptable colour, capable of stealing the show or being an unobtrusive accompaniment when chosen in its paler forms. There are golden plants to use in all aspects and sites of the garden. Give golden plants a dark background which really enables them to shine.

The Mood

The mood is sunshine, the feeling is one of well-being. Use gold in the garden to uplift the spirits. Optimism at its peak. The light at the end of the tunnel. Bright and dazzling, or subdued and mellow. A blaze of sunshine or a single ray. A beacon or a glimmer. Use it to vie with the sun, or to brighten shade. The clouds have been dispered, never to return. The skies are blue, the future is bright.

The Style

Anything you want, you got it. From conifer, heather, grass or herbaceous beds, to modern herbaceous plantings. From Italian palatial splendour to hip Chelsea. From bog garden right into light woodland and back to xeriscaping, you can have it in yellow. You can dangle daisies by the dozen in a dozen different ways. Dazzle or pale by the moonlight. Yellow is modern, its alive and fresh and waiting for innovation. This colour does not stand in the shadows. Although found on the ubiquitous wallflower, it is not a colour to timidly lurk in the shadows waiting to be discovered. Gold has presence.

The Palette

Yellows blend together well. Yellow borders in the past have tended to rely heavily on flowering herbaceous perennials, many of them from the daisy family, where we often find the strongest yellows. However, with new golden foliage plants coming on stream at a fast rate, it is possible to make the yellow border a feast of spectacular foliage, in sun or shade, by the water's edge or in a dry, water-starved area.

The Plants

Use foliage and flowers from all classifications for your required setting, such as annuals, perennials or shrubs. Excellent golden leaved trees are not few in number, many can be pruned back to form shrubs in a small space. There are now more yellow-leaved shrubs than ever before and many new ones are improvements on older cultivars. There are zillions of herbaceous perennials, many late-flowering ones which are needed for late colour. Many golden grasses, wholly or gold variegated in leaf, or golden in their inflorescence, valuable for their airy effect to contrast brilliantly against more solid foliage.

Above: The Enchanted garden designed by Chenies, a golden garden at Hampton Court Flower Show.
Golden echoes reverberated throughout the planting.
Below: A hot sunset border.

Plenty of golden-leaved plants suit specific areas such as the rock garden, bog garden, woodland garden, dry area and so on. Golden flowered bulbs abound in spring and add a sunshine carpet when the sun itself is still relatively weak.

This is an ideal palette for cut flowers. Many yellow flowered plants are suitable for floral arrangements.

The Golden Haze Effect

One of the best gold effects is had by planting *Stipa gigantea*, with the evening sun, its papery inflorescences on wand-like stems truly shine golden making a wonderful structural statement alone or in the border. It is pure delight shimmering and waving in the breeze, a sure fire eye-catcher in summer. Surround the grassy tussocks with more gold-leaves or flowers to bring the sunshine aura down to ground level. This needs a bit of room for best, airy effect, and looks stunning against a darker background. *Stipa tenuissima* or *Chionochloa conspicua* have much the same effect on smaller plants.

The Inspiration

Ideas as ever, come to the fore at the Chelsea Flower Show where there is usually at least one golden garden on view to the public. This is echoed later in the year at the Hampton Court Flower Show.

In 2003, I created award-winning gardens at both the Northwest Flower Show held in Seattle and at the San Francisco Flower Show, both with a theme of gold and black and with the emphasis on foliage.

Inspiration is found by visiting gardens with colour themes and visiting shows. Breeders are working hard to bring more colourful foliage into our gardens. We can look to interior decorating for inspiration too. A quick flick through a paint chart is a good starting point. Be wide open to new ideas and different ways of using plants.

MIDAS TOUCH

The golden rule is not to overdo it

Too much golden yellow will look like a beacon, so temper strong yellow and use it in proportion. A little goes a long way, scatter and keep its use in check. From creamy yellow to deep sunshine yellow, it is a colour which is simplicity itself to use. I prefer the lighter tones, as deep yellow can often shout too much. It is far easier to incorporate a drift of a paler lemon, such as *Cephalaria gigantea*, or the smaller *Scabiosa columbaria v ochroleuca*, than a drift of deep yellow *Rudbeckia*. Yellow, in its many shades, is superb with green, excellent with black, purple, violet and blue. Acid yellow looks good with vivid magenta and cerise. Look to the flower colour of the usual yellow foliaged plant, it is often blue, and this is a superb companion colour. Blend gold into your borders, it will lighten the effect of darker greens and lift the whole planting out of the ordinary. Gold is easily worked into the border, and taken vertically to cover fences or other structures, it is readily used in containers, waterside plantings or edible landscapes. This book concentrates mainly on yellow foliage and not flowers, although there are recommendations for these too. Yellow foliage plants have become increasingly popular as gardeners seek more diversity among foliage colour in gardens. Early cultivars tended to scorch in sun, newer ones are more scorch-resist and you can aid this by keeping plants moist at the roots, and often by offering a little overhead midday shade.

Choose plants carefully for the gold look, avoid weak coloured plants. Siting is important with coloured foliage. If planting in full sun, stay clear of plants which scorch and burn and make sure yellow foliage colour can be retained in shade. Excessive use of gold is supposed to indicate that the user wants to be noticed. We do not want everything to turn to gold, nothing is good in excess. A touch of white or a hint of blue will help things along splendidly.

GOLDEN TOWN GARDEN

A small town garden with seating and entertaining areas and enough interest in the borders to display many different kinds of golden plants including a grass bed, two small trees, a mixed shrubby and herbaceous border, a pergola dripping with gold, and several large blue containers brimming full of golden plants to match the season, with secondary hints of blue and purple.

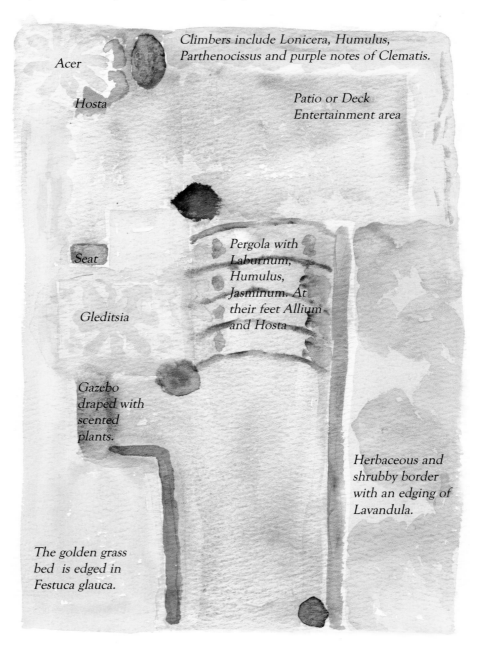

Climbers include Lonicera, Humulus, Parthenocissus and purple notes of Clematis.

Acer

Hosta

Patio or Deck Entertainment area

Seat

Pergola with Laburnum, Humulus, Jasminum. At their feet Allium and Hosta

Gleditsia

Gazebo draped with scented plants.

Herbaceous and shrubby border with an edging of Lavandula.

The golden grass bed is edged in Festuca glauca.

28

DESIGNING WITH GOLD

The brightest colour in the garden, wield its power with care

Remember that large herbaceous borders and large plants belong in a large garden. Always bear in mind the scale of plants. This is not to say that one cannot put big plants in a small garden, you can and should, carefully sited. Take care overall, to do things on a less grand scale, within the boundaries and limitations of your plot.

I really admire single colour borders. The concentration of colour is mesmerizing. Yellow can be used in this way when we blend its many hues. It is also a great highlighter, a full stop of intense bright colour, or an exclamation mark of acid yellow. Its paler hues blend terrifically well into most colour schemes. Yellow sits well on green foliage. Yellow-foliaged plants are perfect in front of a dark background and one of the best companions to other coloured foliage, be it green, blue, bronze or black.

Carex elata 'Aurea'

GOLD ON GOLD

Deep sunshine yellow to acid lemon and palest mellow yellow

Wherever you wish to make a golden garden, simply pay attention to the different hues, combine different types of foliage and texture and blend in all aspects of yellow plants with colour echo, not just flowers and foliage. When planting with a single colour it is important to think about all these things so much more than in a multiple colour garden. With one colour the eye is drawn in to consider more carefully the juxtaposition of plants. This is where the tremendous palette of yellow comes into its own. All the tints and shades and all the different types of foliage come into play.

Yellow is a warm colour in many hues which blend perfectly to make a monotone garden. It also has many partners in the spectrum. Make it hotter by adding orange and red, make it cooler but brighter with violet and blue. Greens are a great background.

Bright borders are popular in New Zealand and Australia and southern California and the sunshine states of the U.S. which have the right light for a yellow garden. They are popular in the U.K. too for a different reason - to brighten shade and those oh so grey skies and chase away the blues. Hot colours advance, making a garden look smaller, so they need to be used very carefully in a small garden. Striking, dramatic use of bright colour is perfect for today's outdoor lifestyle.

29

Warm colour borders are season long, starting with bulbs breaking through early bright coloured foliage, summer shrubs and roses, annuals, herbaceous perennials and climbers, autumn leaf colour and winter conifers and heathers.

Try the feathery foliage of *Tanacetum parthenium 'Isla Gold'* with *Hosta 'Sun Power'* and *Thuja 'Rheingold'*. This idea is easy to adapt, there are several different *Tanacetum* you could use, the same applies to *Thuja* and hundreds of golden *Hosta*. It is also adaptable as to how you use it. Do you need a circle, create it as a circle. A long rectangle? Splendid, buy several *Thuja*, you could even have different ones, and create an avenue of them, surrounded by one hosta, or a mix of varieties and the *Tanacetum*. This planting has great contrast of texture and form and the *Tanacetum* has yellow button daisies too.

Humulus lupulus 'Aureus' is a little rampant, but provides a sunny backdrop for the small leaves of *Berberis thunbergii 'Aurea'*, the flowering honeysuckle *Lonicera 'Graham Thomas'*, the gigantic proportions of *Hosta 'Sum and Substance'* and small leaved *Lamium maculatum 'Aureum'*. This really is tone on tone, something I love playing with in design. It works because of the different texture of the foliage plants. The large-leaved *Humulus* and the tiny round leaves of the *Berberis*, and those fabulous big *Hosta* leaves are dying to be treasured companions.

One of my favourite golden-leaved plants is *Sambucus racemosa 'Sutherland Gold'* not only for its colour, but also for its beautiful jagged leaves which look rather feathery when they are very young, they have a slight reddish edge to them which glows in the light. This makes a great combination for the dark green leaves of *Ligularia 'The Rocket'* which has spires of golden flowers echoing the colour of the elder, but much deeper. Team this with a golden *Hosta* such as H. *'August Moon'*, it will look good all season long when soil is kept moist.

In damp, light shade try *Dicentra spectabilis 'Goldheart'* with *Hosta 'Gold Standard'* and *Lamium maculatum 'Beedham's White'* at their feet.

Gertrude Jekyll is still at the heart of most English herbaceous colour-themed borders. Not many of her designs remain intact, but many designers echo her theory and vision. One garden which is still extant in the U.S. is Glebe House in Woodbury, Connecticut. There is a deep and very long (I found measurements ranging from 300ft to double that on the Glebe website) English style mixed border designed in 1926. The design was not actually used until 60 years later when the original design was found by Beatrix Farrand. The border is planted with typical Jekyll cottage style flowers. *Delphinium, Dahlia, Lilium, Cleome, Alcea* and other cottage style plants. An alluring allee of roses leads one into the rose garden and a small kitchen herb garden.

Jekyll worked with famous architect, Edward Lutyens. Lutyens was married to Emily Lytton, daughter of the Viceroy of India whose family owned Knebworth house. Jekyll and Lutyens designed some of the gardens of this beautiful house. Many of these have been accurately restored including the gold garden which contains various yellow-leaved and flowering shrubs and plants. This garden has a dark green yew (Taxus) hedge and a central round pond.

Hakonechloa and Tiarella

The golden garden at the Village Green, Cottage Grove, Oregon, USA

Stachys byzantina 'Primrose Heron', Myosotis, Caryopteris x clandonensis 'Worcester Gold', Symphytum are just some of the golden plants in this very special garden creating a golden carpet in spring.

31

The best known example of a golden border is probably Hadspen Garden, Somerset. In this well-known garden, *Anthemis tinctoria 'E.C. Buxton'* and *'Kelwayi'* hold their daisy flowerheads and sway in the breeze, colliding with the daisyheads of *Rudbeckia hirta 'Irish Eyes'* which becomes dominant in autumn. Spires of *Linaria dalmatica* rise behind *Potentilla recta 'Pallida'*. The beacon in this border is *Lupinus 'Chandelier'*, deadheaded for continuous long-season bloom accompanied by plates of *Achillea 'Moonshine'*. As the latter finishes flowering, the space is filled with *Argyranthemum 'Jamaica Primrose'* and *Tropaeolum majus*, a yellow nasturtium which keep going until first frosts. *Bupthalmum* and *Thymophila*, two more members of the daisy family are also used in repeat plantings. *Spartium junceum* is covered in pea-like bright flowers and grown as a backdrop to *Rosa 'Graham Thomas'* with *Digitalis lutea*. *Alchemilla mollis* and green fennel are link plants. Tiny amounts of blue rest the eye in the form of *Brunnera macrophylla* in spring and *Geranium pratense* later. This border is at its best in summer. I visited it once in July and it had absolutely no sizzle left in it.

A glorious golden garden exists at the Village Green in Oregon, U.S. Created by Cindee Eichengreen, this garden is an absolute treasure. I visited in late spring 2003 and witnessed the unfurling of this garden as it shook off its winter shroud. The garden has a planstman's eye with regard to choice of plants and how they are used. I adored *Stachys byzantina 'Primrose Heron'* partnered with *Origanum vulgare 'Crispum'* (golden oregano), watched over but not overshadowed by *Acer platanoides 'Princeton Gold''* one of my favourite trees, a real eyecatcher! Another grouping consists of handsome shrubs such as *Lavatera olbia 'Variegata'*, *Caryopteris x clandonensis 'Worcester Gold'* and *Hypericum 'Summer Gold'* chosen for their yellow leaves and flowering attributes, intermingled with honeyed tones of *Aquilegia 'Mellow Yellow'*, bright *Veronica prostrata*

'Aztec Gold', variegated *Symphytum* and golden grasses such as the ever-adorable *Carex elata 'Aurea'*. This is a young garden and one well worth visiting. It is planted in memory of Cindee's grandmother who created a golden garden for her when she was younger. One of a series of colour gardens created at the Village Green.

There is a lovely yellow border opposite a black border in a garden not too far from me, which opens for the National Gardens Schemes, where Mrs. Griffiths has used her expert plantsman's eye with form and colour, texture and shape to create an exquisite garden. These borders still look good in September.

Yellow can also be used singly in many situations. It is an excellent colour to use at the end of a garden or long tunnel, to focus the eye. Create a golden tunnel of *Laburnum* for spring, *Humulus lupulus* for spring-summer, golden-leaved *Jasminum officinale* for summer. A welcoming frame to the house door is had with *Jasminum* and *Lathyrus chloranthus* with golden *Lilium* at their feet.

Gold on gold at the NW Garden Nursery, Oregon

32

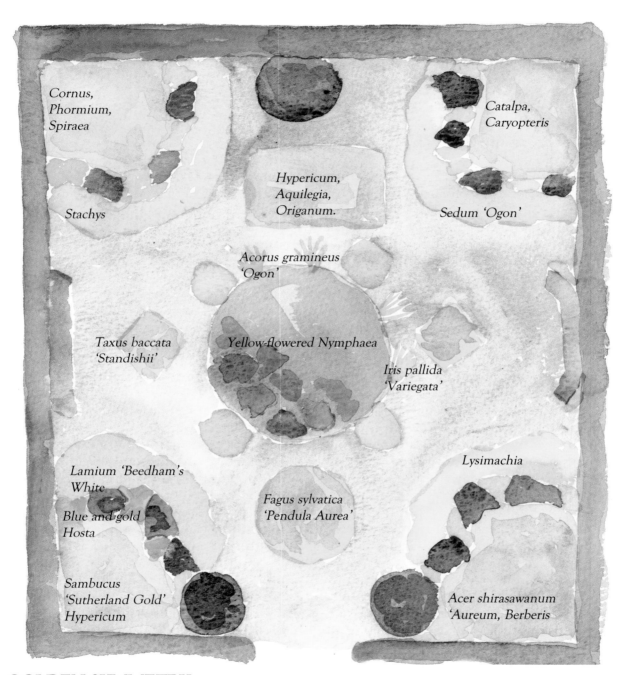

Cornus,
Phormium,
Spiraea

Catalpa,
Caryopteris

Hypericum,
Aquilegia,
Origanum.

Stachys

Sedum 'Ogon'

Acorus gramineus
'Ogon'

Taxus baccata
'Standishii'

Yellow-flowered Nymphaea

Iris pallida
'Variegata'

Lamium 'Beedham's
White

Lysimachia

Blue and gold
Hosta

Fagus sylvatica
'Pendula Aurea'

Sambucus
'Sutherland Gold'
Hypericum

Acer shirasawanum
'Aureum, Berberis

GOLDEN SYMMETRY

Gold with touches of sapphire on a dark Taxus, yew, background. The circular pond is a central feature with glistening yellow-flowered Nymphaea against golden grasses and Iris. Seating is blue, a bench and a fragrant arbour. Two large blue-green pots and one at the far end of the garden complete the picture.

33

SAPPHIRES AND GOLD

The blue of the heavens from which the radiant warmth of the sun descends to earth

We can apply Gertrude Jekyll's comment about the blue garden 'hungering for something of palest-lemon yellow' and turn it around. The yellow garden hungers for a splash of blue. One has to be careful which blue one chooses. Colour echo is the key here. Plants with yellow foliage often have blue flowers such as *Caryopteris x clandonensis 'Worcester Gold'*. Use the flower tone to colour echo, selecting further flowers and foliage in the same shade. Silver-grey foliage found in *Artemisia* and *Lavendula* offers subdued contrast. At Munstead Wood, Gertrude Jekyll used a palette of pale and soft blues with white and soft yellows surrounded by an abundance of soft silvery greys. In the middle of the planting scheme colour would become stronger but never garish. It is still a great colour combiantion. This lady knew the art of mingling; colour groups and plant groups were at once separate yet intermingled with all the artistry she possessed. Her attention to colour, form, texture and overall design was impeccable.

Cool blues look delightful with palest lemon yellow, stronger blues go with stronger yellows. One can work equally well as a highlight to a bed of the other. Yellow with violet provides the most startling contrast. These colour contrasts can be used to lead into the second colour in plantings of colour islands within a bed. For example a yellow and blue bed could be planted with drifts of different yellow hues, with the odd blue highlight, mingling into a blue bed in the centre with the odd yellow highlight, then back to yellow again with a touch of blue.

Combinations within this colour range are highly successful in spring. *Myosotis sylvatica* is a very overrused combination but an extremely effective one with yellow tulips.

A bed of hosta with spires of mauve, *Allium 'Globemaster'* is a pleasing combination beneath a golden tree such as *Laburnum anagyroides 'Aureum'* for golden foliage or *L. x watererii 'Vossii'*, the best choice for flowers, draping its blossoms to greet the plants beneath.

In summer pale to strongly coloured yellow *Verbascum* spires such as the charming, paleish *V. 'Letitia'* vie for attention with the equally delectable *Delphinium* (à la Joan of Arc, staked) with the foliage attributes of *Spiraea* and *Caryopteris x clandonensis 'Worcester Gold'* and a bed of *Limnanthes douglasii* at their feet. *Delphinium x grandiflorum 'Blauer Zwerg'* is quite compact and not as liable to flop, *D. semibarbatum* (*zalil*) is yellow but not such a good grower.

Humulus lupulus 'Aureus' can form a golden backdrop for a foreground planting of the splendid shrub, *Philadelphus coronarius 'Aureus'* and blue *Geranium 'Orion'* with *Centaurea 'Gold Bullion'* (cornflower) and *Nigella damascena* (love in a mist). An elegant combination is usually found in any combination of blue foliage with a yellow foliaged counterpart and a variegated yellow and gold leaved plant. Use *Juniperus squamata 'Blue Carpet'* with *Erica carnea 'Foxhollow'* and *Euonymus 'Blondy'*. Another favourite threesome is *Melianthus major* which is such a fabulous foliage plant in itself, looking superb in autumn with the green and gold striped *Canna 'Striata'* (*'Pretoria'*) which will be lit up from the late summer sun in the right position and the immense golden *Arundo*, this combination also looks good with purple-leaves of *Dahlia 'Moonfire'*, *Canna 'Australia'* and *Ricinus communis 'Carmencita'*. This planting will need plenty, and I mean plenty of room.

Pots large and small in blue look stunning planted together each with a different golden grass. These are a must on any patio, the new *Ophiopogon 'Spring Gold'*, a yellow-leaved form, *Milium effusum 'Aureum', Acorus gramineus 'Ogon', Deschampsia 'Tatra Gold', Hakonechloa macra 'All Gold'*. This is always an easy way of keeping a stunning display, anything not in tip top condition can easily be moved out of the way. Pots can also be used round the garden, and are perfect for placing next to seating areas. Grasses combine well with late flowering daisies such as *Rudbeckia fulgida v sullivantii 'Goldsturm'*. A golden prairie grass bed is easily made with a combination of daises and grasses.

Mellow tones are found in *Achillea 'Moonwalker', Perovskia 'Blue Spire', Scabiosa columbaria v ochroleuca*. In spring add *Primula 'Blue Jean'* (polyanthus) and the palest primrose, *P. vulgaris 'Double Sulphur'*.

The blue and yellow border at Penshurst Place, Kent is best seen in mid May. This is a stunning herbaceous border. A mile of yew hedges divides the gardens into rooms.

Purple Salvia mingles with a purple Heuchera with Lamium 'Beedham's White' and a gold-edged Hosta at their feet.

JET AND GOLD

Yellow shines against strong colours

Not a scheme for the faint-hearted, but what glorious use of colour. Black, purple and gold is a favourite colour scheme with me. A hint of red, a purple flower or a dash of orange can alter this dramatically, giving a look of dying embers at the end of the night. Good strong golds become radiant as they glow against equally strong purples to blacks.

Known as the Purple and Gold border, perhaps the most famous of Mrs. Reiss's schemes at Tintinhull, Somerset. Lush foliage with variegated *Cornus alba 'Spaethii'*, splendid for its red stems in winter, mingles in with purple, copper and bronze foliage. *Berberis thunbergii 'Atropurpurea Nana'* and *B. x ottawensis 'Superba'* are grown not only for their deep purple foliage but also their colour echoes of red and yellow berries picked up by foliage and flower in the border. A dark-leaved elder finds its place here as a backdrop and links the stronger purples and golds. Penelope Hobhouse, who worked at Tintinhull in the 1980's said of this border, that had she been re-working it, she would have taken out the golden elements. Yet the gold is the bright hint of a gleam amongst glaucous blue, purple, and the reds and pinks of roses.

What I would take out would be the reds and pinks. The roses to use in this setting are surely *R. 'Golden Showers'* and *R. 'Graham Thomas'*, along with the pale lemon-yellow *Lonicera periclymenum 'Graham Thomas'* (I am very partial to Mr. Thomas, though I never met him) and the foliage of *Lonicera nitida 'Baggesen's Gold'*. Add the latest in 'black' shrubs, *Sambucus nigra 'Black Lace'* and *Actaea racemosa 'Brunette'* (*Cimicifuga*) along with new releases of *Physocarpus, Spiraea, Choisya, Jasminum and Hydrangea*. Add spiky *Phormium 'Evening Glow'* and *'Dusky Chief'* plus the laxer *'Platt's Black'* and golden grasses such as *Milium* to highlight shady corners. *Dahlia 'Moonfire'* and *'Yellow Hammer'* will work hard until the first frosts. Clothe walls with *Lonicera, Clematis* deep and dark such as *'Etoile Violette'* and the *viticella* types, bright *Humulus lupulus 'Aureus'* and dark *Parthenocissus tricuspidata 'Veitchii'* which goes out in a red glow equivalent to the blaze of a glorious sunset. A fabulous dark-light garden.

This happens to be one of my favourite colour schemes and what first attracted me to yellow-leaved plants was their sympathic association with the dark colours I love so much. The darks serve to make the yellows brighter, and vice versa.

Many new shrubs have a dark or light counterpart. There are dark and golden elders, looking very special with *Physocarpus 'Diablo'* which has a golden partner too. There are gold and purple forms of *Cotinus, Hypericum* and *Weigela.* I have given many examples throughout the book of using these three colours together in Hot Partners.

Black and Gold container created by PW

Sambucus racemosa 'Sutherland Gold' and Physocarpus opulifolius 'Diablo'

SUNSET GOLD

The last rays of warmth of a splendid Indian summer

Getting hot. This is quite a shocking combination and one often sees recommendations that it is perhaps best used sparingly. Yet, in the past few years hot borders have become very favoured in England. These are often late season borders at their best from July onwards, employing as they do, many late season herbaceous perennials. Hot, sunshine gardens are found at many English estate gardens and National Trust properties and other famous gardens. Like any other sheme, done to perfection, it's great.

At Hunstrete House, Bath, the gardens have recently been renovated and now include a hot border. The style of the double 60 feet by 6 feet wide borders is eminently English. Red, yellow and orange dominate with the emphasis on later flowering perennials. Plants include *Anthemis 'Sauce Hollandaise', Canna 'Striata' ('Pretoria'), Coreopsis 'Moonbeam', Helianthus 'Lemon Queen', Rudbeckia fulgida v sullivanti 'Goldsturm'* and *Stachys byzantina 'Primrose Heron'*.

There is a dramatic hot border at Gowan Brae, Burradoo, NSW, Australia, a skilful blend of colour below the wide, informal steps at the end of the croquet lawn. Impressive use of flower and foliage.

The Botanic Garden at Winterbourne, University of Birmingham, U.K. has a red, orange and yellow border too spreading hot rays of sunshine throughout the garden.

Kiftsgate Court in Gloucestershire also has a yellow border, in existence since the 1950's. Primarily foliage with an emphasis on shape and form intermingled with herbaceous plants in cool blue and hot yellow and orange. Amongst the featured plants are *Acer, Euphorbia, Hemerocallis, Hypericum, Lilium, Viola* and golden grasses. The wonderful *Rosa 'Graham Thomas'* adds its fabulous yellow roses to the picture. Royal blue *Delphinium* have been selected without a trace of mauve to fit in with the scheme. The border looks at its best in July.

This border has a magnificent view to the north, on a clear day, Wrekin, 60 miles away in Shropshire can be seen.

Vibrant reds, oranges and yellows are the colours selected by Vita Sackville-West for her personal sunset garden at Sissinghurst Castle, Kent in the 1930's. This cottage style garden in lively colours is designed simply as two crossing paths with four quadrants planted in shimmering perennials. *Taxus baccata*, planted in 1934 stands as sentry at each corner. There is lots of lush green in this garden too and it relies heavily on herbaceous perennials looking fabulous in July, with enough staying power to the end of the season. Sunset shades of *Aquilegia* (columbines), *Antirrhinum* (snapdragons), *Viola x wittrochiana* (pansies), *Dianthus barbatus* (sweet williams) and *Alcea rosea* (hollyhocks) make their cheerful presence felt in typical cottage garden style.

The famous French impressionist painter, Monet, planted sunset colours at his garden in Giverny, France. The border has been kept to the original planting and can still be visited. Monet exploited the low light of sunset which glows in early evening. The garden includes yellows and oranges using *Helianthus* (sunflowers), *Tithonia rotundifolia* (Mexican sunflower) and *Tagetes* (marigolds). Yellow is used year round from spring bulbs to herbaceous late-flowering perennials. The famous water garden looks like molten gold with the reflection from the golden curtain of a weeping willow and the fiery autumn tones of *Liquidamber*. In late spring *Paeonia x lemoinei* glows against the dark foliage of *Mahonia*, which will take its turn to glow in late autumn.

Orange is bold and looks best on bold plants such as the wide cupped bowls of large, oriental poppies, the bigger, the better. *Oenothera* is not one of my favourites, but I make an exception for the outstanding colour found in *O. versicolor 'Sunset Boulevard'*. *Geum 'Borisii'* is a plant I have not used for years, and writing this, I realise how much I miss it. It is an exquisite orange. So too, the strong tone of *Potentilla 'William Rollison'*. *Dahlia 'David Howard'* is one of the best of the bunch, which will add oomph to any late season border, lovely orange flowers sit atop near black foliage. Another oomph plant is the bronze-leaved, *Lychnis x arkwrightii 'Vesuvius'*, molten lava just pours from the flowers of this short-lived perennial. Underplant with *Tulipa 'Golden Artist'* and the lily-flowered *T. 'Ballerina'*. Allow the Californian poppy, *Eschscholzia* to self seed its blaze of orange flowers through the border against attractive blue-green, feathery foliage which will add just the right note of contrast. Lilies are always good to add to any border, there are many hot orange lilies, I like *Lilium henryi* and *L. lancifolium* (tiger lily). *Euphorbia griffithii 'Dixter'* is valuable for its fiery, burnt orange bracts. *Crocosmia* and *Kniphofia* come in many shades of orange as well as yellow and red, making valuable additions to a late season border. Terrific *Canna 'Wyoming'* with its brilliant orange flowers over bronze foliage will add height to the garden. The climbing perennial *Tropaeolum 'Ken Aslett'* with its orange-red flowers make a perfect background. It needs protection from frost.

Here is a fine chance to add sumptuous tones of apricot, amber, peach and cream. *Digitalis 'Sutton's Apricot'* available from seed is a lovely soft tone. This is picked out in the gorgeous colours of *Rosa 'Alchemyst'*, and repeated in *Dahlia 'Amber'* and *Verbascum 'Helen Johnson'* in flower and in the tremendous tones of *Heuchera 'Amber Waves'* in leaf. Bronzey *Libertia peregrinans*, *Viola 'Irish Molly'* and *Carex comans* bronze echo the tones further. *Potentilla fruticosa 'Daydawn'* adds a shrubby effect.

For a sunset threesome, plant vibrant *Crocosmia 'Star of East'* with *Kniphofia 'Sunningdale Yellow'* and *Meconopsis cambrica 'Frances Perry'*, the poppy will self seed, but not as much as the yellow type, and this one is silk, crinkle-handsome!

The bright orange of Papaver, the rusty, fiery glow of Euphorbia 'Dixter' and the bright foliage of Carex elata make for excitement in the garden. This is the very special and colourful Liz Deck's garden in Oregon.

EMERALDS AND GOLD

Refreshingly bright yet cool

As fresh as a spring morning in the sunshine, cool as a soft summer breeze, never fading in autumn and evergreen in winter, green makes a staunch partner for yellow. Many would opt for green and yellow, a safe, quiet and peaceful colour combination with little drama and certainly no shocks. These two colours are excellent partners. They live together happily, in great harmony. Green makes yellow more restful, it quietens and tones it down.

There are a profuse number of plants with yellow flowers and green foliage. Some act as great link plants between yellow and green, such as *Alchemilla mollis* and *Bupthalmum salicifolium*. Add to this the large number of gold-green variegated plants and you have a huge choice of varied material to fill the garden. Gold variegated plants, like their wholly yellow counterparts, can be variegated in all shades of yellow. A creamy yellow edge such as that found in *Brunnera macrophylla 'Hadspen Cream'* is quite delicate and an easy blender. The variegation is really beautifully etched. On the other hand one can find very strongly variegated plants with bright yellow blotching or margins. So too, with the greens which range from chartreuse, a shade very close to some of the yellows, through lime to emerald and so on to the darkest bottle greens. Creamy variegation goes well with blues, greens and stronger yellows. Green makes yellow acceptable to many people, in the right combination. Well-clipped topiary or yew hedging is a respectable dark background for yellow, and the one most favourably used in English gardens. Each green finds a perfect match in one of the yellows.

At Barnsdale Gardens in Rutland, England golden plants are used throughout the garden, but perhaps the most noticeable use is in the conifer bed. Golden conifers are blended exquisitely with others of sympathetic hue. The overall effect is very pleasing. There is also an oustanding companion planting here with a variegted *Euonymus, Humulus lupulus 'Aureus'* (golden hop) and the glaucous foliage of *Rosa glauca*. Planted in a corner as it is, one could miss this, and it is worthy of more than a passing glance. *Humulus lupulus 'Aureus'* is also a feature of one of the small town gardens. A lovely example of use of colour and texture. The gardens here have delightful plant combinations, some of the best I have ever seen.

Golden conifers glow at Sandringham against a background of greens

The golden garden at Bosvigo House and Nursery features a clipped golden Ligustrum cone, Ligularia 'The Rocket, Hedera, Symphytum x uplandicum 'Axminster Gold', Alchemilla mollis with a good mix of white flowers and a hint of blue.

PEARLS AND GOLD

Jewel tones to treasure in the garden

Yellow in all its hues is a great partner for white. This is an enchanting colour scheme. Pale yellows, pastels and silver with a hint of white was one of Gertrude Jekyll's favourite combinations. White adds lightning splashes to the sunshine, both colours glow. A hint of mauve or blue will add a lot to this palette. Many white plants are not pure white, but verging on cream, the palest of pale yellows. A subdued palette of cream, pale yellow and white daises intermingle with *Lysimachia ephemerum* and the spiky bracts and cone shapes of *Eryngium giganteum 'Silver Ghost'* (*Miss Wilmott's Ghost*), its silvery-white hue glowing against the sunshine palette. Golden *Alstroemeria* and *Achillea 'Moonshine'* add a gleam with a patch of *Viola tricolor* echoing and deepening their hues.

Grey leaves as Jekyll honestly called them are more often referred to as silver these days, they include fine foliage plants such as *Eryngium alpinum 'Superbum'*, *Artemisia*, *Stachys byzantina*, *Cynara* and *Convolvulus cneorum*. Blue-silver hosta look perfect for the hint of blue in such a scheme.

Digitalis lutea and *Thalictrum flavum* make a nice partner for tall, airy *Cephalaria gigantea*, with creamy-yellow *Digitalis grandiflora* and white roses.

Think clotted cream, ice-cream, vanilla and other pale tones which are so rich in their own way. Used to excess they can be quite decadent. They serve to subdue the startling quality of pure white. White will also take a little of the dazzle away from strong yellow and make it much more palatable. White is one jewel in the crown of yellow.

One of the loveliest new plants I came across is *Deutzia 'Chardonnay Pearls'* with yellow foliage and white pearls of buttons which open to starry flowers.

Sutera 'Pearls n' Gold' also has the same effect of little pearls amidst the variegated foliage.

At the National Trust property Angelsey Abbey, there is a planting of yellow and white plants known as the Narcissus garden. Two *Koelreuteria paniculata*, Golden Rain trees stand in the lawn.

At Bosvigo House, The Vean garden is formal in design with a tremendous colour scheme of gold, white and a hint of blue. A large golden conical, perfectly clipped *Ligustrum* (privet) stands amonst a bed of white and yellow flowering plants, with Alchemilla making an easy transition. The variegated foliage of the flamboyant and desirable *Symphytum 'Axminster Gold'* draws the eye.

The creamy white variegated leaves of Daphne 'Brigg's Moonlight', a perfect pearl in the garden

EARTH SHADES

Back to nature with mother earth

Yellow blends well in its mellow hues of ochre and amber with earth tones such as sienna, brown and deep rusty orange. Browns and bronzes proliferate amongst the daisy family. Rust brown to orange *Helenium* (Sneezeweed) and *Helianthus* (Sunflower) combine with rusty *Kniphofia*. *Spiraea* has autumn tones which fit in with this colour scheme well.

Say brown to most gardeners and they will probably shudder. *Anthurium*, in any shade, are not to be sniffed at, they come in shades of coffee and chocolate brown. Fabulous glossy, ritzy, high class tropicals, lifting brown out of the mundane.

Disliked by many, but one of England's most planted roses is *R. 'Whisky Mac'*. Its tones of rich gold, apricot and amber are combined with glossy, deep green foliage. Its deep, heavy perfume also recommends it and it is very floriferous. A newer rose is also perfect for this scheme, *R. 'Hot Cocoa'* PPAF, is a good grower with silky petals shaded chocolate-orange to dark red with a deep rust-orange reverse. A vigorous plant with good disease resist. Colour of this rose can change according to growing conditions and climate. *R. 'Amber Queen'* has shapely flowers in clusters of rich amber-yellow, a useful bedding rose.

The bold brown flower spikes of *Typha* mingle at the water's edge with brilliant yellow *Lysichiton americanus*, yellow flag iris and golden hosta.

This is a splendid colour palette to enjoy the autumnal shades of leaves on *Hamamelis* and the like in burnt sugar, toffee and other mouth-watering colours. The sap might not be pumping through those tree trunks, but it sure makes the blood flow through your body to step into a garden full of these wondrous colours.

THE NEON GARDEN

Sunshades are a must

If you want to get really loud, go for vibrant, psychedelic dayglo shades of magenta, cyan, lime green and acid yellow and purple. A garden in these tones will be on view from planet Pluto. Vibrant does not vibrate any more heartily than this. Too much for most gardeners, it is like a Christopher Lloyd taken to extremes. I admire Christopher Lloyd's dashing colour schemes, if he wants to be loud, he is loud. Why not? Colour is there to be used and we might as well break the boundaries and go for it.

In my acid garden, I would plant the magenta blooms on *Geranium 'Ann Folkard'* or the tidier *'Anne Thompson'* both with good yellow foliage, bright *Salvia patens 'Cambridge Blue'*, if you have the right conditions *Meconopsis betonicifolia* is the right shade of blue, lime-green *Kniphofia 'Percy's Pride'*, together with another of my favourite green plants, *Molucella laevis*, chartreuse-leaved *Ipomoea batatas 'Margarita'*, and the green flowered annual *Nicotiana 'Lime Green'*, flamboyantly red hot *Crocosmia 'Lucifer'*, acid-yellow *Euphorbia polychroma*, out of this world spotty variegation of *Farfugium japonicum 'Aureomaculatum'* ready to land on planet Zog, *Aucuba japonica 'Crotonifolia'*, *Canna 'Striata'* (*'Pretoria'*) - catch the morning and evening light on those huge paddle-shaped striped leaves, *Fritillaria imperialis* in zingy orange and yellow, bright yellow crocus, daffodils and tulips, bright yellow *Helenium* and *Inula magnifica* and why not a giant sunflower *Helianthus 'Single Giant'* to tower above and follow the sun, the golden *Centaurea glastifolia*, the yellow foliage of *Fuchsia magellanica 'Aurea'* accompanied by shocking pink and purple ballerinas as they dance against the foliage, *Anemone hupehensis 'Hadspen Abundance'* in all its pink glory for late colour shock, *Dicentra spectabilis 'Goldheart'*, its golden foliage on reddish stems topped with shocking pink hearts combined with *Tulipa 'China Pink'* in late spring as there is nothing else you can do with pink-flowered, yellow-foliaged plants but to give them another splash of divinely bold pink flowers, x *Heucherella 'Sunspot'* is a must in this dazzling border with its bright yellow foliage, and golden grasses just glow and glow. I will stop there. Plant this in drifts, intemingling with each other. I guarantee it will shock. And if you don't like it, you could call it the holiday garden, you plant it, go on holiday and hope it has gone when you come back. It might grow on you!

Dicentra spectabilis 'Goldheart' is perfect for the Neon garden

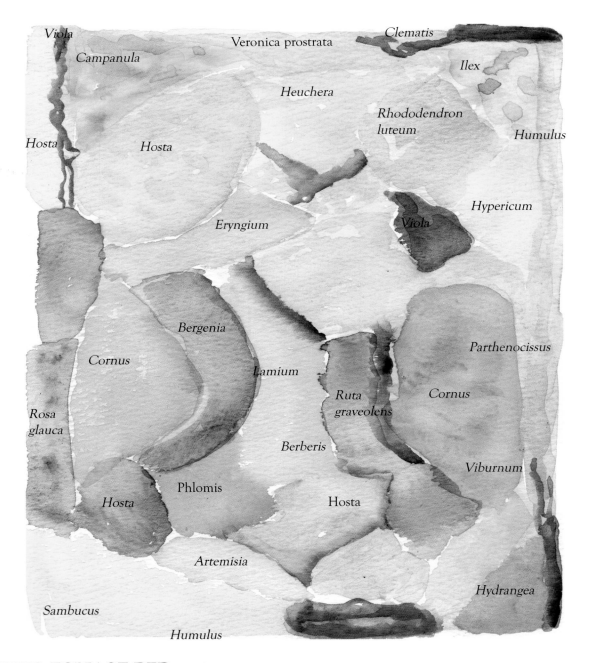

Viola
Campanula
Veronica prostrata
Clematis
Ilex
Heuchera
Rhododendron luteum
Humulus
Hosta
Hosta
Eryngium
Viola
Hypericum
Bergenia
Parthenocissus
Cornus
Lamium
Ruta graveolens
Cornus
Rosa glauca
Berberis
Viburnum
Hosta
Phlomis
Hosta
Artemisia
Hydrangea
Sambucus
Humulus

MIXED FOLIAGE BED

Leaf size and shape and texture is all important here. Incude feathery Sambucus, the large leaves of Hosta, crimpled and crinkled, the tiny leaves of Berberis, and the large leathery leaves of Bergenia against fine Artemisia and spiky Eryngium. Balance the gold with hints of silver through to purple. Look for season long interest. Viola edges the larger plantings.

WHERE TO USE GOLD

Having such a large range of plants, means there are gold-leaved plants for every situation. So wherever you want to use them, you will find you are not restricted by choice. Choose plants which harmonise in colour, yet contrast well in form, texture and shape. Pay attention to when they flower, the soil type and conditions that suits them best. Bear in mind eventual height and you will not fail to create a pleasing garden. Cover any gaps left by summer dormant plants with another behind ready to come forward and drape gracefully. Underplant with bulbs. Keep pots of annuals at the ready to fill gaps.

THE DAMP GARDEN

One of the areas often considered a problem to gardeners. Take advantage of constantly moist soil by creating a dazzling display.

These moisture lovers will relish the constantly wet conditions where other plants would not sit happily. *Petasites palmatus 'Golden Palms'* is King of moisture lovers. *Hosta* and *Ligularia* will enjoy similar conditons teamed with red-flowered, purple-leaved *Lobelia* and dark-foliaged *Cimicifuga* and *Eupatorium* and bronze *Rheum* and *Rodgersia*. Moisture loving *Iris* are good companions here.

SHADY GLADE

Whether a dark corner, bed or light woodland, there are gold-leaved plants that will just illuminate that space. Even in your darkest hour, this area will shine and disperse the clouds. Whether dry or damp shade there are golden plants to suit, coming out of the dark. Many of the golden shrubs are woodlanders. *Hosta* are known as Queen of shade plants.

FOLIAGE MIXED BED

Using foliage in a mixed bed is highly satisfactory. Texture, form and shape abound in flower and leaves. The whole range of tones and shades can be used in such a border. Use spiky *Osmanthus*, the rounded to oval leaves of *Cotinus 'Golden Spirit'* with its exquisite toffee colours in autumn, bright winter *Jasminum* trained low in a corner to interact with bulbs, fabulous shrubs such as golden *Philadelphus*, *Viburnum*, *Hydrangea* and *Physocarpus*, teamed with smaller shrubs such as *Spiraea* for season long interest, *Caryopteris*, useful gold and purple *Berberis* and a shrubby *Cornus*. Herbaceous perennials to include here are *Astrantia major 'Sunningdale Variegated'*, spiky and ghostly *Eryngium 'Silver Ghost'*, soft *Stachys byzantina*, *Geranium*, strap-leaved *Hemerocallis*, given room spires of *Acanthus*, *Thalictrum flavum ssp glaucum*, *Rosa glauca*, *Lilium* and *Dahlia* for late colour. Drifts of bulbs are underplanted for a spring show and *Allium flavum* and *A. atropurpureum* join the show.

THE KNOT GARDEN

I love the formal intertwining hedges which surround the blocks of plants within. The hedges would be gold or gold-variegated, with the choice of slow-growing *Buxus* or faster growing *Lonicera nitida*. A knot garden is not the place to be constantly clipping a fast growing hedge. Golden yew is another possibility, although I prefer this for the cones at corner. *Thuja* or *Chamaecyparis* make the rounded spheres. *Berberis 'Helmond Pillar'* adds height and a dark note to the centre.

Within the framework, plant golden herbs and purple herbs with silver greys.

COLOUR FADE

Start with silver and blue hints found in Artemisia and Eryngium with palest lemon of Potentilla recta 'Pallida' and Achillea 'Anthea', and work your way through ever deeper shades adding touches of ochre to bronze, Carex comans bronze form would be ideal, until you reach the crescendo of fiery tones found in Crocosmia 'Lucifer', just a little of this, a hint of a flame, not a blazing fire, Euphorbia griffithii 'Fireglow', a scarlet and orange poppy, and the deep golds found in Anthemis 'Sauce Hollandaise' and saturated golden Hemerocallis, to go with the deeper blues of Hosta 'Halcyon' and Campanula and Delphinium.

The border is intended for a large garden, ideally 9m x 1.8m (30 ft by 8ft wide).

Allow the plants to mingle, they need to get to know each other well. They do not want to stand alone. Always underplant with bulbs of seasonal interest, Crocus and Narcissus in spring with golden Tulipa to follow, Allium in summer.

Golden mats are formed at the edge by Eranthis hyemalis in winter, Viola in summer, Primula in spring.

Mix texture, form , flower and foliage, there will always be something to catch the eye. Have one or two focal points in the border. A spiky Phormium, a trimmed cone of Ligustrum or Taxus, a rounded mound of Chamaecyparis or Berberis.

46

Gold Plant
Profiles A-Z

ABIES

Handsome, hardy evergreen conifers provide excellent shelter and screening and make wonderful specimen trees. Silver firs go for gold.

HOW TO GROW
Late frosts can damage young foliage. Best in fertile, moist but well-drained soil in full sun. They thrive in neutral to slightly acidic soil with *A. pinsapo* generally tolerating drier, alkaline soils. A site out of cold winds is most appreciated. Quite shade tolerant, especially when young. Z3 and above depending on species. Cultivars are grafted in winter.

A. concolor 'Wintergold' has soft needles of yellow-green during the growing season, turning canary yellow with the onset of colder weather. Makes a pyramidal habit in most soils. This very slow growing form originated in northern Germany. Down to Z3.

A. koreana 'Blinsham Gold' is grown at Kenwith Nursery as a seedling off *A. koreana 'Aurea'*. A small, flat-topped, spreading bush of yellow-gold leaves.

A. koreana 'Flava' (*'Aurea'*) (Wittboldt-Muller) grows at a rate of about 15cm (6") a year, not bad by conifer standards. Especially beautiful in autumn and winter. This gold form may burn when young, but develops scorch resistance with age, but is best in a little shade. It makes a broad globe when young, eventually developing a leader and growing into a broad upright shape. Purple cones can appear on medium-sized specimens. 60cm-1.8m (3-6ft). Z5.

A. koreana 'Goldener Traum' (*'Golden Dream'*) grows into a wide, flat-topped bush with a more subdued colouring which is best in winter. Can become broadly conical in habit. 1m-1.8m (3-6ft). Z5.

A. koreana 'Luminetta' is similar to *'Aurea'* with very pale colouring, striking as an older tree.

A. nebrodensis 'Sicilian Gold' is a golden form of a very rare tree, almost extinct in the wild. A chance seedling spotted by Robert Aebel. Stiff needles bedeck this smallish tree which has a flat crown at maturity.

A. nordmanniana 'Golden Spreader' (*'Aurea Nana'*) is perhaps the best known of the golden firs. A slow-growing dwarf form which can sometimes make a small tree given plenty of time with spreading branches and a flattish top. Its cheering golden leaves are paler beneath. This form exhibits excellent colour in partial shade and is admirable in winter. A choice conifer for any garden offering a vibrant colour accent. Best on acid soil, but is tolerant of other types. 1-1.5m (3-5ft) tall with a spread of 1.5m (5ft). Z5.

A. pinsapo 'Aurea' bears golden foliage which turns green by winter, but some gold can be retained in full sun. The colouring is most prominent on the upper surfaces of new, thick, waxy growth. Not particularly cold hardy. It makes a large shrub or small tree being suitable for chalk soil, but is a slow starter, needs good soil. 3m (10ft). There is also a dwarf form *A. pinsapo 'Aurea Nana'*. Z7.

A. procera 'Sherwoodii' sometimes seen as *A. procera 'Aurea'*, is a golden form with long needles discovered in 1933 at Sherwood Nursery in Portland, Oregon. Young foliage can burn, but this will cease as the plant grows. For a conifer this is a fast grower. 7.5m (25ft).

Hot Partner: Darkest *Cryptomeria*

Cool Companion: plant with blue silver firs.

Abies nordmanniana 'Golden Spreader'

ACANTHUS

Bear's breeches are great architectural plants with wonderful stature in both foliage and flowers. If they have one fault it is that they are hard to get rid of. They need plenty of room. These perennials, mostly from the Mediterranean are well adapted to dry sites and are known to be vigorous.

HOW TO GROW

Any soil in sun or partial shade. In deep, fertile, well-drained soil they will become immense. Divide in spring or autum. Take root cuttings in winter. Z6.

The golden form A. 'Hollard's Gold' (*Fielding Gold'*, *New Zealand Gold'*) has that little extra! Large yellowish leaves deepen in good light giving a golden glow. Colour is best in spring in full sun in well-drained soil, but remain burnished all season. Perhaps more chartreuse than gold in half shade, but a very interesting form and a perfect foil for those purple-mauve flowers in summer. Handsome, architectural Bear's Breeches need careful siting as they can take over and are capable of re-emerging from any scrap of root. Originated in New Zealand in 1992. 90cm (3ft). Z6 in a hot spot or Z7.
Hot Partner: *Canna indica 'Purpurea', Vitis vinifera 'Purpurea'.*
Cool Companion: *Pulmonaria* blue flowered, *Veronica peduncularis 'Georgia Blue', Rosa glauca, Miscanthus sinensis.*
Golden Glory: *Lupinus arboreus* yellow, *Philadelphus coronarius 'Aureus'.*

ACER

Elegance and spectacular colour put maples firmly at the top of the list as specimen trees or as shrubs in light woodland. There is a maple with at least some golden colouring for every garden. Excellent as container plants.

HOW TO GROW

Grow in moist but well-drained soil in sun or part shade, with shelter from winds. Late frosts may kill foliage of *A. palmatum* cultivars.
Graft in late winter or bud in late summer.

A. campestre 'Postelense' is rarely offered, but if you do find it, this slow growing shrub or tree bears golden yellow foliage in spring and summer, preferring dappled shade. It can be hard pruned to make a hedge. 7.5m (25ft) in time. Z5.
A. cappadocicum 'Aureum' has rich, striking butter yellow leaves in spring, turning yellow in summer, early foliage emerges claret. Glossy, palmate leaves give excellent accent on a fine tree. Can be hard pruned in summer to make an eye-catching bush. It will not thank you for exposed, windy sites in dense shade but will thrive on chalk. The species itself also turns golden in autumn. 7.6x3m (25 x 10ft) in 20 years, ultimate height 20m (65ft).
A. negundo 'Auratum' is a slow growing form, bearing bright golden yellow leaves in spring, becoming paler in summer. An undemanding box elder also known as ash-leaved maple. 8m (25ft).
A. negundo 'Aureomargiantum' has green leaves widely margined in gold. Excellent autumn colour on this small tree or large shrub. Can be pruned to keep small. Good on chalky soil. Fast growing when young. 3m (10ft) ultimately 7.6m (25ft).
A. negundo 'Kelly's Gold' holds its golden colour well, this form is more vigorous than *'Auratum'* and less liable to burn in sun, but the golden colour is not as strong, fading more to chartreuse. It was raised in New Zealand before 1989. 10m (30ft). Z4-10.

Above: Acer shirasawanum 'Aureum'   *Below: Acer cappadocicum 'Aureum' x A. campestre*

A. palmatum 'Sango-kaku' (*'Senkaki'*) offers soft yellow autumn colouring on vivid and very conspicuous, coral stems. Its 5-lobed leaves up to 7cm (3") long open orange-yellow. A beautiful specimen. 6m (20ft).

A. platanoides 'Princeton Gold' (*'Prigo'*) PBR is an outstanding tree for yellow foliage. Pure gold leaves shimmer in spring on red petioles. By far the best golden *Acer* I have seen in spring and it holds its colour well into summer. Performs in most soils, but thrives best in moist, well-drained conditions. Quite stunning in sun to partial shade. An exceptional landscaping and specimen Norway maple. 24 carat gold absolutely shimmers in spring. 15m (45ft). Z4.

A. pseudoplatanus 'Corstorphinense' has pale spring yellow leaves through rich yellow in summer and then green later in the season. 10m (30ft). Z 4-10.

A. pseudoplatanus 'Worley' (*Worleei*), the golden sycamore makes a medium-sized tree. Soft yellow-green leaves turn gold, and end the season in green against red leaf stalks. Raised in Germany before 1893. 10m (30ft).

A. saccharinum f lutescens has leaves emerging orange-yellow when young turning soft yellow-green in summer with yellow autumn colour to round off its display. Needs sun to bring out the best colour but is tolerant of a wide range of soil types including poor soils. The species which is fast growing also turns yellow in autumn. 20m (60ft). Z3-9.

A saccharum and its cultivars offer brilliant autumn colouring. *'Goldspire'* is a columnar form which turns bright orange-yellow. *A. saccharinum ssp nigrum 'Green Column'* has bright yellow foliage in autumn.

A. shirasawanum 'Aureum' (*A. japonicum 'Aureum'*) is a slow growing tree or shrub, bearing bright soft yellow foliage, and pendent coral-red flowers. Lovely catching the sunlight, needing some sun to colour but best not in full sun where it scorches. Also appreciates protection from wind. Golden fan-shaped leaves are arranged in tiers on a compact, rounded shrub which slowly grows into a tree in time. Who would not wish to grow a tree known as Full Moon Maple or Moonglow Maple? Good autumn colours of orange and red. Red-winged seeds and petioles set off the colouring. A gem when grown well and worth paying particular attention to soil and siting. Even though it is a little fussy, it is the most planted yellow-leaved *Acer*. Hardy. 3.7-6m (12-20ft). Z6.

Many other *Acer* have superb autumn colouring, chief amongst them are **A. x conspicuum 'Phoenix'**, a snake bark maple with fine golden autumn leaf colour.

Acer pennsylvanicum 'Erythrocladum' has good autumn gold colour. Z5-9.

Acer pycnanthum has yellow autumn colour.

Acer tschonkii bears strong yellow leaves in autumn

Hot Partner: *Berberis thunbergii 'Atropurpurea', Euphorbia amygdaloides 'Purpurea'.*

Cool Companion: *Crocus vernus, Hosta 'Krossa Regal'.*

Acer palmatum 'Sango-kaku'

ACORUS

These are odd members of the *Arum* family, lacking the usual characteristics of spathe and spadix and appearing more like a grass than anything else. Appreciate the arching foliage to its best advantage at the edge of a border. Japanese rushes are easy to grow. The strap-like leaves die off in autumn, leaving behind a small basal tuft of foliage to start over again the following spring.

HOW TO GROW

These waterside plants are best in sun to partial shade in moist soil which must not dry out. Divide rhizomes at the beginning of the season every 3-4 years, pot up and grow on until established before planting out. *A. gramineus* is semi-evergreen. Z5-9.

A. gramineus 'Hakuro-nishiki' is a yellow-leaved evergreen. Neat and sweet. Starts off on the chartreuse side in spring as in the photograph, turning yellower. Has a central tuft of evergreen leaves. 15cm (6").

A. gramineus 'Masumune' is a slow, dense, spreading evergreen with variegated, linear, golden leaves and yellow flowers. Half hardy. 30cm (12").

A. gramineus 'Minimus Aureus', the dwarf golden sweet flag is striking and as sweet as they come, making a slowly spreading clump of tiny golden leaves. Excellent in moist conditions in part sun to light shade. Short and sweet. 7cm (3").

A. gramineus 'Ogon' (*'Wogon'*) *'Oborozuki'* is usually the same in cultivation though I have come across one nursery who claim to have the real thing from Japan bears butter yellow and green coloured striking foliage, an excellent contrast to rounder leaves. Performs best in sun to part shade in moist soil. Its stiff leaves look absolutely glorious in winter. Not completely evergreen but will withstand all but the coldest, severest winters. Excellent in a small half barrel water feature or in a very damp sunny border and a great container plant too. Plantsman and friend Josh Schneider says this is his all-time favourite. An easy and adaptable grass. 25cm (10").

A. gramineus 'Tanimanoyuki', has lime-yellow stripes on each blade. Evergreen in moist conditions. Hardy in SE Ohio. 7cm (3").

Hot Partner: *Bergenia*, green or purple, *Ophiopogon* black, green or near white.

Cool Companion: *Primula denticulata*.

Golden Glory: *Lysichiton americanus*, *Iris pallida 'Variegata'*, *Caltha palustris*.

Acorus gramineus 'Ogon'

Acorus gramineus 'Hakuro-nishiki'

ALTERNANTHERA

Not many of these tropical annuals and perennials are in cultivation. Grown for their foliage effect, when they are seen, it is often in bedding. They are also useful for ground cover and containers. Any period of cold weather sets them back and halts growth.

HOW TO GROW
Plant out after danger of frost has passed in moist, but well-drained soil in full sun for best leaf colour. Can be clipped to maintain compactness. Divide in spring. Take softwood or greenwood cuttings in late summer. Can be grown under glass. Z10.

A. ficoidea 'Aurea' known as parrot leaf, has yellow linear leaves, undemanding and its small, compact size makes it a great plant for containers. 12cm (5").
A. ficoidea 'Bettzickeana' this low-growing calico plant has broad, chartreuse leaves which turn gold in full sun. Will not withstand cold temperatures.
A. 'Gold Thread' has tiny, slim golden leaves. For a windowbox or on the rockery as well as bedding.

Aquilegia 'Mellow Yellow'

AQUILEGIA

These clump-forming, hardy perennials from the northern hemisphere produce basal rosettes of handsome foliage topped by equally handsome flowers. The distinctive, bell-shaped flowers are often known as granny's bonnets. Good in light woodland or the herbaceous border.

HOW TO GROW
Easy from seed when grown in isolation, many come true. A popular subject for hybridising. Grow well in sun or partial shade in any fertile, moist, well-drained soil. Divide named cultivars in spring, but bear in mind roots resent disturbance on this member of the ranunculaceae family. Rather big on self-seeding, so cut off flower heads as they fade if you do not want prolific numbers of seedlings.

A. 'Purple Emperor' (Mike Tristram) has the fascinating combination of nodding, single purple flowers and golden foliage, with red stems to boot. Robust with overwintering power.
A. 'Mellow Yellow' bears pale yellow foliage in spring fades to chartreuse with white, or sometimes pale blue flowers. Excellent in a little shade or sun in reasonably fertile soil. Cut back hard after flowering for a second flush of leaves. As with the one below, from Ray Brown of Plantworld, Devon. 50cm (20").
A. 'Sunburst Ruby' has the astonishing combination of golden foliage and ruby red flowers. Best in sun to light shade. 50cm (20").
A. vulgaris 'Horwood Gold' has soft golden foliage and contrasting blue flowers.
A. vulgaris Vervaeneana Group covers variegated foliage types splashed and flecked with gold. Blue and white flowered varieties are known as *'Woodside'*.
Hot Partner: *Geranium phaeum 'Samobor', Heuchera 'Obsidion', Imperata cylindrica 'Rubra', Cosmos atrosanguineus.*
Cool Partner: *Bergenia,* Ferns, *Campanula.*
Golden Glory: *Bidens 'Golden Goddess'.*

ARUNDO

These are huge plants, make that HUGE. Do I have a problem with this? They are a lot bigger than me! Plant it, big plants are IT. Z7.

A. donax 'Golden Chain' is an admirable gold variegated form needing good soil in a warm position. 3.5m (12ft).

A. formosana 'Oriental Gold' is one stunning grass. Forms large clumps of arching golden foliage that will cause quite a stir. Make a 2m (6ft) statement in gold easily, can reach 3m (10ft). King Midas would be envious. Pinkish white plumes appear in late summer. Best in sun or light shade with average watering. A dramatic accent plant in a large container. Evergreen, hardy to (15-20°F), becomes dormant otherwise. 3.5m (12ft).

Hot Partner: *Canna 'Australia', Ensete ventricosum 'Maurellii', Ricinus communis 'Carmencita'.*

Cool Companion: *Melianthus major.*

Berberis 'Golden Nugget'

BERBERIS

Golden Berberis are outstanding ornamental shrubs for their foliage and autumn fruits. They are a superb accompaniment to darker leaved forms and contrast well with other dark leaved shrubs such as *Cotinus* and *Physocarpus*. Spiny, usually compact, deciduous shrubs make good border plants.

HOW TO GROW

Well-drained soils in full sun to partial shade. Fruiting and autumn colour is better in sun. Root softwood cuttings or take semi-ripe ones in summer. Hardy to -10°F (-23°C). Z. 4-10.

B. 'Bonanza Gold' (Bogozam TM. PBR) is compact and has bright golden foliage with good scorch resistance in semi-shade, having orange new shoots. A cushion forming mound, similar to 'Aurea' but more compact. 45 x 90cm (18 x 36").

B. 'Golden Nugget' (Monlers TM) is an even smaller form with yellow foliage turning orange in autumn. Best colour in sun. Thought to be a seedling from a naturally occurring cross between *B. thunbergii* 'Aurea' and 'Kobold'. 30 x 36cm (12 x 14").

B. thunbergii 'Aurea' is bright yellow in sun, yet greenish-yellow in shade with autumn colour of orange. A few small yellow flowers appear in spring. Position with a little afternoon partial shade to avoid sun scorch. Water well in dry areas.1.2-1.5m (4-5ft).

B. thunbergii 'Aurea Nana' is a delightful dwarf form growing to just 60-90cm (2-3ft) tall. Its bright golden display turns red in autumn.

B. thunbergii 'Sunsation' TM ('Monry') has new growth of greenish yellow, turning sunshine yellow in sun to part shade. Has an unusual reddish edge in autumn.

Hot Partner: *Cotinus coggygria 'Royal Velvet', Tulipa 'Queen of Night'.*

Cool Companion: *Eryngium planum 'Superbum'.*

Golden Glory: *Hosta 'Sum and Substance', Lamium 'Beedham's White', Lysimachia nummularia 'Aurea'.*

Above: Berberis thunbergii 'Aurea'   Below: Berberis 'Bonanza Gold'

CALLUNA

Golden heathers proliferate. One must understand that colour is not persistent. Recent additions have better gold colouring that last into winter without turning orange. These hardy evergreen shrubs are found on acid moorland and heaths and make excellent groundcover. Give afternoon shade in hot climates. Their little bell-shaped flowers attract bees.

HOW TO GROW
Prefer an open site in humus-rich, well-drained, acid soil in full sun. Z5-8.

C. **'Beoley Gold'** has yellow foliage and white flowers in August and September. Looking good in summer and winter. A strong growing form. 35cm (14").

C. **'Boskoop'** with rich golden foliage turning orange-red in winter. Flowers are lilac-pink. 30cm (12").

C. **'Fairy'** has clear yellow foliage which turns orange to bronze in winter with many pale flowers.30cm.

C. **'Gold Carmen'** bears lilac pink flowers and golden foliage deepening in winter. 25-30cm (10-12").

C. **'Gold Finch'** has golden foliage deepening in winter with magenta flowers. 25-30cm (10-12").

C. **'Gold Haze'** flaunts pale gold foliage all year and white flowers in August to October. Upright habit. A J W Sparkes cultivar. 25-30cm (10-12"). Z5-8.

C. **'Gold Knight'** has lavender flowers in late summer with downy gold foliage on a vigorous erect habit. 30-45cm (12-18").

C. **'Gold Spronk'** has clear yellow foliage all year with white flowers in late summer. Upright. 40cm (12-18").

C. **'Golden Blazeaway'** is a sport of *'Blazeaway'*, but unlike its parent, retains its golden foliage into winter. Open erect habit. A superb choice. 35cm (14").

C. **'Golden Dream'** has golden foliage all year with double white flowers in August to September. Erect habit. 25-30cm (10-12").

C. **'Golden Feather'** has feathery gold foliage, turning warm orange in winter with sparse mauve flowers. Feathery foliage is susceptible to windburn. 50cm.

C. **'Golden Max'** has white flowers in July to August with clear yellow foliage throughout the year. Upright habit. 30-45cm (12-18").

C. **Golden Turret'** bears white flowers in August to September above golden foliage. A sport of *'Loch Turret'* found in Scotland. 45-60cm (18-24").

C. **'Guinea Gold'** has vigorous white flowers and yellow foliage all year, a lighter shade than *'Beoley Gold'*. Vigorous. 30-5cm (10-20").

C. **'Ineke'** has golden foliage contrasting with rose-violet flowers. 30cm (12").

C. **'Inshriach Bronze'** bears lemon-yellow foliage in spring, through gold in summer and bronze tones in winter with lilac-pink flowers. 25cm (10").

C. **'Robert Chapman'** has gold foliage through summer, turning orange then finally red in winter and spring with soft purple flowers. 30cm (12").

C. **'Roland Haagen'** (*'Rowland Heagen'*) displays gold foliage which turns bright orange in winter with lilac-pink flowers. 35cm (14").

C. **'Rosalind'** has golden foliage and pink flowers. 30cm (12").

C. **'Serlei Aurea'** possesses dense yellow-green, erect foliage, tipped yellow in summer and autumn, with white flowers on long racemes. 60cm (24").

C. **'Sir John Charrington'** has gold foliage turning orange and red in winter with mauve-pink flowers. 40cm (16").

C. **'Sirsson'** has gold leaves, with orange and red tones in winter when exposed to cold. Pink flowers are borne in midseason on this seedling from the above.

C. **'Sunrise'** bears golden-yellow foliage turning orange-red in winter with purple flowers. 30cm (12").

C. **'Sunset'** has golden early foliage, orange in summer, and finally red in winter with mauve-pink flowers. 25cm (10").

C. **'Wickwar Flame'** has golden leaves with red coppery colouring in winter and mauve-pink flowers in August to October. 50cm (20").

Hot Partner: *Cornus alba 'Kesselringii'*.

Cool Companion: *Abies koreana 'Blue Magic', Juniperus 'Blue Arrow'*.

CALOCEDRUS

This small genus of conifers has some gold surprises. Incense cedar is similar to *Thuja*, branchlets are borne in flattened sprays with scaly, flattened leaves. Male and female strobili are borne on different branches of the same tree and woody cones ripen the first year. Z6.

C. decurrens 'Aureovariegata' has sprays of golden mottled leaves occurring irregularly throughout its branches. Has an attractive two-tone, green-gold effect. Columnar and can be clipped to keep its upright shape. Best colour is in full sun. 3m (10ft).

C. decurrens 'Berrima Gold' is a slow growing, broadly columnar form with orange bark and pale yellow-green foliage, tipped orange in winter. The most golden form, especially in spring. Best with partial shade to prevent sun scorch. Grows 15-25cm (6-10") per year. Has a slightly coarser texture than *Thuja*. Introduced into the U.K. by Sir Harold Hillier from Claude Crowe of the Australian nursery, Berrima Bridge. 2.5m (8ft).

C. decurrens 'Maupin Glow' has bright yellow tipped leaves which can withstand sun. The top of the tree is ablaze with yellow foliage. Upright growth but wider at the base. Found by Greg Rigby in Oregon. Best colour is had in full sun. 2.5m (8ft).

Cool Companion: *Abies concolor Violacea Group, Picea 'Alberta Blue'.*

CAMPANULA

Bellflowers have long been appreciated for their ornamental flowers, and now there are two golden leaved varieties to adorn the garden. *C. garganica* is a perennial rock garden species, and should prove well-behaved. *C. persicifolia* is perennial and needs fertile, neutral to alkaline moist but well-drained soil.

C. garganica 'Dickson's Gold' (*'Aurea'*) has striking golden foliage retained throughout the season but turning more limey in summer. Dainty, upward facing, starry blue bellflowers on 12cm (5") stems in summer. The almost heart-shaped, toothed leaves are best in full sun or light shade at the front of a border or a rock garden. An excellent edger, requiring good drainage. Z5-7.

C. persicifolia 'Kelly's Gold', the golden peach-leaved bellflower, was originally found in Ann Holts' garden on Bainbridge Island in the Pacific Northwest. Brilliant gold foliage shines in spring, retaining its colour well in heat and is the perfect accompaniment to the white flowers, edged in blue in June and July. Best in full sun to partial shade. Cut back after flowering, and it will most likely rebloom. 70cm (28"). Z4-9.

Hot Partner: *Heuchera 'Obsidion', Geranium 'Victor Reiter'.*

Cool Companion: *Myosotis 'Gold n' Sapphires'*

Campanula persicifolia 'Kelly's Gold' with an admirable Astrantia

CARYOPTERIS

Small, showy late season flowering perennial shrubs are grown both for foliage and their attractive flowers. An excellent choice for chalky soils. Grow in any mixed border.

HOW TO GROW
Best grown in well-drained soil and full sun to give splendid colour in the garden. Where summers are cool and temperatures fall below -15°C (5°F) plant against a sunny wall. Root softwood cuttings in late spring or greenwood cuttings in early summer. Z5-9.

C. x clandonensis 'Worcester Gold' is a small perennial shrub with soft golden, lance-shaped foliage emerging in spring, but held throughout the season. Complemented to perfection by plenty of rich lavender-blue flowers in late summer which attract butterflies. Position in sun in well-drained soil, good drainage is the key, will take partial shade. I have been pleased with the performance of my shrub which still looked attractive in October. This really does earn its place in the garden. 90cm (3ft). Z6.

Caryopteris 'Sunshine Blue' courtesy of SpringMeadow Nursery

Caryopteris x clandonensis 'Worcester Gold'

C. divaricata is a choice new variegated form from Japan. Herbaceous with the usual blue flowers for a sheltered sunny spot. 75cm (30").

C. 'Sunshine Blue' (*incana 'Jason'*) PPAF, CPAF bred by Peter Champion in the U.K., this incredibly strong growing shrub has brilliant gold foliage. It claims to be a dramatic improvement on *C. 'Worcester Gold'*, stronger growing, deeper yellow gold foliage and pale blue flowers. Performs well in full sun to partial shade in well-drained, even droughty soils. Stand back and admire! Z5b-8.

Hot Partner: *Weigela 'Wine and Roses'*, *Berberis 'Helmond Pillar'*.

Cool Companion: *Geranium 'Nimbus'*, *Perovskia 'Blue Spire'*, *Buxus sempervirens*, dark evergreens.

Golden Glory: *Spiraea 'Golden Princess'*, *Lonicera nitida 'Baggesen's Gold'*.

CATALPA

Indian bean is a deciduous tree, excellent for light woodland and by the banks of streams. Avoid exposed sites which would leave foliage in tatters. These trees earn their keep threefold for their heart-shaped leaves, clusters of bell-shaped flowers in summer and slender, bean-like pods. Its spreading form is best seen as a specimen.

HOW TO GROW
Grow in full sun, with shelter from strong winds in deep, fertile, moist but well-drained soil. Extra large leaves are obtained when pruned to near base in early spring. Protect from frost in extreme weather. Hardy to -20°C (-29°F). Z5-10.

C. bignonioides 'Aurea' is an enchanting soft yellow-leaved form whose large, heart-shaped foliage is bronze when young. This mop-headed tree is pollution tolerant making it a good choice for city gardens. Panicles of white flowers with yellow and purple markings are only produced in cold areas in very hot summers and are never as fine as the green-leaved variety. The foxglove-like flowers are never produced on young trees. It bears the delightful name of the golden Indian bean tree and makes a medium-sized tree. 10m (30ft).
Hot Partner: *Hydrangea quercifolia.*
Cool Companion: *Juniperus 'Blue Arrow'* or *'Blue Carpet'.*

Cedrus deodora 'Gold Cascade'

CEDRUS

Beloved conifers with fine architectural effect. Their presence in the landscape gives an immediate effect of grandeur and majesty and they are renowned for their longevity. Add to that their branching habit, texture and colour and you have one of the finest large trees for specimen planting in an open area in all but the harshest climates. Male and female strobili are usually borne on the same tree. The males are bright yellow, conspicuous on the flattened branches in autumn. Female barrel shaped cones take two years to mature and break up whilst still on the tree.

HOW TO GROW
Best in full sun in any well-drained soil, including chalk. If double leaders form, cut out the weakest. Cultivars are grafted in late summer or winter. Z6-9.

C. atlantica 'Aurea' is a slow-growing, conical tree with young, golden yellow foliage maturing green. This medium-sized tree has leaves shorter than the type. Makes an ideal lawn specimen for a large garden with all exposed foliage showing as gold. Dislikes salt winds. Unfortunately this does not always grow well but it certainly does not lack grace. 3mx1.2m. (10 x 4ft). Z6-9.
C. atlantica 'Aurea Robusta' has blue undertones and looks really yellow. Mature plants are burn resist and this eventually makes a large pyramidal tree with open, layered branching. Originated in Boskoop, Holland in 1932. 3m (10ft).
C. atlantica 'Glauca Aurea' is distinct from *C. atlantica 'Aurea'* and not as golden, but resists burn all the better for that. Planted in full sun, its blue foliage is dusted with gold. 3mx3m (10x10ft).
C. atlantica 'Golden Dwarf' (*'Aurea Prostrata'*) grows low and golden. This is a lovely form with a graceful dwarf upright habit with horizontal branches. Z6.
C. deodora 'Aurea' is slow-growing with needle-like, striking new yellow foliage becoming greener as it matures. All exposed foliage is gold in spring. The

golden deodar develops a flat top at a younger age than the species. Will take somewhat dry soil. As a superb specimen tree, this deservedly earns a position where it can take centre stage. 5m (15ft). Z6-10.

C. deodora 'Aurea Well's Select' makes a conical specimen quicker than *'Aurea'* with good yellow foliage. Found as a seedling in Mt. Vernon at Wells Nursery, U.S. Best in full sun. 4x2.5m (14x8ft).

C. deodora 'Aurea Pendula' the golden weeping deodor has a wonderful, graceful habit with leaves yellow during late spring and summer turning greener in winter. Growth is upright with weeping branches from the central trunk. 3m (10ft).

C. deodora 'Deep Cove' is a semi-dwarf, narrow column with foliage beginning yellow, changing one month later to white, then becoming greenish. Found by Gordan Bentham in B.C., Canada. Best colour is seen in full sun. 3x1.2m (10x4ft).

C. deodora 'Gold Cascade' has a lovely, cascading habit with yellow new growth. Highly ornamental, compact weeping form like a small *'Aurea'*. Best in full sun. Originated in Australia. 60x45cm. (2ftx18").

C. deodora 'Gold Cone' is a fast growing, narrowly upright form with very yellow foliage, held well throughout the year. Being narrower than many cultivars it is more suitable for a small garden. Stems are pendulous at the tips. Best in full sun. An excellent selection, found by Goddard in B.C. Canada. 3x1.2m (8x4ft).

C. deodora 'Gold Mound' is bright yellow, forming a low, broad pyramid with dense foliage which will appreciate a little room to develop. Can be sheared to keep foliage tight and neat. Found by Goddard in 1985. 2.5x2m (8x6ft).

C. deodora 'Gold Nugget' is extremely slow growing, but worthwhile for its good golden colour which is scorch-resist. A dwarf, pendulous form raised in Australia. Grows only 2-5cm (1-2") a year.

C. deodora 'Golden Horizon' is a vigorous, flat-growing, spreading, prostrate type with yellow foliage sometimes suffused green if grown in sun, but blue-green in shade. Needs protection from cold winds.

Remove any occasional terminal shoots. Easy to keep in shape, it layers gracefully over itself to make a large, yellow mound. A Dutch raised selection made by Vliet Nursery in 1975. Z6. 1.2x1.8m (4x6ft).

C. deodora 'Harvest Gold' exhibits nicely golden foliage, making a large specimen.

C. deodora 'Klondike' bears greenish yellow colouring in summer on pendulous, yellowish stems, and looks much better in its winter clothing of bronze-gold. Not quite as hardy as some. Discovered by Goddard. 3x2.5m (10x8ft).

C. deodora 'Scott' makes a rounded bush having a golden sheen.

C. deodora 'Vink's Golden' is a broad mounding selection found as a broom in Tasmania. Its yellow foliage has blue-grey undertones. This dense, pyramidal form is eye-catching for its layered appearance which is graceful. It makes a decent, compact specimen superior to *C. deodora 'Aurea'*. Plant away from strong winds. 7x4m (22x13ft).

Cedrus deodora 'Gold Cone'

CENTAUREA

This mat-forming perennial enjoys moist, well-drained soil. Avoid rich, fertilised soils. In cool, northern climates, this can spread quite rapidly by rhizomes. Sparse rebloom may occur late season, if finished flowerheads are cut back immediately. Attractive to bees and butterflies.

HOW TO GROW
Herbaceous perennial cornflower is delightful in dry to medium wet, well-drained soil. Divide every 3 years.

C. montana 'Gold Bullion' selected in the U.K, has bright gold foliage and complimentary blue flowers in May-June. Best in full sun with free draining soil, preferably a raised bed, where this perennial cornflower will make mounds of delightful golden foliage 40 x40cm (16x16"). Cut back after flowering for a second flush of flowers. Solitary, fringed, rich blue cornflowers on long stems cannot be overlooked. Excellent in the cottage garden or in any border. Z4.

C. montana 'Horwood Gold' (Hopleys) is a Peter Adams version of the golden-leaved Knapweed. 60x60cm (2x2ft)
Hot Partner: *Kniphofia 'Orange Crush', K. 'Bees' Sunset'*
Cool Companion: Yellow *Nasturtium, Caryopteris x clandonensis 'Worcester Gold'*.
Golden Glory: *Achillea 'Moonwalker', Digitalis lutea, Aquilegia 'Mellow Yellow'*.

CEPHALOTAXUS

Golden leaved plum yews are quite rare. Foliage is similar to *Taxus* on these evergreen conifers. In general needs shade, but leaf colour on the gold varieties will be lost. Hardy Japanese plum yews exhibit tremendous natural variation. Male flowers are produced in clusters. Female plants produce fruits consisting of a single hard seed with a fleshy green covering. Make useful hedges given shelter from cold, drying winds.

HOW TO GROW
Appreciate dry to moist soil in partial shade to sun. Tolerant of hard clipping, hedges can be trimmed in early summer. Greenwood or semi-ripe cuttings of terminal shoots can be taken in summer. (-10°F to 0°F). Z6-9.

C. harringtonii 'Fastigiata Aurea' has foliage variegated or margined yellow. Z5.
C. harringtonii 'Korean Gold' (*'Ogen'*) is a gold-leaved sport of *'Fastigiata'* with new growth yellow on a loosely fastigiate form with erect, medium growth. Introduced by Barry Yinger in the 1980's, originally from Japan. Best in a sunny position needing a little shelter, but note it is subject to burn in hot climates. 3m (10ft). Z5.
Companions: Plant with other conifers.

CERATOSTIGMA

A hardy deciduous shrub, thriving in light soils and full sun. Needs shelter from frost and cold winds. A lovely addition to the golden garden or to any shrubby area. This is one of those admirable shrubs valued equally for foliage and flowers.

HOW TO GROW
In a sunny, sheltered border, or against a warm, sunny wall. Well-drained soil in full sun, a light soil is best. Prune in early spring. Root softwood cuttings in summer. Layer in autumn.

C. willmottianum 'Desert Skies' (*'Palmgold'*) PBR is a spectacularly vibrant golden form aglow with blue flowers from late summer. An open-branched, spreading shrub with lance-shaped leaves. 60cm (2ft) height and spread.
Cool Companion: *Eryngium bourgattii 'Oxford Blue'*

CHAMAECYPARIS

Many of these hardy, evergreen conifers are highly suitable for the small garden as dwarf forms abound. Young plants are usually conical, but spread and differ with age. Foliage is usually frond-like and flattened. They do not resent disturbance and even small specimen trees can be moved. False cypress have male and female strobili on the same trees. Tiny males are usually yellow or red. Cones normally mature in the first year. Useful as a hedge.

HOW TO GROW

Tolerant of full sun or partial shade and a wide variety of soils, but best on neutral to slightly acid, moist well-drained soils. They are tolerant of, but slower growing on dry chalk. Trim between late spring and autumn. Prefer deep loamy soil in full sun with protection from cold winds. A humid atmosphere suits them, although they are quite adaptable. Root semi-ripe cuttings in late summer. *C. obtusa* cultivars are grafted in late winter or spring. Hardy to -20°F. 5-8 unless noted otherwise. Cold wind blown sites in Z5 will mean losses, plant in a sheltered site.

C. lawsoniana 'Alumnigold' glows on the uppermost growth, shading to green at the base of the plant.

C. lawsoniana 'Aurea Densa' bears dense, pale golden foliage making a neat column. Flattened, densely packed sprays of foliage are stiff. An excellent choice for a large rock garden. Raised by Rogers', Red Lodge Nurseries, Southampton. Small, slow-growing bush eventually reaches 2m. (6ft).

C. lawsoniana 'B.D.Edginton' is a rich, gold-yellow upright specimen. An old variety which does not burn. 5x2m (16x6ft).

C. lawsoniana 'Brilliance' will be yellow all year round in a sunny position. Conical habit. 2x1m (6x3ft).

C. lawsoniana 'Broomhill Gold' bears bright gold foliage. A sport of *Erecta Viridis* and very similar in its erect habit, making a slow-growing, medium-sized tree of compact growth when young, broadening in

maturity. Good colour in summer, greenish in winter. 60x30cm (2 x 1ft).

C. lawsoniana 'Cream Gold' makes a smaller and more compact form than *'Ellwood's Gold'* and is of a brighter colour especially in spring. 1m (3ft).

C. lawsoniana 'Dutch Gold' has bright, golden-yellow foliage in a neat and tidy, upright pyramid. 3m (10ft).

C. lawsoniana 'Ellwood's Gold' is a slow, compact, upright form for sun or part shade having sprays tipped in gold to give a glow to the whole. 1.5m x 60cm (4x 2ft).

C. lawsoniana 'Ellwood's Gold Pillar' is a narrow, columnar dwarf with feathery golden foliage. 75x25cm (30x10").

C. lawsoniana 'Erecta Aurea' bears golden foliage making a small upright, rounded column in the shape of a candle flame. Tends to scorch in full sun. This slow-growing form with a compact habit was raised in Holland in 1874. 2m (6ft).

C. lawsoniana 'Gold Flake' has upright, conical growth with open sprays of green foliage mottled yellow, much more green than yellow. A sport of *'Ellwoodii'* which arose at Konijn Nursery, Holland.

C. lawsoniana 'Golden King' makes a medium-sized, conical tree with bright yellow foliage which turns bronze in winter. This seedling from *'Triomf of Boskoop'* was raised in Holland before 1931.

C. lawsoniana 'Golden Pot' (*'Pot of Gold'*) is a slow-growing golden sport of *'Pottenii'* with wonderful soft foliage that reminds me of a teddy bear. Very bright yellow in summer. Eventually grows into a broad cone. 1.5m (4ft).

C. lawsoniana 'Golden Showers' is a compact form with yellow outer leaves, tinged blue interior leaves. Up to 1.8m (6ft).

C. lawsoniana 'Golden Wonder' is bright gold all year making a broad pyramid. Best in full sun. A medium sized tree raised in Holland in 1955. 2.5x1m (8x3ft).

C. lawsoniana 'Grayswood Gold' has yellow foliage and makes a slender upright column which is excellent for a hedge. 1.5m (4ft) Maximum height 5m (15ft).

Above: the dense and lush golden conifer hedge at Barnsdale
Below: Chamaecyparis 'Nana Lutea'

Chamaecyparis pisifera 'Filifera Aurea' at Tony Avent's Plant Delights' Nursery garden. Courtesy of Charlene Harris.

C. lawsoniana 'Hollard's Gold' ('*Darleyensis*') displays yellow foliage without burning. Graceful, weeping branches bear clusters of blue cones in autumn. Conical habit. 5x4.2m (16x15ft).

C. lawsoniana 'Jonesii' will suit sun or shade and still hold its yellow colour well. Upright pyramidal habit. 2x1m (6x3ft).

C. lawsoniana 'Lanei Aurea' (Lane) is narrowly conical with feathery, gold-yellow foliage above, greener beneath which sets off a dark green yew background to perfection. Changes to bronze-gold in winter. Raised by Lane's of Berkhampstead in 1938.

C. lawsoniana 'Lemon Queen' bears a pyramidal column with pale lemon and green foliage, similar to '*Golden Wonder*'. A semi-dwarf, conical habit with juvenile and adult foliage make this an interesting addition to a rockery. Best in part shade, it may burn in full sun. 3.7m (12ft). Z4.

C. lawsoniana 'Lutea' is a narrow form with yellow golden foliage in pendent sprays. This medium sized older cultivar has a columnar habit with a drooping top after 10 years when it comes into its own. 15m.

C. lawsoniana 'Lutea Nana' is a small bush with golden foliage in short, flattened sprays. Capable of surviving lower temperatures than most. 2m (6ft).

C. lawsoniana 'Lutea Smithii' is a slow growing conifer eventually making a medium sized tree of conical habit. Its spreading branches are golden-yellow in large, drooping, horizontal sprays.

C. lawsoniana 'Miki' has yellow to dull yellow colouring on a broadly conical habit. Protect in very cold areas and do not overwater. 3m (10ft).

C. lawsoniana 'Minima Aurea' is a dwarf variety with two-tone foliage, rich golden on the upper and yellow underneath. Good colour year round, but intense in winter. Compact and very hardy, it makes a handsome oval mound, conical at the tip, soft to the touch. An excellent choice for a rock garden, raised at Red Lodge Nursery. Needs free draining soil but avoid drying out when young. 90cm (3ft).

C. lawsoniana 'Southern Gold' this slow growing lemon form looks best in part shade. Makes a pyramidal plant which dislikes salt winds. 2m (6x4ft).

C. lawsoniana 'Springtime' PBR is a dwarf, rounded bush with soft, light yellow-green foliage all year in sun or part shade. Young growth is especially attractive on this sport of '*Elwoodii*'. 90cm (3x2ft).

Chamaecyparis lawsoniana 'Miki' below
C. lawsoniana 'Minima Aurea' right

Chamaecyparis lawsoniana 'Treasure Island'

C. lawsoniana 'Winston Churchill' is a broadly conical tree with dense, rich golden foliage all year round. Makes a small to medium-sized specimen raised in Sussex before 1945.

C. lawsoniana 'Yellow Transparent' bears young foliage which is yellow, appearing transparent in summer when backlit by the sun, bronzing in winter. Hardy and easy away from coastal areas, making an attractive narrow column. A slow-growing sport of *'Fletcheri'* raised in Boskoop in Holland around 1955. 1.8mx80cm (6ftx32").

C. lawsoniana 'Yvonne' makes a narrow pyramid with gold-yellow foliage, hardly losing any of its colouring all year in full sun. 2x1m (6x3ft).

C. nootkatensis 'Aurea' (now renamed *Xanthocyparis nootkatensis*) has yellow young foliage, maturing to yellow green, exhibiting subtle variation on a conical form which will eventually grow into a dense, compact tree of medium size. Its horizontal branches tipped in yellow, are pendulous at the ends. Will lose colour in too much shade. 3m (10ft).

C. nootkatensis 'Van der Aker' is an extremely narrow form of yellow Alaskan Cedar, making a fantastic vertical accent. 6mx30cm (20x1ft). Z5.

C. obtusa 'Aurea' has flattened sprays of golden foliage with green interior, on a conical tree. Denser foliage than *'Crippsii'* but not as elegant. Introduced from Japan in 1860 by Robert Fortune. 2.5m (8-10ft).

C. obtusa 'Aurea Nana' has twisted, fan-shaped foliage in strong gold throughout the year. A lovely specimen with swirling foliage. 60-90cm (2-3ft).

C. obtusa 'Confucius' has bright gold growth in spring, with older foliage being dark green. It makes a dense, irregular cone and has a layered look with its whip like foliage. Originated in New Zealand and is apparently more cold tolerant than other cultivars. 1.2-1.5m (4-5ft).

C. obtusa 'Crippsii' has rich, bright golden new growth, fading to yellow-green making a slow-growing excellent conical tree with loose and airy growth which is best in full sun. Frond tips curve downwards gracefully on this handsome and elegant plant.

C. lawsoniana 'Stardust' is a slow-growing, broadly conical form with fern-like, sulphur yellow foliage bronzing at the tips. A superb specimen tree raised in Holland. Makes a good hedge or specimen, but is unsuitable for a very small garden unless you want the shears constantly in hand. 3x1.2m (10x4ft).

C. lawsoniana 'Stewartii' makes an elegant, medium sized, conical tree with flattened sprays of bright golden foliage. Very hardy older cultivar whose base becomes broader with age. Excellent wind and burn resistance. Good drainage essential. 3.5m (12x8ft).

C. lawsoniana 'Treasure' is a dwarf green conifer with patches of yellow, mainly to the edges of leaves. Very attractive, glows at the edges.

C. lawsoniana 'Treasure Island' is a sport of the above making a tiny mound of feathery foliage.

C. lawsoniana 'Westermanii' is a beautiful yellow variegated form which does not burn. Flexible tips project out and are gracefully pendulous. 3x3m (10x10ft).

Chamaecyparis pisifera 'Aurea Nana'

A good specimen. Takes full sun in Oregon and N. England. Raised by Thomas Cripps of Tunbridge Wells before 1899. Not quite as hardy as *'Aurea'*, but a much finer cultivar. 1.5m (5ft). Takes a lifetime to reach 15m (50ft). There is a specimen almost that size at Sedro Woolley, Skagit County, WA, USA.

C. obtusa 'Devine's Golden' is a lovely golden dwarf introduced by Bill Devine. Very slow growing upright form which eventually develops a leader.

C. obtusa 'Fernspray Gold' has ferny, golden foliage on a slow-growing form which is very attractive with its twisted, fern-like branches. Best in partial shade. Resembles *'Tetragona Aurea'* but lemon rather than orange and with a broader habit. 1.8m (6ft).

C. obtusa 'Gold Drop' (Ed Rezek 1974) shows its golden colouring best in summer, a dwarf form which will take full sun. Tight and compact.

C. obtusa 'Gold Lace' is a sport from *'Youngii'* found at Cedar Lodge making a bright golden dwarf shrub in full sun for best colour. The name comes from the swirling foliage. 1.5x1.2m (5x4ft).

C. obtusa 'Golden Fairy' (Springarn) is a dense dwarf, making a bun-shaped dome with yellow-golden foliage. 50cm (20").

C. obtusa 'Golden Fern' has lovely dense, feathery golden foliage. A mutation of *'Fernspray Gold'* exhibiting juvenile foliage, slower but more branched. This is a delightful choice dwarf. Needs afternoon shade in hot areas. Originated in Australia. 50cm (20").

C. obtusa 'Golden Filament' is sunburn resist and has bright gold foliage. Very dwarf and similar to *'Golden Sprite'*.

C. obtusa 'Golden Nymph' (Springarn) is a compact, very dwarf form making a flattened cone with excellent gold foliage.

C. obtusa 'Golden Pillar' (Henry Weissenberger) is a narrowly columnar form with bright golden foliage which does not burn.

C. obtusa 'Golden Pygmy' (Springarn) is a low form with loose feathery foliage looking delightfully golden. Grows around 4cm (less than 2") a year.

C. obtusa 'Golden Sprite' (Springarn 1979) is a real slow dwarf, with rich golden foliage, shading to green at the base which burns in full sun so it will appreciate afternoon shade. An excellent subject for a trough. After ten years this will only have reached the size of a canteloupe melon. That's slow! A seedling of *'Gracilis Aurea'* raised before 1967.

C. obtusa 'Golden Whorl' ('Tsatsumi Gold') bears golden swirling foliage on a flat, globose shape. Adult foliage is tufted.

Chamaecyparis obtusa 'Kameini Hiba'

C. obtusa 'Goldilocks' has rich sprays of golden foliage against the darker green leaves.

C. obtusa 'Gracilis Aurea' is worthy of inclusion in the garden for its gold foliage and spreading, slow growing form. 4.5m (15ft) x 3m (10ft).

C. obtusa 'Kameini Hiba' makes a delightful small, irregular golden dome with both threadlike foliage and crested shoots. Tolerates sun fairly well without burning.

C. obtusa 'Keraldo' makes an irregular, spreading, broad shrub with foliage highlighted in pale yellow, similar to 'Crippsii'. Originated in the garden of Prince Wolkonsky at Keraldo, Brittany, France.

C. obtusa 'Lemon Twist' is a vigorous golden yellow variegated form with twisty, contorted foliage. Fairly fast grower.

C. obtusa 'Lenny's Star' is a dwarf with irregular tufted foliage showing golden in full sun. It has an upright habit ideal for a narrow border. Selected at Cedar Lodge. 80x40cm (32x16").

C. obtusa 'Little Marky' is a pale yellow, cone-shaped plant with small, flat sprays of foliage.

C. obtusa 'Lutea Nova' is similar to 'Crippsii' but more open growing with a lacier effect. Its bright yellow colouring is sensitive to sun when young. 2.4x2m (8x6ft).

C. obtusa 'Lycopodioides Aurea' has an open habit making an irregular rounded form. New foliage is twisted and fanned in bright gold throughout the year. 60cm (2ft).

C. obtusa 'Lynn's Gold' ('Golden Ceramic') is an upright growing pyramidal shape, very dwarf. New foliage is bright gold, holding well. Will resist burn even in full sun. Displays attractive purple hints in winter when it turns more orange-yellow. Slow.

C. obtusa 'Marian' forms an upright conical with cupped sprays of yellow foliage.

C. obtusa 'Marie's Gold' this golden sport comes from 'Mariesii' and has a dwarf, globose habit.

C. obtusa 'Meroke' is a Joe Reis selection made in 1960. It makes very narrow, upright, conical growth with a slight twist with good golden colouring in sun.

The tips really glow on this burn resist plant with conspicuous red stems. 1-1.5m (3-5ft).

C. obtusa 'Nana Aurea' is not to be confused with 'Aurea Nana', well, how confusing can it get??? This is not as gold, although many cannot tell the difference, this is probably because the plants have been sold under either name. Loose foliage, good for a rock garden. 50cm (20").

C. obtusa 'Nana Lutea' has bright gold foliage all year which is fairly sun-resist. It makes a compact, dwarf bush very slowly, which can be enhanced by pruning if desired. A sport of 'Nana Gracilis Aurea' raised in Holland in 1966. Growth rate can be increased by grafting at the expense of a little loss of compactness. It is slower growing than 'Nana Aurea'. 35cm (14").

C. obtusa 'Pygmaea Aurescens' makes a small spreading bush with loose sprays of yellow-bronze foliage at its best in winter. Sprays are arranged in flattened tiers on this sport of 'Pygmaea' which was found in Holland before 1939.

C. obtusa 'Regina Gold' makes a semi-dwarf with a pyramidal habit developing into a pagoda shape as it matures. Quick to establish with golden foliage.

C. obtusa 'South Shore' is a small form exhibiting tight, crested gold foliage in bright, golden yellow.

C. obtusa 'Sunspray' is a selection from New Zealand with gold tipped foliage on dense ferny sprays. An irregular upright with swirled foliage reaching 2.5m (8ft) in time.

C. obtusa 'Tetragona Aurea' has bright, moss-like sprays of gold foliage in full sun, greening in shade. Makes an irregular branched tree, angular in appearance. Associates well with heathers. This is a very colourful conifer, the winter effect is a variegated one of gold, yellow, cream, green and bronze. An old cultivar from Japan, introduced in 1870. 2x1m (6x3ft).

C. obtusa 'Verdoni' makes a dense, pyramidal landscape specimen in time. Its golden foliage is scorch-resist in any situation and it is a dependable choice for smaller gardens. Faster growing than many. 1.5x1m (5x3ft).

C. pisifera 'Aurea' bears young yellow foliage changing to soft green in summer. Introduced in 1861 from its native Japan by Robert Fortune.

C. pisifera 'Aurea Nana' is a slow-growing, dwarf, flat-topped, evergreen. Consistently rich yellow and eminently suitable for a rock garden to 1m (3ft).

C. pisifera 'Bright Gold' is a selection of gold threadleaf cypress similar to *'Golden Mop'* with very bright colouring and a dense, globose habit. Retains its colouring year round.

C. pisifera 'Filifera Aurea' has very attractive, slender, fine-textured foliage on drooping stems forming a pyramidal mound to ground level. Its striking foliage is best used as an accent plant, bearing in mind that it will burn in full sun. This attractive form with golden colouring usually needs an annual trim. Slowly makes a dense mound. 3m (10ft), in time capable of reaching 12m (40ft), spread of 4.5m (15ft).

C. pisifera 'Filifera Aurea Nana' produces pendulous, golden-tipped whip-like foliage and branches in a dwarf, irregular mound. This has a soft look and feel to it and is best in full sun. 90-120cm (3-4ft). Z4.

C. pisifera 'Gold Globe' makes a small golden globe.

C. pisifera 'Gold Spangle' is a threadleaf type, with good gold colour, sun resist, and a conical, upright habit with graceful, drooping branchlets. Sparkles,

Chamaecyparis obtusa 'Verdoni' below
Chamaecyparis pisifera 'Filifera Aurea' above

looking exceptionally good in winter. Its rounded habit makes it suitable for a rock garden or in the border. Tolerant of most soils. A sport of *'Filifera Aurea'*, remove any reverting shoots. 1m (3ft).

C. pisifera 'Gold Thread' is a brilliant yellow form which only turns green in deep shade. Neither does it burn in full sun. Branchlets have an attractive weeping habit. Eventually develops a central leader and reaches 1.8x1m (6x3ft).

C. pisifera 'Golden Mop' ('Mops') is a slow growing, golden, thread-leaved evergreen with long, trailing branches and stringy leaves, eventually reaching 90-120cm (3-4ft). The brightest gold of all, may burn in full sun. Makes a superb focal point in the garden.

C. pisifera 'Golden Pin Cushion' is a tiny, slow growing golden form making a spreading mound in full sun. Under 1m (3ft).

C. pisifera 'Goldilots' forms a conical shape but can be sheared to globose form. It remains gold all year round. Foliage has the texture of *C. obtusa*.

C. pisifera 'Juniperoides Aurea' makes a dense, globular dwarf with golden foliage which is green in summer. Gold and attractive in winter. 60cm (2ft).

C. pisifera 'Lemon Thread' the yellow-lemon thread-like foliage is graceful and drooping. Broadly conical in shape. Sensational in full sun, but avoid over-exposure in hot climates. Choice. A sport from Mitsch Nursery, Oregon in 1965. 1.2m (4ft).

C. pisifera 'Minima Aurea' has foliage with a golden sheen. A tight little cushion, originally from Vancouver, B.C. Needs full sun for best colour.

C. pisifera 'Plumosa Aurea' ('Gold Dust') is fast-growing with a bright gold colour at first fading to a soft yellow-green, stained bronze-yellow. Attractive feathery appearance which has instant appeal. Introduced by Robert Fortune in 1861.

C. pisifera 'Plumosa Aurea Compacta' slowly makes a dwarf, dense conical bush. Its soft yellow foliage is at its best in spring.

C. pisifera 'Plumosa Flavescens' slowly forms soft domes of juvenile foliage, with the pale sulphur colouring greening up in summer. Introduced around 1866 by Philip von Siebold. 1m (3ft).

C. pisifera 'Squarrosa Aurea' juvenile foliage persists on this yellow-tipped form, in contrast to the lime-green interior needles. Lovely soft texture appreciates protection from wind. Has an upright, broad habit which is best in sun to partial shade. 1-1.5m (3-5ft).

C. pisifera 'Squarrosa Aurea Nana' is a dwarf, slow-growing form of dense, compact habit with yellow foliage which pales in winter.

C. pisifera 'Squarrosa Lutea' has very bright yellow-white foliage at the tips in a compact habit with upright growth. Slightly denser foliage than 'Squarrosa Aurea'.

C. pisifera 'Squarrosa Sulphurea' makes a small to medium tree, broadly conical in habit. Sulphur yellow foliage is at its best in spring.

C. pisifera 'Strathmore' has yellow thread-like foliage, especially to the tip ends.

C. pisifera 'Sungold' bears thread-like foliage on a mop form which resists sun scorch even in full sun, but then it is not as bright as 'Golden Mop' as foliage matures to lime-green. Makes a semi-dwarf flat globe. Arrowhead Alpines (U.S.) claim this is indestructible. 60x60cm (24x24").

C. pisifera 'Tsukama' has young foliage which is yellow giving the effect of a yellow tipped shrub.

C. pisifera 'Vintage Gold' is no fools gold, but the real foliar variety of gold, all year round on a compact, slow-growing conifer in sun to part shade. 60cm (2ft).

C. thyoides 'Aurea' is from Belgium, dating from 1874. Its bright golden foliage turns bronze in winter. Makes a conical plant. Its loose and airy foliage benefits from pruning when young.

Hot Partner: *Cryptomeria 'Black Dragon', Chamaecyparis thyoides 'Heatherbun'.*

Cool Companions: *Picea pungens glauca*, heathers.

Chamaecyparis pisifera 'Golden Mops'

Chamaecyparis pisifera 'Strathmore'

CHOISYA

C. ternata, related to *Citrus* and found in Mexico and the very south-west of N. America, is cultivated for its leaves and orange blossoms, which are pitifully few on the golden-leaved cultivars. This evergreen shrub has leaves which are aromatic and is best against a wall or in a shrub border.

HOW TO GROW
Best in fertile, well drained soil in sun or part shade. Root semi-ripe cuttings in summer. Z7-11.

C. 'Goldfingers' (*Limo*) PBR (Peter Moore 1996) a promising golden cultivar after ten years of breeding work. Narrow, aromatic yellow foliage and infrequent white, fragrant flowers flushed pink on this aromatic evergreen. Foliage is of a softer yellow than *'Sundance'* which is one of its parents and leaves have narrower and shallower toothed leaflets. 1.5m (5ft).

C. ternata 'Sundance' (*Lich*, also known as *'Brica'* and *'Moonsleeper'* in Europe) PBR is, in my opinion, a very overrated plant, usually looks sickly, intended to be golden in sun, greening in shade. When grown well, I have seen this looking superb, its golden rounded foliage shining, but it so often looks chloritic or is placed in too much shade, where it turns green, that it is perhaps best avoided. Needs careful siting. Rarely flowers in anything but a warm, sunny site and needs protection in cold winters. Introduced by Blooms of Bressingham. 1.5-1.8m (5-6ft).
Hot Partner: *Clematis viticella 'Etoile Violette'*, *Cryptomeria*.
Cool Companion: *Ceanothus 'Blue Jeans'*, *Ruta graveolens 'Jackman's Blue'*, *Clematis eriostemon 'Blue Boy'*.
Golden Glory: *Rosa 'Maigold'*.

Choisya 'Goldfingers' left
Choisya ternata 'Sundance' below

CORNUS

Ornamental in so many ways, dogwoods or cornels are easy in cultivation. Valued for their foliage, flowers or bracts, attractive tree bark or colourful winter stems on shrubs with the onset of colder weather. They are all season plants with year round interest, looking excellent against a dark backdrop.

HOW TO GROW

Enjoy rich, moist soil, well-watered until established. Flowering dogwoods prefer fertile, humus-rich, well-drained, neutral to acid soil in sun to part shade. Others are tolerant of a wide range of soils and conditions. Root greenwood cuttings in summer or take hardwood cuttings of colourful winter stem types in autumn. Z2-10 depending on species.

C. alba 'Aurea' so rarely seen in gardens, yet so worthy of inclusion. Bears showy golden foliage followed by red tinged autumn colours and glowing red stems in winter. Plant this for season long interest. Hardy and tolerant of damp sites. Hard prune in late March for excellent red stem colour. Prefers sun, but is tolerant of shade where leaf colour will be greener. To get the benefit of both leaves and red winter stems, prune only a proportion of the stems each spring. Suitable for light well-drained soils as well as heavy clay. A true golden ray of sunshine when planted to catch the evening sun. Easy. 3x3m (10x10ft). Z4-9.

C. alba 'Spaethii' is another notable form of red-stemmed dogwood for its golden and green variegated leaves. All season shrub with wonderful winter coloration of stems. 2x2m (6x6ft).

C. alternifolia 'Golden Shadows' TM (W.Stackman) is a magnificent variegated shrub. The natural habit of Pagoda dogwood is a delight in itself. The horizontally tiered branches are enhanced by leaves with a broad lime central zone bleeding into a wide yellow margin. Best in moist, retentive soil that is well-drained in partial shade. 2-2.5m (6-8ft) tall and wide in 10 years. Z3-9.

C. controversa 'Janine' is a variegated form of giant dogwood. Leaves are brightly coloured yellow with a green centre on this fast growing tree. Large white flowers in May to June are followed by fruits which ripen to black in September. 13m (45ft).

C. florida 'Golden Nugget' has bronze gold yellow margins on its leaves with white flowers.

C. kousa 'Gold Cup' has a yellow centre to its leaves. White flowers. *C. kousa* flower later than *C. florida*.

C. kousa 'Gold Star' bears deep green leaves with a large central yellow blotch. In autumn the centre turns red and the margin purple. Chinese dogwood makes a slow-growing, large, elegant shrub with plentiful white flowers and rich autumn colouring. Takes 10 years to reach 6m (20ft). Z5-8.

C. kousa 'Sunsplash' the bright variegated gold and green leaves are the sunshine on this slow growing variety. Tolerates sun better than other variegated types. Dense, fairly upright growth. Medium-sized white flower bracts. Autumn colours of red and burgundy will blaze in low sunlight.

C. mas 'Aurea' is a yellow-leaved Cornelian cherry. Foliage emerges gold, looking bright throughout summer, but fading in heat. Flowers are yellow too, borne on naked twigs in February on this large shrub or small, densely branched tree. Bright red fruits are borne in midsummer. Exfoliating bark adds immense interest in winter. 6m (20ft). Z6-9.

C. nuttalii 'Gold Spot' is a very unusual form of mountain dogwood with leaves spotted and mottled yellow on mature leaves, which can be almost all gold by the end of summer. Not immune to anthracnose, but spectacular nevertheless. *'Eddiei'* is probably the same thing. Medium sized trees, they have yellow foliage in autumn sometimes flushed red. Flowering twice a year, most prolifically in summer with conspicuous white bracts.

C. sanguinea 'Winter Beauty' is worthy of mention for its bright orange-yellow shoots. Leaves are pale yellow-green in summer, turning orange-yellow in winter. This is a Dutch selection of the common hedgerow dogwood.

C. sericea 'Bud's Yellow' (*alba*) resembles the better known *'Flaviramea'* but is said to be more resistant to twig canker which causes unsightly brown patches on stems. Z5.

C. sericea 'Flaviramea' (*alba*) bears young shoots of yellow to olive-green and is a very effective winter plant, particularly when seen with the red-stemmed dogwoods. A good choice for moist or wet soils.

C. sericea 'Hedgerow Gold' (*alba*) was found on the Oregon and Washington border in the U.S. Young leaves have a yellow margin which turns creamy white. Keeps its variegation well in shade. Deep red stems. 1.5m (5ft).

C. sericea 'Rosco' (*stolonifera* or *sericea 'Kelsey Gold'*) has bright yellowish green leaves, bronze when young, spreads into a large clump. Red stemmed. 60-90cm (2-3ft). Z5-10.

C. sericea 'Sunshine' makes a large suckering shrub with yellow or yellow-margined leaves, lime in shade.

C. sericea 'White Gold' has white margined leaves with bright yellow stems, it is a white variegated form of *'Flaviramea'*.

Hot Partner: *Salvia guaranitica 'Black and Blue'*.
Cool Companion: Dark evergreens.

Corydalis flexuosa 'Golden Panda'

CORYDALIS

Grown for their delicate, fern-like foliage and fascinating flowers, *Corydalis* are hardly in need of any other attribute to bring them into the garden. Yet, here they are with gold leaves adding the perfect foil. The delicate look of both flower and foliage belie the hardiness of these superb plants. Enjoying cool climates where they can remain in flower, though normally thought of as summer dormant and highly valuable in the spring garden.

HOW TO GROW
Moist, fertile soil in sun to part shade. Divide *C. flexuosa* in autumn. Z5.

C. flexuosa 'Golden Panda' PPAF bears green spring leaves infused gold as they mature contrasting with slender, tubular, cobalt blue flowers held above the foliage. Preferring a summer cool climate in moist but well-drained soil. 20cm (10"). Z5.

C. scouleri 'Forest Angel' at almost 1.5 (5ft) high is impressive with its golden ferny, foliage. It spreads by underground rhizomes and is capable of covering a large area. The golden form of this U.S. native was found by Chuck Pavlich on a mountainside in Washington State, U.S.

COTINUS

Admirable hardy deciduous shrubs with season long interest and fabulous leaf colour. A very handsome golden shrub to add to the garden, you simply have to make room for this. Leaves will only scorch in extremely dry conditions, so keep this moist at the roots. Pruning is unnecessary except to encourage fresh new growth and larger leaves and does restrict the height of the plant.

HOW TO GROW
Well drained soil in full or part sun. Layer in spring or root softwood cuttings in summer and be patient.

C. **'Golden Spirit'** (*'Ancot'*) (Sanders) PBR forms a medium sized shrub covered in yellow rounded leaves throughout the summer. If soil is not too dry this will not burn in full sun. Having whitish pink plumes and autumn colours of coral, orange and red, this really earns a place in the garden. Raised in Holland. 2-2.5m (6-8ft). Z4/5-8.
Hot Partner: *Berberis 'Helmond Pillar', Physocarpus opulifolius 'Diablo', Rosa 'Robin Hood', Hypericum 'Albury Purple'.*
Cool Companion: *Geranium 'Nimbus'.*
Golden Glory: *Leycesteria formosa 'Golden Lantens'.*

Cryptomeria japonica 'Sekkan Sugi'

CRYPTOMERIA

Gold forms of *Cryptomeria* are very sought after. Thick, fibrous red-brown bark enhances leaf colour nicely and makes for effective accent plants. Can be successfully coppiced. Male and female strobili are borne on the same plants and cones mature the same year. Withstand strong winds and are reliably hardy, but do prefer a sheltered site.

HOW TO GROW
Easily cultivated, especially in moist, well drained soils, including chalk. Root ripewood cuttings in late summer or early autumn.

C. japonica **'Antique Gold'** is yellowish green in summer and antique gold in winter. It bears soft, juvenile foliage. Very adaptable and suitable for areas with high rainfall where soil is well-drained. Dislikes salt winds. 5.5x2.5 (16x8ft).
C. japonica **'Barabits Gold'** is an upright, weeping form with yellow foliage. 90cm-1.8m (3-6ft).
C. japonica **'Elegans Aurea'** will eventually make a small tree of elegant habit. Its green foliage turns more yellow in colder weather, and will only bronze in very cold weather. Erect, bushy habit.
C. japonica **'Golden Promise'** displays almost white young foliage and is very eye-catching in spring and summer. 50cm (20").
C. japonica **'Lemonade'** is a large specimen tree distinguished by lemon foliage. Colour is enhanced by colder weather. Quick growing. 7x2.5m (22x8ft).
C. japonica **'Sekkan-sugi'** is fairly slow-growing with plumose, creamy-yellow young foliage turning almost white in winter, showing well against darker, older foliage. Makes a graceful, medium sized tree of a very pale colouring. Quite unusual, distinct and yet easy to grow. Give afternoon shade in very hot areas, rarely burns. Upright oval shape.1.5-1.8m (5-6ft).
C. japonica **'Sekka-sugi v sinensis'** is conical when young becoming rounded with pendulous branches and yellow-green leaves.

x CUPRESSOCYPARIS

Hardy evergreen, coniferous trees, providing dense screening in a short time. The leyland cypress is the cause of many arguments with neighbours, arising from the size of the vigorous, fast-growing green types, left unpruned. 30m (100ft) makes for a lot of shade! Keep the shears handy. On poor soils a cutting can reach 15m (50ft) in 16 years. Golden forms are less vigorous and highly decorative. Growing conditions are similar to *Chamaecyparis*. Good for coastal areas and chalk soils.

HOW TO GROW
Appreciates sun and deep, well-drained soil, but is tolerant of part shade. Easy to transplant. Never cut into old wood when pruning. Trim hedges 2-3 times a season. Root semi-ripe cuttings in late summer. Has recently been renamed *x Cuprocyparis leylandii*. Z6.

x C. leylandii 'Castlewellan' (*'Galway Gold'*) produces sprays of pale yellow young foliage. Older foliage tends to bronze. Slower growing than green forms which are too vigorous for small gardens. Gold tones are most noticeable in spring, continuing into summer. A strong growing form in a free-draining position. Raised in 1962 at Castlewellan, Co. Down from *Cupressus macrocarpa 'Lutea'* and *Chamaecyparis nootkatensis 'Lutea'*. 5m (15ft). Z6.

x C. leylandii 'Golconda' (*'Gold Pride'*) has brilliant white-gold foliage on a slow growing cultivar. Broadly conical habit making a large shrub or small tree.

x C. leylandii 'Gold Rider' (van Gelderen) this Dutch introduction has bright yellow golden foliage retained on feathery sprays all year. Makes a slower growing hedge or useful as a single bush. 2m (6ft).

x C. leylandii 'Robinson's Gold' (*'Mellow Yellow'*) has bronze-yellow foliage in spring, maturing to golden-yellow and lime-green. Full sun and moist, well-drained soil. This seedling was raised at Belvoir Castle. Co. Down in 1962 and represents a better golden form than *'Castlewellan'*.12m (40ft). Z5.

CUPRESSUS

Not quite as hardy as the false cypress, *Chamaecyparis*, needing shelter from cold winds. These evergreen conifers are well known for their easy-to-recognise, conical habit. Male and female strobili are borne on the same tree, globular cones mature in their second year, remaining on branches for several years. They dislike transplanting in open ground, so are better pot grown. Also dislike being clipped and never recover if cut back to old wood.

HOW TO GROW
Tolerant of many conditions with the exception of wet soils, much preferring dry soils. Several species will grow on chalk. Root semi-ripe cuttings in late summer. Z7-10.

C. arizonica v glabra 'Aurea' makes a broadly conical tree handsomely suffused with yellow during summer, paling into autumn and winter. Originated in Australia.

C. arizonica v glabra 'Golden Pyramid' this slow grower makes loose, bushy pyramidal growth with dull yellow colouring especially at leaf tips. Shear to keep in a neat column. Best in full sun. 4x2m (12x6ft). Z7-8.

C. arizonica v glabra 'Lutea' is not the darkest, but has pale lemon colouring to the ends of its branches.

C. macrocarpa, the Monterey cypress native to just two groves in the Monterey Bay, California where it is almost extinct, is useful for hegding or screening, affording privacy to the garden. Excellent specimen trees, tolerant of dry conditions in sandy soils. Best in full sun. In windswept coastal areas it develops irregular, contorted shapes. Hardy. Z7.

C. macrocarpa 'Aurea' is a vigorous broadly conical tree with long, golden spikes of foliage spreading almost as horizontal as tall.

C. macrocarpa 'Aurea Saligna' has elongated foliage on weeping, horizontal branches tipped in gold. Fast growing to start. Low growing to 1.2x1.3m (4x4ft). Z7.

C. macrocarpa 'Brunniana' is somewhat columnar with bright yellow colour fading to green, retained better in sun. Will tolerate dry sites. Trim only lightly. Not as wide as other golden *macrocarpa*. 5m (10ft).

C. macrocarpa 'Conybeareii Aurea' is a small, wide-spreading tree with a loose conical habit, bearing drooping branches with yellow or yellowish green branchlets. Similar to *Chamaecyparis pisifera 'Filifera Aurea'* in habit, raised in Australia.

C. macrocarpa 'Crippsii' ('*Sulphurea*') has stiffly spreading, horizontal branches with short, stiff branchlets, creamy yellow at the tips when young.

C. macrocarpa 'Donard Gold' came from Slieve Donard Nursery in 1935 as an improvement on '*Lutea*'. Its rich, deep yellow foliage clothes a medium-sized, conical tree. A lovely upright fast-growing form which is best in sun. 3-5m (10-15ft).

C. macrocarpa 'Dudley' is a sport found in New Zealand with finer foliage than other *macrocarpa*. Deep yellow burns in sun, in semi-shade it is pale gold to bright yellow. 6x1.5m (20x5ft).

C. macrocarpa 'Fine Gold' is a fast growing specimen with bright yellow foliage in sun. 8mx5m (25x16ft).

C. macrocarpa 'Gold Spread' is highly ornamental with bright golden foliage spreading across its compact form without a central leader. An excellent golden ground cover in all but the coldest areas. Suitable for coastal areas. Raised in Australia in 1950. 1x3m (3x10ft).

C. macrocarpa 'Goldcrest' is narrowly conical with dense, feathery juvenile, gold to lime green foliage. Suitable for coastal areas. A desirable lawn specimen with irregular but upright stately growth. Can even be grown indoors as a pot plant given sufficient bright light. Excellent as a screen. A superb golden form from Treseder of Truro in 1948. 5m (16ft) tall and 2.5m (8ft) wide.

C. macrocarpa 'Golden Cone' makes a dense, conical tree with golden foliage.

C. macrocarpa 'Golden Pillar' makes an upright, narrowly conical golden small tree which is highly attractive. Suitable for coastal areas. This bright golden yellow form was raised in Holland before 1950. Compact form for all but the smallest of gardens. 3mx1.5m (10x5ft).

C. macrocarpa 'Horizontalis Aurea' ('*Lambertiana Aurea*') is an exceptional bright yellow form. 5x3m (16x10ft).

C. macrocarpa 'Lutea' has soft gold foliage becoming green on a tall, conical habit. Makes a good hedge when clipped. Can grow to 24m (80ft).

C. macrocarpa 'Sunshine' is a semi weeping, fast growing form with bright yellow foliage all year round. Makes an attractive large tree. 7x4m (20x13ft).

C. sempervirens 'Swane's Gold' is narrowly upright making a tall, slender column with pale yellow or greenish yellow foliage in some shade. An attractive Australian cultivar which originated in 1944 at the Swane's Nursery in Sydney. A seedling variant from *C. sempervirens 'Stricta'*. It needs protection when young and full sun all day to retain its best colouring. Makes a good golden vertical accent and is an excellent choice for small gardens. Also perfect for a container. A favourite with me. 3m (10ft) and just 50cm (20") wide. Z7.

C. torulosa 'Aurea' is an open, semi weeping form with bright golden foliage. Attractive. The Kashmir golden cypress is not hardy and in frost-prone areas can be grown under glass. 3.5x2m (11x6ft).

Hot Companion: *Tulipa 'Queen of Night'*, *Solenostemon 'Merlot'*.

Cupressus arizonica v glabra 'Lutea'

75

DESCHAMPSIA

Wonderful hardy grasses with golden, airy panicles which mix easily into the border or a wildflower garden. Grow in dry to damp, neutral to acid soil in sun or partial shade. The fine texture needs to be appreciated against a dark backdrop, but hair grass has uses in the border, rock garden, by the edge of water, and in containers. With ample moisture will tolerate hot, dry conditions. Seedheads can be left on the plants in winter and are useful for dried flower arrangements. Bring movement to the garden in the slightest breeze. Low maintenance.

HOW TO GROW
Grow in dry to damp, neutral to acid soil in sun or partial shade. Divide in mid spring or early summer. Z4.

D. cespitosa 'Goldgehaenge' (*'Gold Shower', 'Gold Pendant'*) is often seen in the U.S. and is making its way into select catalogues in England. Its golden panicles are stupendous against the darkish green leaves. Inflorescences are weeping and look superb in the breeze. Best in shade to part shade.1.2m (4ft).

D. cespitosa 'Goldschleier' (*'Golden Veil'*) has dark green leaves with airy panicles ageing to bright shimmering yellow. 1.2m (4ft).

D. cespitosa 'Goldstaub' (*'Gold Dust'*) is a shorter variety with large, golden panicles. 30-60cm (1-2ft).

D. cespitosa 'Goldtau' (*'Golden Dew'*) is a compact form with silvery reddish brown spikelets ageing to golden yellow. Fine textured, dark green foliage. From Germany, this selection blooms two weeks later than most other cultivars. 75cm (30").

D. flexuosa 'Tatra Gold' (*'Aurea'*) has arching bright yellow-green, thread-like leaves and golden bronze tinted panicles which shimmer in the evening light in midsummer. Prefers acid soil. Gold dust drifting in the breeze! 50x20cm (20x8").

Hot Partner: *Bergenia purpurascens, Ligularia 'Britt-Marie Crawford', Helleborus 'Queen of Night', Viola 'Bowles' Black'*.

Cool Companion: *Hosta 'Pineapple Upside Down Cake'*.

Deschampsia 'Tatra Gold'

DEUTZIA

This is one of the most fantastic recent introductions of gold-leaved shrubs, an incredible colour breakthrough. *D. gracilis* make bushy shrubs with attractive tapered leaves. Hardy, elegant and easy to grow. Plant this now!

HOW TO GROW
Reasonably fertile, not too dry soil, preferably in sun, although can tolerate some shade. Softwood cuttings in summer, hardwood cuttings in autumn.

D. 'Chardonnay Pearls' (*gracilis 'Seward'*) PPAF, CPAF (Wood, USA) has vibrant, sunshine bright gold leaves which are burn resist. Perfect in full sun to part shade. Adaptable as to soil, needing moderate moisture. Growth is strong and compact on this wonderful shrub. This is so elegant, so cool. Numerous white pearl like buds burst into star-shaped flowers in spring. Adds season long colour. See it and want it, I fell in love with this at first sight. Easy to grow. 90cm (3ft). Z5-7.
Hot Partner: Purple low groundcover.
Cool Companion: Blue, white echoes.

DICENTRA

Long a garden favourite, the golden form of *Dicentra spectabilis* was selected by Sandra and Nori Pope of Hadspen House and Gardens, U.K. Such fabulous flowers should be grown in any garden, add gold leaves with the same fern-like grace as the species and you have a real winner. Plant amongst later developing shrubs which will fill the gap left by this summer dormant perennial. Excellent in moist woodland and equally stunning in the border.

HOW TO GROW
Dies back earlier in dry soils, but is tolerant of sun in moist soil. Intolerant of wet in winter. Early growth can be damaged by frosts. Divide in early spring or after leaves have died down. Take root cuttings in winter. Z3-9.

D. spectabilis 'Goldheart' PPAF PVR is a superb combination of dancing pink hearts and yellow, ferny leaves in spring and all summer. A little shade is required to avoid scorching. This has deservedly proved a very poular recent introduction. 90cm (3ft).
Companions: *Tulipa* in white, pink or black.

DIOSMA

Evergreen, heath-like shrubs related to *Coleonema*, natives of South Africa. Excellent rock garden plants. Drought and wind tolerant, providing easy year round colour in a sunny spot. Planted widely in New Zealand. Of interest as a flowering shrub and as a foliage plant providing bold ground cover. Has a myriad of uses, prominently placed on a bank, in a patio pot, as a low hedge or clipped into a ball.

HOW TO GROW

Best in full sun in well-drained soil. Tolerant of drought and heat. If it begins to drop its leaves it is too dry.

D. ericoides 'Sunset Gold' (*Coleonema pulchrum 'Sunset Gold'*) bears vibrant yellow foliage and tiny pink flowers on a dwarf shrub with densely arranged leaves in spring and summer. Foliage is scented when touched. Summer long and into autumn its prominent attraction is its golden foliage. In winter there is apple green foliage and from early spring a profusion of tiny pink flowers. Forms a rounded mound which is easily clipped to shape. 60cmx1.2m (2x4ft).
Hot Partner: *Aeonium 'Schwarzkopf'*, let it come through the ground cover. Edge with dark succulents such as *Sempervivum 'Black Mountain'* or *Jovibarba 'Chocoleto'*.
Cool Companion: *Agapanthus 'Black Pantha'* or *'Bressingham Blue'*.

EPIPREMNUM

Pothos is a climber native to the Solomon islands. In forests it scrambles up trees. Also known as Devil's ivy. A large climbing aroid of immense proportions and the ability to spread itself around. Adult plants are quite vigorous and send out aerial roots. Z10.

HOW TO GROW

Under glass in full or filtered light. Outdoors in fertile, well-drained soil in full sun or partial shade. Tip prune in spring to promote branching.

E. pinnatum 'Aureum' has many synonyms. Golden pothos, also known as centipede tongavine or golden philodendron is an attractive, scandent vine with golden lance-like leaves creating a tumbling display from a large basket, but more usually used to scramble up other plants. Easily grown. Leaves to 60cm (24") long. Erect cream spathes can sometimes appear but soon wither. Listed as an invasive weed in Florida.10m (30ft).
E. aureum 'Hawaiian' is golden leaved with better substance.
E. radicans 'Variegatum' bears leaves striped with yellow and cream. In good light this will produce clusters of carmine flowers.

ERICA

Popular for their year round colour. Most *carnea* types lose their golden foliage in cold weather, turning orange. I have attempted to list those that retain their golden colour well. Many heaths have yellow-tipped foliage in spring and summer. *E. arborea* cultivars can be pruned hard during April. Hardy species make good ground cover. Best with some afternoon shade in hot climates. Z6-8.

HOW TO GROW
Lime haters thrive in acid soil, especially well-drained, sandy soils. They flower best in full sun, although tolerant of some shade. Some winter flowering species and cultivars such as *E. carnea, E. erigena, E.terminalis* and *E. x darleyensis* will grow in lime soils. Prune after flowering. Root semi-ripe cuttings in mid to late summer. Mound layer in spring.

E. arborea 'Albert's Gold' (*'Arnold's Gold'*) bears dazzling, golden foliage but rarely produces its white flowers in spring. Upright, vigorous tree heather forming a large shrub to 2m (6ft).

E. alpina 'Estrella Gold' is a very hardy form with bright yellow young foliage making a small shrub. Recommended by Lichen of Paintbox Plants for keeping its colour well in winter.

E. carnea 'Aurea' has bright gold foliage particularly in spring but also into summer with deep pink flowers, paling to almost white.

E. carnea 'Barry Sellers' has yellow foliage which turns orange in cold weather with deep pink flowers which mature to magenta. 30cm (12").

E. carnea 'Foxhollow' I have grown for years and it is a plant I would take with me to a new garden. It makes an easy mound of yellowish-green foliage, becoming yellow tinged red in winter with a profusion of pink flowers.

E. carnea 'Golden Lady' admired by friend, Lichen of Paintbox Plants, California. Keeps its colour well on a low, compact form with white flowers. 30cm (12").

E. carnea 'Golden Starlet' has bright yellow foliage in winter, more lime in summer with white flowers.

E. carnea 'Westwood Yellow' is fairly upright and compact in growth, displaying yellow foliage and shell-pink flowers. 30cm (12").

E. ciliaris 'Aurea' has straw-yellow foliage in summer, deepening in winter. 25cm (10").

E. cinerea 'Celebration' has prostrate foliage of a deep gold during summer and autumn, becoming lime green in winter with white flowers.

E. cinerea 'Golden Hue' bears pale yellow foliage tipped orange-red in winter with amethyst flowers. 35cm (14") and spreading to twice as wide.

E. x darleyensis 'Jack H. Brummage' has pale golden foliage, tinged red in winter with deep pink flowers on short spikes. 30cm (12").

E. erigena 'Golden Lady' has bright golden yellow foliage but watch for wind burn. White flowers are produced on this compact plant. 30cm (12").

E. x griffithsii 'Valerie Griffiths' is a bushy, upright plant with yellow foliage in summer turning golden-yellow in winter with pale pink flowers. 45cm (18").

E. lusitanica 'George Hunt' has bright yellow leaves, requiring a sheltered site. Will succumb to frost. A tree heath which is earlier flowering than *E. arborea*.

E. vagans 'Valerie Proudley' bears bright yellow foliage and white flowers on long sprays in July to October. 15cm (6") making a dwarf, dense bush.

Hot Partner: *Cornus alba 'Kesselringii', Imperata cylindrica 'Rubra'*.

Cool Companion: *Liriope muscari* and *Hebe pinguifolia 'Pagei'* with blue *Picea pungens glauca*.

Golden Glory: *Cornus stolonifera 'Flaviramea'*.

Erica carnea 'Foxhollow'

FAGUS

Noble trees excellent in landscape. I am very partial to purple beech and the golden forms hit the same note. They have the same delicacy found in the purple forms. Best colour is found in spring.

HOW TO GROW
Suitable for any well-drained soil and notable for tolerance of acidity or alkilinity in its extremes and will thrive in exposed sites. Z4.

F. sylvatica 'Aurea Pendula' is a stiffly weeping tree of slender, elegant growth, the same in form as *'Pendula'*, bearing golden yellow leaves that scorch in full sun and are apt to lose their rich colour in deep shade. Very slow growing, making a dwarf tree with branches hanging almost parallel with the main stem. There is an outstanding specimen at the Trompenburg Arboretum in Holland. Originated as a sport around 1900. 12x1.5m (40ft by 5ft wide).

F. sylvatica 'Dawyck Gold' bears new leaves suffused with gold, fading to green in summer. A second flush of new growth makes a delightful contrast. Its habit is like *'Dawyck'*, slender and fastigiate with dense foliage, and the colouring is similar to its other parent, *'Zlatia'*. Since it greens up, this does not need to be grown in shade and makes a fantastic vertical accent. Raised by J.R.P. van Hoey-Smith in 1969. There is a fine specimen at the Sir Harold Hillier Gardens and Arboretum which has reached 14m (2000). 15x1m (45x3ft). Z4.

F. sylvatica 'Luteovariegata' (*'Aureovariegata'*) has leaves variegated yellow with light gold margins which sometimes bleed into the central green area. The yellow fades as summer progesses.

F. sylvatica 'Rohan Gold' is a very attractive fern-leaf beech with gold-green foliage, young gold colour contrasts with the lime green mature leaves. Similar to *'Rohanii'* but much more vigorous. Exceptionally beautiful tree. Raised in 1970 by J.R.P. van Hoey-Smith. 3x1m (10x3ft).

F. sylvatica 'Zlatia' has young yellow leaves slowly turning green. Slow growing with a conical habit. Originated in Yugoslavia, the name comes from the Serbian for gold, this form having been introduced into horticulture by Professor Dragasevic in the early 1890's. 15m (45ft).

FALLOPIA

Mile a Minute plant is not everyone's idea of a desirable hardy climber, rampacious as it is. But if that rampant climber were golden leaved, would that make it more bearable? Needs a strong, durable support. Do remember to prune in early spring.

HOW TO GROW
Poor to moderately fertile soil, moist but well-drained in full sun to partial shade. Take heeled, semi-ripe cuttings in summer or hardwood cuttings in autumn.

F. baldschuanica 'Summer Sunshine' (*'Acofal'*) (*Polygonum*) (Paul Hutchinson) PBR discovered as a sport, this Russian Vine has bright red stems and attractive golden, heart-shaped leaves, holding their colour well. Bears creamy white to pink tinged flowers in summer and autumn. Ideal for covering fences and walls quickly and attractively.

It will usually smother any partner and is best used to cover an unsightly wall or area. A deciduous climber so there is no winter growth. Could be teamed with winter jasmine which will provide golden colour when the vigorous Russian Vine is taking a well earned rest.

FESTUCA

Grasses are finally getting the appreciation they deserve, thanks to superb cultivars such as this. Fescues are normally known for the excellent range of blue grasses, however, this is a fine, golden example for well drained soil in sun. Its tufted, bright leaves are perfect for the edge of woodland, and by stream margins in temperate areas. Provides great contrast with alpines in the rock garden.

HOW TO GROW
Moderately fertile, dry, well-drained soil in full sun. Divide and replant every 2-3 years in spring. Z4.

F. glauca 'Golden Toupee' is a fantastic hardy golden grass, put it to use in a rock garden or at the front of the border. Its spiky, golden-yellow foliage is a pleasure year round. It is a great 'hair-do' plant for containers. Also highly suitable for mass plantings. Best colour in summer. 30cmx20cm (12x8").
Hot Partner: *Imperata cylindrica 'Rubra'*.
Cool Companion: *Festuca glauca 'Elijah Blue'*.

FILIPENDULA

A hardy, clump-forming, perennial shrub keeping its colouring best in light shade. Attractive strongly-veined, pinnate leaves on this admirable woodlander. Bears dense corymbs of fluffy whitish flowers in summer. Golden-leaved meadowsweet thrives in boggy conditions where it will provide a useful bright accent, especially in spring. Superb in a moist woodland setting.

HOW TO GROW
A moisture lover suited to the waterside in full sun or partial shade. Likes moderately fertile, leafy soil. Divide in autumn or spring. Take root cuttings from late winter to early spring. Z3-8.

F. ulmaria 'Aurea' is best in partial shade where it will truly shine. Outstanding colour on deeply dissected, deeply veined leaves. Keep extremely moist and this perennial will exhibit best colouring in spring. White flowers in summer, remove flowerheads and as soon as flowering has finished cut down to the ground for an autumn show. 90cm (3ft). Hardy to -30°F (-35°C).
F. ulmaria 'Variegata' has a central splash of gold.
Hot Partner: *Hydrangea serrata 'Preziosa', Geranium phaeum 'Lily Lovell'.*
Cool Companion: *Lythrum salicaria, Lysimachia clethroides, Miscanthus sinesis 'Gracillimus'.*
Golden Glory: *Geranium phaeum 'Golden Spring', Corydalis flexuosa 'Golden Panda'.*

Filipendula ulmaria 'Aurea'

FORSYTHIA

Recent breeding programmes have brought us not just improved flowering shrubs, but gold leaved ones too. Once only valued for their bright early spring flower colour, winter jasmine can now also be used for their golden leaves. The bright flowers are carried on naked twigs. Useful for hedging.

HOW TO GROW

These hardy, deciduous shrubs are adaptable to many soils and easily transplanted. Tolerant of part shade, although full sun is best. They withstand urban conditions, so make an excellent town garden shrub. Easy on maintenance, prune immediately after flowering if necessary. Root greenwood cuttings in late spring or early summer, or semi-ripe cuttings in late summer. Flower buds can be damaged in Z5, although the plant will survive. Z5-9.

Below: Forsythia 'Fiesta'
Right: Forsythia koreana 'Suwon Gold'

F. 'Fiesta' has bright gold variegated leaves edged in green and a reddish tinge to the new stems. The gold leaf colour remains even in sun. It has the disadvantage of being shy-flowering. Originated with Duncan and Davies, New Zealand. 1.2m (up to 4ft).

F. x intermedia 'Evergold' bears gold leaves which are retained all season long.

F. x intermedia 'Goldleaf' maintains its bright gold leaves all season. Leaves emerge lime, quickly changing to gold even in part shade. A strong grower in woodland, where its golden leaves brighten every corner all season long. The golden flowers in spring become secondary. 1.5m (5ft).

F. x intermedia 'Golden Times' bears bright yellow young leaves which later become green in the centre with creamy-white margins whilst some leaves remain all yellow. Shy-flowering variety can scorch in sun.

F. koreana 'All Gold' is a sport from *'Ilgwang'*. Its leaves are uniformly gold. 1.5m (5ft).

F. koreana 'Suwon Gold' is another gold leaf cultivar.
Golden Glory: *Corylopsis pauciflora, Ilex 'Milkboy', Euonymus 'Blondy', Symphytum 'Axminster Gold'*.

FRAGARIA

These stoloniferous perennials, normally spreading by runners are well known for their delicious fruits - strawberries. Excellent in the herb border, container or hanging basket, a colourful addition to the potager or patio.

HOW TO GROW
Grow in fertile, moist but well-drained soil.

F. **'Golden Alexandria'** is an ornamental, runnerless alpine strawberry having bright gold leaves and small white flowers with the usual tasty small fruits all summer long. Kept anything but dry, the leaves will not scorch and colour is better and brighter in good sun. Excellent container and patio plant. Edible plants are always most welcome in the garden. Developed by Mike Tristram of Binsted Nursery, Sussex.

Fuchsia magellanica 'Aurea'

FUCHSIA

Wonderful hardy shrubs, and the tender, basket types are perhaps even more attractive in their way. *F. magellanica* is the hardiest species. Valued for both foliage and flower. The hardy types need sun to flower well, but make handsome foliage shrubs in shade.

HOW TO GROW
Enjoy good, deep fertile soil. Plant deep especially in frost-prone areas, and it behaves like a herbaceous perennial. Best colour in full sun. Above 4°C (39°F) fuchsia are capable of remaining evergreen. Provide a deep winter mulch. Cut back to the base in frost-prone areas. Root softwood cuttings in spring, semi-ripe cuttings in late summer with bottom heat. Z7-10.

F. **'Genii'** has attractive, burnished, golden leaves highlighted by red stems, bearing small red and purple flowers in single tubes. In light shade and full sun, this dwarf hardy hybrid, usually grown for its foliage effect really shines especially when fresh or in summer, fading to green in autumn. Excellent in a container, or in light shade. Almost hardy. 50cm.

F. **magellanica v gracilis 'Aurea'** is a vigorous shrub with golden-yellow foliage. Avoid excessive heat and sun. Blooms from late spring to first frosts in full sun. Most probably the same as above.

F. **magellanica v molinae 'Sharpitor Aurea'** (1974) is brightly variegated with gold and soft green with pale pink flowers. Vigorous even in dense shade where it is an effective brightener. Slow growing, late flowering variety with profuse blooms. 90cm (3ft).

F. **magellanica v molinae 'Enstone Gold'** (Dawson 1986) bears single flowers with the tube tinged green, whitish pink sepals and palest lilac corolla against variegated green and gold foliage. 120cm (4ft).

Tender basket types include **'Golden Herald'**, **'Golden Marinka'** and **'Golden Treasure'**.

Hot Partner: *Dahlia 'Arabian Night'*, *Petunia*, *Verbena bonariensis*, *Phormium 'Dusky Chief'*.

Golden Glory: *Hakonochloa m. 'Aureola'*, *Milium*.

GERANIUM

You would think that with the number of cranesbill cultivars that abound, there would be more with golden leaves, and I had to put my golden nose to the ground to find most of these, as only the first two are well-known. These handsome herbaceous perennials in leaf and flower, add a splash of light to the border. Favourites with many people and rightly so. Margery Fish was not joking when she said, 'if in doubt, plant a Geranium'. They merge into any scheme and offer long season interest without troubling the gardener for too much attention. The following are easy to grow in the border, easy maintenance.

HOW TO GROW

Moderately well-drained soil in full sun or partial shade. Most soils are tolerated except boggy areas. Removing old stems and leaves encourages a second flush. Divide in spring. Take basal cuttings in spring and root with bottom heat.

Geranium 'Anne Thompson' above
G. 'Ann Folkard' bottom left

G. 'Ann Folkard' bears yellow leaves, greening with age, with purple magenta flowers having a central black blotch. Use the rangy, lax stems to best advantage by growing through other plants. I grow it over purple and pink flowered hebe where it blends well. A good performer in full sun or part shade, floriferous from May to November. On this and the one below, I go for the flowers rather than the gold foliage. 30x1.5m (12x60"). Z5-9.

G. 'Anne Thompson' (Alan Bremner) the breeder must have had a desire to contain the lax stems, because this is a neater yellow-leaved hybrid, with similar shocking magenta flowers. Very heat tolerant in sun to light shade, performing in southern California. Reputedly slightly hardier than its parent. 30x90cm (12x36"). Z4-8a.

G. 'Blue Sunrise' PPAF (Hans Kramer) is also known as 'Verguld Saffier', bred in Holland, this is a wonderful hybrid from 'Buxton's Variety' and 'Ann Folkard'. Its golden foliage is topped by blue flowers with a white eye and it appears to be the most compact form. Becomes greener. 30x45cm (12x18"). Z5.

G. 'Catforth Cadenza' is a golden-variegated leaved *pratense* type which arose as a chance seedling at Catforth Gardens. Bright gold and green leaves emerge in spring, fading but retaining some variegation. Typical blue flowers.

G. maculatum 'Heronswood Gold' has golden leaves which hold their colour all season. 30x40cm (12x16"). Z5.

G. x monacense 'Claudine Dupont' has yellow spring foliage, fading by summer.

G. x oxonianum 'Spring Fling' PVR is spectacularly variegated in spring with leaves of yellow, cream and green with a pink-red internodal flush. Colour fades by summer, but is certainly a delight in spring. Pink flowers are borne in May to October. One of the neatest plants of this type. 35cm (14").

G. phaeum 'Golden Spring' from Robin Moss and Judith Bradshaw, National Collection holders in the U.K. has pale gold foliage in spring that fades quite quickly to a more typical *phaeum* leaf. Maroon flowers. 45x50cm (18x20"). Z2-3.

G. phaeum 'Mrs. Withey Price' from Jerry Flintoff has a nice golden flush to the young leaves which become mid-green with small red blotches. Reflexed flowers are mid lilac with a mauve ring. 45x60cm (18x24"). Z2-3.

G. phaeum 'Ring of Fire' bright yellow spring foliage is highlighted by a central ring of fiery red dots. In mid-late spring, deep pink reflexed petalled flowers sit atop the foliage. Best in light shade, looks tarnished in sun. Turns greenish yellow in summer. Josh McCullough spotted the sport at Heronswood Nursery, U.S.
Hot Partner: *Heuchera 'Velvet Night', Salvia officinalis 'Purpurascens', Viola 'Molly Sanderson'.*
Cool Companion: *Kniphofia 'Little Maid'* in sun.
Golden Glory: *Euphorbia 'Lambrook Gold'.*

GLEDITSIA

Excellent for town and city gardens, the honey locust is tolerant of atmospheric pollution and poor soils. Valued for their delightful, pinnate foliage and in the honey locusts this can be magnificently golden.

HOW TO GROW
Grow in full sun in fertile, well-drained soil with shelter from winds in spring and early frost. Bud in summer or graft in late winter. Fully hardy. Z3-10.

G. triacanthos 'Sunburst' (*G.t. 'Inermis Aurea'*) makes a quick-growing, elegant, thornless, specimen tree with good burnt gold foliage in spring. In summer the foliage turns lime green providing good contrast between young and older foliage, before a final blaze of yellow to end the season. Bears distinctive horizontal, zigzag branches. The usual long brown pods of the species are not produced on this small to medium, mop-headed tree. This fast growing tree is best in sun and foliage looks best in spring, when opening leaves unfurl on bare branches. It can defoliate easily in drought or temperature changes. Introduced in 1957, and still deservedly very popular. 12m (40ft), spread 10m (30ft).
G. triacanthos 'Skyline' and *G. t. 'Stevens'* turn golden yellow in autumn.

Hakonechloa macra 'Aureola' and Plectranthus

HAKONECHLOA

Deciduous, clump-forming grasses. Use for the beautiful effect of movement in the slightest breeze in containers or the border or the edge of woodland. Slow to establish, but worth every effort. Cascading foliage has the waterfall effect and is very graceful. Grow it with virtually everything, these fine grasses are superb in pots, and are equally at home at the front of the border. They seem to be the perfect companion plant.

HOW TO GROW

A hardy woodland grass from Japan which tolerates sun or partial shade and requires humus rich, moist, well-drained soil. Best variegation is usually found in partial shade. Z5-10.

H. macra 'Alba Aurea' is a delicious variegation of green, yellow and white. Z5.

H. macra 'All Gold' bears incredible, golden upright, spiky foliage looking excellent in containers. This will be even more planted than the very popular form below. 20cm (10"). Z6.

H. macra 'Aureola' has brilliant yellow, bamboo-like foliage spreading slowly in a mounded form which is superb in so many situations, but best in partial shade. Foliage is often red flushed in autumn. Adorns the garden with its graceful, cascading form. 30cm (12"). Z5.

Hot Partner: *Bergenia cordifolia 'Purpurascens'*, *Lychnis x arkwrightii 'Vesuvius'*.

Cool Companion: *Hosta tardiflora*, *Corydalis flexuosa*.

Top: H. macra 'Alba Aurea'
Centre: H. macra 'All Gold'
Bottom: H. macra 'Aureola'

HEBE

First rate ornamental, evergreen garden shrubs, include a golden cultivar with the appearance of a conifer, which is frost hardy. Wonderful in the mixed border or rock garden. Invaluable for seaside plantings as hedging. They make good container plants too and are pollution tolerant.

HOW TO GROW

Mainly from New Zealand, they succeed in any well-drained site in neutral to slightly alkaline soil. Sun or partial shade with shelter from cold, drying winds. Z6

H. 'Karo Golden Esk' is a dwarf whipcord hebe with yellow-green to golden foliage. This was a naturally occurring hybrid found by Dr. Brian Molloy on a tributary of the River Esk, Canterbury, New Zealand. 80cm (32").

Hebe ochracea 'James Stirling'

Hebe 'Katrine' is a creamy-yellow variegated variety.
H. ochracea is a dwarf, densely branched shrub with the unusual colouring of old gold. From the mountains of the South Island in New Zealand, it is often found labelled as *H. armstrongii*, which has greener branches and pointed leaves. White flowers appear in July and August.
H. ochracea 'James Sterling' is a dwarf, compact form with rich ochre-yellow leaves, looking good in winter, but never with the elegance and grace of the typical form. Stout branches are best left unpruned. Smallish white flowers are rarely seen in cultivation. Looks like a conifer. 45cm (18") and a spread of 60cm (24").
H. odora 'New Zealand Gold' is a form whose young growths are tipped bright yellow to contrast with the green leaves and white flowers.
Hot Partner: *Helenium, Helianthemum.*
Cool Companion: *Salvia officinalis 'Icterina'.*
Golden Glory: *Hypericum 'Summer Gold', Juniperus communis 'Depressa Aurea'.*

HEDERA

Yellow leaves can scorch in full sun, yet sun brings out the best colouring on variegated ivies, so choose a north-facing aspect. Gold ivies tend to be more slow growing. I really like the gold-leaved 'Buttercup', but most of the golden cultivars are variegated.

HOW TO GROW

Thrive best in lime soils. Variegated types grown in acid soil are not as pronounced and throw up green shoots. For climbing types, once anchored to a wall they take off quickly, anchoring takes around a year. Well watered sites best, tolerate average to dry in moderately fertile soil.

H. helix 'Amberwaves' bears 5 lobed yellow leaves with a dense overlapping habit. Raised by Russell Wendell in the U.S. Holds its yellow colouring better in shade than many other cultivars of this colouring. Self branching.

H. helix 'Angularis Aurea' is a gold ivy with variegation not showing in young plants. A large climber with glossy leaves, unsuitable as groundcover.

H. helix 'Buttercup' (known as *'Golden Cloud'* in Europe) is my personal favourite, a superb golden ivy. Allow its 5-lobed large leaves to climb a wall in sun to bring out the best colouring, as shade ground cover it will not shine at all. Some shoots are green and these, rather than gold, root easily when propagating this variety. A slow-growing ivy. Will not burn in a Midwest U.S. winter. 1.8m (6ft).

H. helix 'California Gold' has green and yellow leaves which are blotched and speckled.

H. helix 'Flavescens' bears uniform yellow leaves at first marked with green veins, then becoming greenish. Slow growing, small heart-shaped leaves.

H. helix 'Goldchild' has a golden margin when young and is suitable outside on low walls but performs better as a houseplant ivy. A sport of *'Chicago'*.

H. helix 'Goldcraft' bears yellow leaves with a green splash in the centre. Good in pots. Z8, possibly 7.

H. helix 'Goldstern' (*'Goldfinger'*) has variegated gold, five-lobed leaves with a dense habit.

H. helix 'Goldheart' (*'Oro di Bogliasco'* but better known by its synonym, as it is included here) has to be the best known gold cultivar, much overused. Dark green leaves have a splash of gold in the centre. Best grown as a wall ivy. Cut out all-green shoots as they appear. Shade tolerant without losing its colouring. Attractive when grown well. Z 7.

H. helix 'Golden Carpet' is a yellow form of *'Shamrock'*.

H. helix 'Golden Ingot' is a popular variety with bright variegation, having golden-yellow leaves, splashed and blotched green and lime.

H. helix 'Gold Knight' originated in Denmark and is remarkable for its pale-yellow colour which develops with age, especially in good light. Best indoors.

H. helix 'Golden Snow' is distinguished by yellow and white variegation. Makes a good houseplant.

H. helix 'Jake' Gold is a sport from *'Lightfinger'* with small, single lobed, almost heart-shaped leaves which are bright yellow on a dense, bushy, compact plant.

H. helix 'Light Fingers' has attractive, yellow arrowhead shaped leaves.

H. helix 'Midas Touch' is a vigorous ivy with bright yellow variegation on a base of bright green on heart-shaped, three lobed leaves. A variation with slightly recurved leaves is often found as *'Golden Curl'*. Excellent in mixed baskets or containers.

H. helix 'Nigra Aurea' has yellow young leaves and older dark green variegated foliage.

H. helix 'Northington Gold' is noted for its almost complete yellow leaves, a slightly weak grower. A tiny blotch of green is apparent on some of the leaves.

Previous page: Hedera 'Gold Ingot'
Above: Hedera 'Goldchild'
Below Left: Hedera 'Sulphur Heart'

H. helix 'Sally' has lemon leaves, spotted and splashed in mid-green.

H. helix 'Sterntaler' has new growth of yellow to chartreuse, being a typical ivy leaf with a slight curl.

H. helix 'Steven' is a golden yellow variety with five irregularly shaped lobes and a crinkly edge.

H. colchica 'Sulphur Heart' is not as deep colouring as *H. helix 'Goldheart'* and much easier to blend into the border as it does not shout too loud. Z6-11.

H. helix 'Sunrise' is a traditional ivy leaf in golden yellow. A good grower.

H. helix 'Ursula' is a yellow-green form of *'Shamrock'*.

Hot Partner: *Clematis 'Jackmannii', Hedera helix 'Glymii', Parthenocissus tricuspidata 'Veitchii'.*

Cool Companion: *Hedera 'Gloire de Marengo', Ceanothus 'Gloire de Versailles'.*

HELLEBORUS

The stinking hellebore is not, as one would expect from its botanical and common name, a smelly individual unless its leaves are bruised. The poor thing is even known as dungwort. From midwinter to midspring it pleases with its flowers and this one has foliage in a very attractive hue. Champions of shade gardens. Hardy perennial.

HOW TO GROW
Neutral to alkaline soil in full sun to dappled shade. Incorporate plenty of leaf mould and organic matter when planting. Mulch annually in autumn. Best raised from seed as *H. foetidus* is not suitable for division. A proportion of seedlings will come true, especially if the plants have been grown in isolation.

H. foetidus 'Chedglow' (*'Gold Bullion'*) is a gold-foliaged form of *H. foetidus* which originated in the garden of Major Soden and was introduced into horticulture by English nurseryman, Martin Cragg-Barber. Spidery, evergreen leaves are gold almost outshone by the soft yellow flowers in early to mid winter. Needs a bright but sheltered position. Has good intense colour which needs careful siting. 30cm (12"). Z5.

H. foetidus 'Chedglow Variegated' is variegated in yellow and green.

Hot Partner: *Cornus alba 'Kesselringii', Heuchera 'Ebony and Ivory'.*

Cool Companion: *x Fatshedera lizei*

Golden Glory: *Mahonia aquifolium 'Apollo', Heuchera 'Amber Waves', Narcissus, Tulipa.*

Heuchera 'Amber Waves'

HEUCHERA

These evergreen and semi-evergreen perennials from north America are valuable additions to any garden. Essential and excellent foliage plants to have in your garden. Stunning as ground cover, fabulous in a container and what an eye-catcher at the edge of the mixed border. The rose pink flowers are attractive too, expect bees to gather.

HOW TO GROW
Grow in fertile, moist but well-drained soil in sun or partial shade. Mulch to prevent root heaving in cold weather. Divide in autumn.

H. 'Amber Waves' PPAF is a stunning amber-gold foliage variety with ruffled leaves. Light rose coloured flowers take second place. First class beauty deserves to be in every garden. This will turn heads. The tints and tones will tempt and tantalise and this will always be commented upon and coveted. A superb new introduction and an amazing leaf colour break from Dan Heims. Excellent companion to gold and dark plants. 20cm (8"). Z 5-11.
H. 'Marmalade' is definitely sweeter than sugar!
Hot Partner: *Carex comans bronze*
Cool Companion: *Oxalis spiralis 'Aureus'* excellent, yellow-green and butterscotch tones not hardy, these two are perfect container partners.

x HEUCHERELLA

This interesting intergeneric hybrid is an absolute dazzler in the garden. If grown in full sun, consistent moisture is of extreme importance. Afternoon shade is more important in hotter climates. Removing fading flowers will result in additional blooms.

HOW TO GROW
Humus-rich soil fairly moist but well-drained soil in full sun or part shade. Divide every 3-4 years. Where ground freezes, apply a mulch to prevent root heaving. Z4-9.

x H. 'Sunspot' PPAF, EUPVR makes an amazing 45cm (18") wide clump of golden, maple-like foliage with an attractive central pattern of red veining. Topped in late spring with pink flowers on red stems. Intense colour fades to straw yellow in summer. An incredible creation, bred by the one and only Dan Heims, Terra Nova nursery introduction. Well-drained soil will keep this beautiful plant in tip top condition. Most effective en masse, but if you only have room for one, get it now. Suitable for rock gardens, borders, open woodland and an excellent edger to paths or walkways. The hottest cool plant! 20cm (8").
Hot Partner: Heuchera 'Obsidion'.
Cool Companion: *Heuchera 'Amber Waves'*.
Golden Glory: Hakonechloa macra 'Aureola' or 'All Gold'.

Heuchera 'Marmalade'

x Heucherella 'Sunspot'

HOSTA

Ostentatious, lush foliage. Sculptured and textured hosta leaves are desirable as groundcover and edgers as well as specimen plants. Luminescent, golden leaves will glow in the shade, for many the aristocrat of shade plants, they are becoming more and more sun tolerant. It is in sun that you will normally obtain the best colour on a yellow hosta. Excellent for groundcover under deep-rooted, deciduous trees, in a mixed or herbaceous border and by water. Representative of gold and yellow in all its differing hues. Remember that hostas show their true selves when they are mature, around 5 seasons. Lap up that bold, sunshine foliage and enjoy the flowers too.

HOW TO GROW

Grow in fertile, moist soil, well-drained in dappled shade to part sun, some newer varieties are extremely sun tolerant, look for good leaf substance. Appreciate shelter from cold, drying winds.

Divide large clumps in spring to autumn. Plant in humus rich soil, adding fertiliser each spring just before the shoots come through. Water well especially during dry spells, they are not drought tolerant and appreciate a mulch annually to conserve water. Pray for no slugs, or put down slug deterrent on February 14th as does holder of one of the National Collections, Roger Bowden, in Devon, England. So, there you have it, the ideal Valentine's gift for hosta lovers is slug deterrent! Easy to grow. Z 4-10.

Aden, long recognised as the Hosta King and deservedly so, but I admire the breeding work being done by Ron Livingston, his plants are absolutely knockout and I am so pleased to give these plants greater exposure.

The flowering foliage plant has come of age, put on its party frock and stepped out to bask in sunshine. Truly glorious plants which deserve to be in every garden.

H. 'Abiqua Recluse' (Walden West 1989) is fairly sun tolerant with heart-shaped, corrugated, glossy gold leaves and pale violet flowers on leafy scapes in July to August. This vigorous, large leaved clump is greener in shade. 45cm (18") tall with a spread of 75cm (30").

H. 'Abiqua Zodiac' (Walden West) bears large, eye-catching, bright gold leaves worthy of a spot in the border. Near white flowers are held high above the attractive mound.

H. 'Aftergow' (Livingston) makes a small mound of horizontally held folded and rippled, bright golden leaves with white backs and great substance. Plant and enjoy its prominence. A Livingston masterpiece. I just love this guy's hostas, they are brilliant.

H. 'Ahamo Gold' (Geissler 1970) bears light gold crinkled leaves on a compact plant. Has white bell-shaped flowers on 50cm (20") scapes with viable seed.

H. 'Alabama Gold' (Suggs 1986) has gold crinkled leaves, with a tendency to burn in full sun. Upright grower with round to heart-shaped leaves which are puckered and slightly cupped. Lavender flowers.

H. 'Alice Gladden' (Ward 1998) is a gold variety that will appreciate at least morning sun, greening up in shade. Near white bell-shaped flowers in July.

H. 'Alice in Wonderland' (Malloy) bears broad, golden-yellow leaves with a deep green border, holding its colour well throughout the season. Pale lavender fertile flowers.

H. 'Alison' (Ward 2000) is a superb golden variety with well-crinkled leaves, not easy to find.

H. 'All Gold' (NR) has golden leaves with good substance appreciating some sun.

H. 'Alpine Aire' (E.Minks) makes a dense mound of pointed leaves emerging chartreuse and turning gold in sun. Similar to *'August Moon'* which is one of its parents. Fertile lavender flowers in July-August.

H. 'Amber Tiara' (Walter Gardens 1998) has golden, pointed, slightly wavy leaves with lavender flowers in summer. Lovely spring colour on a small mounding variety with thick leaves which is great at the front of the border. Bears purple and white striped flowers. 30x50cm (12x20").

H. 'American Gold Cup' (Wade NR) has lightly corrugated golden leaves, best in light shade.

H. 'Amy Elizabeth' (Zillis) a sport of *'Gold Drop'*, is of small stature to 20cm (8") tall with a spread of 30cm (12"). The small, pointed, heart-shaped gold leaves with a green margin have great substance. In July lavender flowers are borne on 35cm (14") scapes.

H. 'Anne Arett' (Arett 1975) is an exquisite dwarf yellow best in open shade where its ruffled, lance-shaped leaves will shine. Deep purple tubular flowers add to the spectacle. A variegated mutation of *'Subcrocea'* but quite viridescent.

H. 'Archangel' (Zilis, NR) has golden leaves which are deeply veined and bears pale lavender-white flowers.

H. 'Aspen Gold' (Grapes/AHS 1986) bears almost round, cupped and corrugated leaves of gold with a green frosting, having heavy substance. Dramatic texture similar to seersucker that takes some sun. This was one of the first golden, puckered types and is still widely grown, even though it is a little on the slow side. Keep moist for sun tolerance. Pale lavender flowers are carried on 50cm (20") scapes in July. 50x90cm (20x36").

H. 'Atom Smasher' (Livingston) has fabulous wavy, lancifolia-type leaves of pure, intense gold. Its lavender flowers are followed by bright red and yellow pods which are simply amazing. Fast growing and fertile. A superb and dazzling variety. Will blow your mind!

H. 'August Moon' (Langfelder/Summers 1968) has large, golden, deeply veined leaves and is a vigorous grower. Spring leaves are like the pale moon rising, then in summer leaves are longer and brighter in colour. This popular variety exhibits excellent texture, tolerating some sun. Best in bright light with 4-5 hours of morning sun. Holds its colour well until frost. Fertile white flowers from July to August. Easy to obtain and to grow. 50cm (20") tall, and almost twice that in width.

H. 'Baja Sunset' (Livingston) is what golden gardens are all about. This amazing hosta has more glow than a glowworm in low, evening or morning light.

H. 'Bengee' resembles *'Aspen Gold'* when mature with crinkled and cupped leaves and near white fertile flowers.

H. 'Big Dipper' (Kuk 1995) makes a large, semi-upright mound of golden-yellow leaves with a glaucous touch to both top and underside. Moderately cupped, corrugated and wavy with heavy substance. Lavender flowers.

H. 'Birchwood Parky's Gold' (Shaw/AHS 1986) has gold, heart-shaped leaves to 5cm (3") across, needing sun to colour well. Emerges greyish and you think it will never make the golden grade, but it does, and has earned its place as a classic. Makes excellent, vigorous groundcover with crinkled leaves. Quite good slug resist foliage. Lavender, bell-shaped flowers in summer. 45cm (18") tall, almost twice that in width.

Hosta 'Atom Smasher'

Hosta 'August Moon'

Above: Hosta 'Baja Sunset' planted with Lamium
and Myosotis. For a gold echo use Lamium
'Beedham's White' and Myosostis 'Gold n'
Sapphires'.
Right: Hosta 'Blond Elf'

H. 'Bitsy Gold' (Savory 1985) has very narrow, pointed lance-shaped gold leaves forming a spreading clump with lavender flowers on 15cm (6") scapes in July. This mini quickly makes a dense mound 45cm (18") wide.

H. 'Blackfoot' (Plater-Zyberk/Solberg) has electric light bulb spring foliage. Its spoon-shaped leaves have dark petioles. A stunning, vigorous plant with lavender flowers.

H. 'Blaugold' (Klose) this is not variegated gold and blue, but reputed to be the first golden-leaved hosta with bluish flowers, open-pollinated in Germany.

H. 'Blond Elf' (Aden) is a sport from 'Fresh' with golden-yellow leaves making a small clump. Small, lance-shaped pointed leaves have closely spaced veins offering good texture. This fine addition to the front of the border will pale in low light. Its small stature makes it a good subject for a rock garden. Lavender flowers in profusion. 20cm tall, 55cm wide. (8x22").

H. 'Bold Ruffles' is as handsome as something crinkly can be. Good gold colouring.

H. 'Bright Glow' (Aden 1986) has leaves emerging chartreuse but quickly turning gold. Makes a small, neat dense mound with excellent slug resistance owing to its heavy substance. Near white flowers are borne on 50cm (20") scapes in June on this fertile, rapid growing *tardiana* type. 30cmx 90cm (1x3ft).

H. 'Bright Lights' (Aden/Klehm) makes a vigorous small to medium plant with heavy substance in the puckered, bright gold leaves which have an attractive, wide blue-green margin. Good grower and performs well in the southern areas of the U.S. Near white flowers are borne in June to July on 60cm (24") scapes. An elegant *tokudama* type. 45cm (18").

H. 'Cadillac' (Skrocki/Avent 1998) makes a small mound to 25cm (10") tall with a spread of double that displaying lightly cupped, corrugated roundish, golden yellow leaves with a medium green margin and near white flowers.

H. 'Captain Kirk' (Brill) a sport of 'Gold Standard' with a dark green margin and a yellow centre which holds its colour well. Heavier substance than its parents, very thick leaves and a good grower, topped by lavender flowers.

H. 'Cardwell Yellow' (Krossa/Ruh 1981) is a small yellow variety.

H. 'Centerfold' (G.Kamp 1994) has a mounding habit with yellow-gold, corrugated leaves with slightly wavy margins with a light gloss on both sides. Has good substance. Near white tubular flowers are borne on 45cm (18") scapes. 60x120cm (2x4ft).

H. 'Cheatin' Heart' (Zumbar 1995) is a miniature form with a spread of three times its height, the deep gold leaves are truly bright and have a slightly wavy margin and the light pink-purple fertile flowers are held aloft on 17cm (7") scapes. Has red speckling on the petioles and scapes. This rapid increaser looks orange-gold in the sun.

H. 'Chelsea Ore' (Chelsea Physic Garden 1989) has pure gold deeply veined leaves with a slight, darker margin. Leaves are slightly wavy and pointed on a *plantaginea* type.

Hosta 'Bold Ruffles'

Hosta 'Chinese Sunrise'

H. 'Cherry Tart' (Altarra Scheer) is so bright and light, its lance-shaped leaves are upward growing, and it almost looks like this hosta could get up and dance, especially when you see those red petioles that bleed into the leaf. Has that come hither look to beckon passers by to take a closer look. Wow!

H. 'Chesterland Gold' (Zilis/Ruth 1997) bears bright pointed, smooth, lightly veined leaves. Good colouring on this sport from the fabulous *'Paul's Glory'*. Topped with lavender flowers.

H. 'Chinese Gold' (Wade NR) exhibits wavy, pointed yellow-green leaves.

H. 'Chinese Sunrise' (Alex Summers) is a *lancifolia* type (parentage unrecorded) with glossy, gold leaves having a narrow green border with a tapering point. Emerging early in the season but fading to pale green in midsummer. Lavender flowers appear late in the season on tall scapes. 35x60cm (14"x2ft).

H. 'Chiquita' (M.Eisel 1979) has bright yellow leaves turning lime green as the season progresses. 60x120cm (2x4ft).

H. 'Choo Choo Train' bears attractive heavily rippled edges to its wonderful bright gold leaves. Excellent with cool blues. Soft lavender to white flowers top this large leaved specimen. 55x150cm (22x60").

H. 'Christmas Gold' (Seaver) cupped, seersucker leaves of a nice lemon-gold which take sun, with a delightful glaucous bloom. The undersides are glaucous pale green. Bell-shaped flowers of palest lavender are borne in mid season. Has distinctive purple seed capsules. 45x60cm (18x24").

H. 'City Lights' (Aden 1978) has yellow heart-shaped leaves in a class of their own. Fertile bell-shaped white flowers are carried on 1m (3ft) scapes above the large mound of intensely corrugated foliage with good substance. A radiant specimen. 35x90cm (14x36").

H. 'Community Chest' (Malloy) bears golden-yellow leaves, smooth and pointed.

H. 'Copa Cabana' (Terpening, NR) exhibits light gold, oval and deeply veined leaves.

H. 'Cracker Crumbs' (Solberg 2002) is a sport of *'Shiny Penny'* with bright golden leaves and a shiny dark green margin. This miniature form exhibits good substance and growth and is excellent for containers. Lavender flowers in July.

H. 'Cup of Gold' if your cup runneth over, try this golden variety with puckered, yellow-green leaves, will probably take a little sun to turn yellow. Nice texture.

H. 'Curious Yellow' (Livingston) was named for its unusual shade of yellow-gold ruffled leaves. Delicate purple flowers vie for attention.

H. 'Dalton's Pick' (Terpening) has crinkled, puckered golden leaves which are rounded, exhibits good texture. Its bright yellow colouring takes quite a bit of sunshine in upstate New York.

H. 'Dance With Me' (Hansen/Shady Oaks) 'Are you asking?' 'I'm dancing'. A great line from the opening of the Liverbirds with Polly James (A British comedy series that ran for years). This is a great sport from *'Summer Music'*. Its heart-shaped leaves are framed in dark green. Makes a vigorous clump with good substance finished off with lavender flowers. Reverse colouration of *'Last Dance'*.

H. 'Darwin's Standard' is a sport of *'Gold Standard'* with yellow, rugose leaves broadly margined in glossy apple-green to blue. Good substance with a definite sheen in sun or shade. White-lilac flowers.

H. 'Daughter of Ledi Lantis' (M.Seaver, NR) has gold-green puckered foliage, similar to *'Midas Touch'*. Distinguished by its wonderful texture. 90cm (30").

H. 'Dave Stone' (Summers) has bright gold foliage having deep green margins. Leaves are nicely veined. Near white flowers. A sport of *'Piedmont Gold'* makes an outstanding specimen.

H. 'Dawn' (BHHS/Bond 2000) makes a dainty mound of beautiful, oval, bright yellow wavy leaves. Purple funnel shaped flowers have bluish anthers. A stoloniferous variety holds its colour longer than *'Hydon Sunset'* with which it is sometimes confused. Best in light shade. 20x30cm (8x12").

H. 'Dawn's Early Light' (Petruszyn 1988) has deep veined and puckered golden leaves with good texture. The colour is lost in summer as it changes to chartreuse. A golden *tokudama* with good colour in spring in light shade. Lavender flowers on 90cm (30") scapes. 50cm (20").

H. 'Daybreak' (Aden 1986) bears large brassy gold, puckered, heart-shaped leaves of thick substance with conspicuous veining. Heavy leaves are almost bad weather proof. Distinguished by light undulations to the leaf and a turned down tip. The 30cm long, slightly shiny leaves form a flattish mound to 65cm (26") tall and more than double the spread. Topped by lavender flowers on long scapes in August. Superb, hard to beat colour which is a parent of many yellows. 50x90cm (20"x3ft).

H. 'Day Dream' is a sport of *'Sea Dream'* with moderately rugose, yellow-gold leaves which hold their colour well with slightly rippled margins. Petioles have a distinguishing red spot at their base. This makes a good mound above which lavender flowers are held on tall scapes. 25cmx90cm (10x36").

H. 'Dee's Golden Jewel' (Walek 1996) has heart-shaped, pointed, lightly cupped golden foliage which appreciates being in sun without losing its colour. Leaves have a glaucous bloom on the underside and beautiful substance. This stoloniferous variety has an upright habit and is slow growing. Near white flowers are an added bonus in June to July. 45cm (18").

H. 'Delia' (Ford 1995) this sport from *'Golden Prayers'* exhibits good light golden foliage with a medium green edge to each leaf. Has great substance on a small mound suitable for the small garden. Near white flowers. 15cm tall and 45cm wide (6x18").

H. 'Delta Dawn' (Vaughn) has large corrugated, golden-chartreuse, creamy white edged leaves which hold their colour until frost. Bears light lavender flowers in spring. 45cm (18").

H. 'Devon Gold' (Bowden,NR) bears tiny, oval butter yellow leaves, excellent in a rock garden or sink. Best in shade, certainly not for direct sunlight as it scorches. Purple flowers. Attractive, will brighten any shady spot. 15cm (6").

H. 'Dick Ward' (Hatfield) is a sport of *'Zounds'* with admirable golden leaves edged nicely in green. Good texture and makes a good wide clump eventually, topped with lavender flowers. 35x90cm (14"x3ft).

H. 'Dorothy's Brass Band' (Benedict) not too brassy, this is a quiet gold with cupped, slightly veined and crinkled leaves.

H. 'Doubloons' (Zilis/Zumbar 1995) has bright gold leaves with good substance, making a large mound above which near white flowers are carried on 90cm (3ft) scapes. 50cmx1.15m (20x45").

H. 'Drawn Butter' (Belle Gardens) has slightly shiny, butter-yellow foliage starting out greenish. Leaves with good substance have a rippled margin and are slightly wavy. Pale purple flowers. Makes a semi-upright clump.

H. 'Eaglet' (Benedict, NR) has gold, pointed wavy leaves needing some sun.

H. 'Early Times' (Neo Plants) with glaucous yellow leaves is a sport of my favourite variegated hosta *'June'*. Holds its colour well to complement the lavender flowers.

H. 'El Dorado' (M. Seaver) absolutely glows gold and has great staying power. It makes a compact mound 60x90cm (2x3ft).

H. 'Electroglow' (Zilis) medium gold, heart-shaped leaves with heavy substance are the good characteristics of this plant with lavender flowers.

H. 'Electrum Stater' (A. Malloy 1997) is a fast-growing sport from *'Abiqua Recluse'* having shiny gold leaves with a white rippled margin. This forms a mound of slightly wavy and corrugated foliage. Fertile pale lavender flowers are borne on long scapes. 30x60cm (12x24").

H. 'Ellie Bee' (Brinkerhoft/Ruh 1996) has elegant, gold-chartreuse, wavy pointed leaves.

H. 'Elvis On Stage' (Livingston) move over Elvis, even the King himself (and I am a big Elvis fan) was not as dazzling as this hosta that takes centre stage. Utter glowing glory, flashy corrugated yellow leaves are in the spotlight here. Attractively tapered and rippled they outshine everything else. Good substance. Gold hostas do not come any better than this. Applause please for the King of *Hosta*!

H. 'English Sunrise' (Zilis) is an all-gold sport of one of my favourite hosta *'June'*. Heart-shaped leaves prefer sun, but colour will fade by midseason. Contrasting lavender flowers are on show in July-August above a mound of 35cm (14") high foliage with a spread of twice the height.

H. 'Eternity' (Wilkins 1995) bears shiny, slightly cupped leaves which are held upright beneath the white flowers in July to August. Its upright growing habit brings a little sunshine into the garden.

H. 'Evening Magic' (Zilis 1988) has lovely golden-yellow puckered leaves with distinguishing white margins. Good substance and texture. 40x55cm (16x22").

Hosta 'Elvis On Stage'

H. 'Excitation' (Aden 1988) has yellow cordate leaves with wavy edges making a nice small mound useful as groundcover. Good pale lavender flowers. 20cm (8").

H. 'Eye Catcher' (Goodwin 1996) bears yellow-gold leaves which are deeply cupped and intensely corrugated with pale purple fertile flowers. Makes a medium to large clump with changing flushes in leaf colour in some sun, offering electric bright foliage in spring. 30x60cm (1x2ft).

H. 'Fan Dance' (Benedict 1987) has leaves that retain more gold when placed in part shade with morning sun, in full sun they bleach to parchment, with shade to cream with a dark green edge. Bears light lavender flowers in midsummer. Not the goldest of plants, but quick to make medium-sized mounds. 35cm (14").

H. 'Fascinator' (Wilkins/Owen 1989) has a golden yellow leaf with a green margin developing as the season progresses. Lavender flowers are carried on 90cm (3ft) scapes. 35x90cm (14x36").

H. 'Fat Cat' (D.&J.Ward 1996) has corrugated, yellow-gold leaves with slightly rippled margins. Tubular flowers are near white and are borne on 105cm (42") scapes. 90x1.5m (30x60").

Hosta fortunei f aurea

H. 'Five o' Clock Shadow' (Solberg 2000) exhibits large golden, deeply veined leaves with green variegated edges. This sport of *'High Noon'* shines with a couple of hours sun in the morning. Lavender flowers in June.

H. 'Fort Knox' (Wilkins 1989) bears veined, vase-shaped bright yellow, large leaves with good, heavy substance. Shining radiance in shade and will take quite a lot of sun making an excellent specimen plant. Lavender flowers appear in July on 90cm (3ft) scapes. 60cm (24") tall with double the spread.

H. fortunei v albopicta (Miquel 1869) bears bright butter yellow leaves edged in green in spring, turning all green later. Lilac flowers. Light to full shade.

H. fortunei f aurea (*'Twinkles'*) (von Siebold/Hylander) has vivid butter yellow emerging leaves, slowly turning green later. Wavy, luminous foliage makes a striking clump with upright growth. Best in shade. Lavender flowers. 35x60cm (14x24").

H. 'Fragrant Gold' (Aden 1982) bears yellow-green leaves with a green central line, maturing gold. Thick, heart-shaped leaves are undulated. Scapes of funnel-shaped lavender-blue flowers which have some fragrance are borne in summer. Thrives in sun or light shade. 45x90cm (18x30").

H. 'Fried Bananas' (Solberg 1994) Grow it just for the name, I love bananas. A sport of *'Guacamole'*, bearing shiny gold leaves in good light above large, fragrant (yes sweet-smelling hosta) near-white flowers in August. Quick to make 75cm (30") wide clumps in sun to light shade, so give it a little room to spread its thickly veined leaves and it will make a great accent plant. Heat tolerant. 45cm (18"). Z3-9.

H. 'Frills' (Benedict, NR) is a golden, frilly variety.

H. 'Frosty Morn' (E.Lachman 1993) is best in light shade where it will brighten any area with its gold leaves. The thick, corrugated leaves have a white back. Light lavender flowers appear in late summer above the 60cm (2ft) wide clump. 25cm (10") tall. Z3-9.

H. 'Fruhlingssonne' (Klose, NR) has pale gold, lightly veined and pointed foliage.

H. 'Gaiety' (Aden 1986) has bright yellow leaves with a narrow white margin and a green central line. White flowers are borne in July to August on this medium sized clump. Performs best in light to full shade. 23x45cm (9x18").

H. 'Garden Party' (Solberg/Zilis 2002) is a sport of *'Golden Sculpture'* making a large, upright mound of rounded, golden leaves with a thin, deep green margin. Its puckered and cupped leaves resist sun burn and it makes a spectacular clump given a little time.

H. 'George Smith' (Smith) is a superior golden *sieboldiana* type with near white flowers. 40-45cm (16-18").

H. 'Gilt By Association' (Summers/Walek 2000) has golden leaves, deeply veined and further distinguished by white undersides and purple-red petioles. Fades to green. Foliage is slightly wavy and arching. Lavender to blue flowers in July to August on contrasting yellow scapes shaded in red to top and base make this a most unusual hosta which is sun tolerant and should be added to your collection post haste.

H. 'Glorious' (Livingston) is a lovely graceful plant with thick, glossy, waxy, undulating leaves which turn golden in sun. Small but a fast grower. Bud and scape bases are vibrant red. Lavender striped flowers.

Hosta 'Glorious'

Hosta 'Glory'

H. 'Glory' (Savory 1985) forms a golden mound with green veins and ruffled edges to the thick leaves. 30cm (12") high and 60cm (24") wide with light purple flowers on 45cm (18") high scapes in late spring to summer. Best in part sun for golden glow. Makes a statement en masse. Z3-9.

H. 'Gold Bullion' makes a medium clump of gold leaves with lavender flowers. 40cm (16").

H. 'Gold Cadet' (Aden 1974) has wavy, veined golden leaves on a small plant. 20-25cm (8-10"). Pale purple fertile flowers.

H. 'Gold Chip' (Wade, NR) has cupped golden foliage with a definite point to the rounded leaves.

H. 'Gold Cover' (Vaughn 1982) has deeply veined, slightly cupped leaves on a small plant.

H. 'Gold Cup' (Aden 1978) has an incredible puckering to the golden cupped leaves with a pale reverse. Will green up in too much shade. Makes a medium clump topped by near white, bell-shaped flowers. I like this one, has good substance. 45cm (18").

H. 'Gold Drop' (Anderson 1977) has good gold foliage making small mounds to 20cm (8"), with many lavender to white flowers in midseason. The smooth, miniature, heart-shaped leaves need sun to colour well, otherwise they tend to look chartreuse rather than gold. This *venusta* type multiplies quickly and stays neat with a spread of 30cm (12").

H. 'Gold Edger' (Aden 1978) makes a fast growing, dense mound 20cm (8") high with a spread of 40cm (16"). Thick, pointed foliage needs sun to bring out the soft, medium-gold colouring. Lavender-white flowers are borne in abundance on 55cm (22") scapes in June to July. A good choice for groundcover.

H. 'Gold Glory' (Lydell 1995) has gold, deeply veined and slightly puckered, cupped leaves having a slightly shiny leaf top on a medium plant. Tubular pale lavender flowers.

H. 'Gold Haze' is a *fortunei f aurea* cross with *sieboldiana*, but holds its colour better than its golden parent. Very attractive upright grower. Lilac flowers.

Hosta 'Gold Haze'

H. 'Gold Pan' (Aden 1978) has fabulous, very puckered and cupped foliage exhibiting good texture. White flowers. 45cm (18").

H. 'Gold Petite' has delightful, wavy, lance-shaped leaves.

H. 'Gold Rajah' has large, seersucker leaves topped by white flowers. 50cm (20").

H. 'Gold Regal' (Aden 1974) bears pointed, overlapping, yellow-chartreuse leaves which are held upright in the style of *'Krossa Regal'* with contrasting, very attractive fertile, purple-mauve flowers on 105cm (42") scapes in July. Has puckered and deeply veined leaves offering excellent texture. This stately, compact variety with dense, overlapping foliage offers its best colour in plenty of morning sun, can take until June to July to show its golden tones. Reaches 40cm (16") and has a spread of twice its height.

H. 'Gold Rush' is a New Zealand golden *sieboldiana* with off-white flowers making a favourable clump of crinkled leaves in time. Pale flowers.

H. 'Gold Seer' (Aden 1972) has immense seersucker texture on pointed leaves. 40cm (16").

Hosta 'Goldbrook Gold'

H. **'Gold Standard'** (P.Banyai 1976) is a classic hosta with emerging green heart-shaped leaves turning gold, bordered with a dark green margin. Will green up in shade, but just a little early morning sun gives the best colour. This *'Hyacinthina'* sport is late to emerge and reaches 50cm (20") tall with a spread of 140cm (55"). The violet-lavender flowers appear in August on long scapes. Too much sun and the centre will turn white and burn; too much shade and it will look green. 50x90cm (20x30").

H. **'Goldbrook Gold'** (Bond) Sarah of the goldfinger has this seedling from *H. sieboldiana*, displaying puckered gold leaves with a white back and white flowers. A little slow to establish, best in dappled shade. A handsome mature plant.

H. **'Golddigger'** has deeply puckered and pointed, golden foliage. Rounded to oval golden leaves.

H. **'Goldee'** (Whitmore) has moderately corrugated, golden-yellow leaves, with scapes of lavender flowers.

H. **'Goldsmith'** (E.Smith/BHHS 1988) has superb colour in its veined, pointed and cupped leaves.

H. **'Golden Anniversary'** has gold leaves to 25cm (10") wide which green up later in the season. Lavender flowers.

H. **'Golden Bouquet'** (Benedict) has deeply veined and corrugated, puckered foliage displaying excellent texture.

H. **'Golden Bullion'** (Bennerup/Ruh 1989) needs a little shade to display its golden, corrugated leaves to advantage. Emerges chartreuse, becoming yellow. Flowers are nearly white on long scapes in midseason. Its thick leaves are quite pest resistant.

H. **'Golden Canopy'** (Asch) has butter-golden leaves with good corrugated and puckered texture. White flowers are carried well above the foliage.

H. **'Golden Cascade'** (Benedict 1984) has veined, pointed, golden leaves. Makes a dense mound of slightly wavy leaves. Attractive.

H. **'Golden Delight'** (Kuk 1994) has very nice substance to its large, golden foliage.

H. **'Golden Dorothy of Richland'** bears deeply veined, shapely cupped leaves.

H. **'Golden Empress'** (Kuk 1990) has pale gold, heart-shaped, deeply veined and pointed foliage with a slight wave to the edges. Lavender flowers in June.

H. **'Golden Fantasy'** (Benedict) has excellent corrugated leaves.

H. **'Golden Fascination'** (AHS 1986) has deeply veined pointed foliage. Pale lavender flowers in July attract attention to this medium sized clump.

H. **'Golden Fountain'** (Dishon 1993) has lance-shaped, veined leaves.

H. **'Golden Friendship'** (H.Gowan 1991) the rounded, cupped, upright leaves of this beauty emerge chartreuse soon to turn medium gold with prominent veins. Lavender flowers appear in July on tall scapes. 47x90cm (19x36").

H. **'Golden Gate'** (Petryszyn/Brincka 1994) forms an attractive large specimen 65cm (26") by 135cm (52"). Its shiny corrugated foliage is strongly marked with prominent veins and lightly rippled margins. The gold colouring is richer in summer. Lavender flowers are produced in July.

H. **'Golden Ghost'** (Plater-Zyberk/Meyer, NR) exhibits elegant pointed, lightly veined foliage which emerges chartreuse and turns gold with some sun.

H. **'Golden Girl'** (K.Anderson 1982) has corrugated, cupped leaves with good colouring.

H. **'Golden Medallion'** (Eisel/AHS 1984) is slow to form a clump of cupped, heart-shaped, puckered gold leaves to 15cm (6") long. Thick leaves emerge chartreuse and colour is best in sun. Off white flowers are borne in summer. 35x60cm (14x24").

H. **'Golden Nugget'** (1969) bears slightly corrugated, pointed leaves.

H. **'Golden Oriole'** (E.Smith/BHHS 1988) has attractive pointed, wavy yellow foliage to 20cm (8") long and just 7cm (3") wide. Steals the show in spring, then turns greener. A medium-sized clump with lavender flowers.

H. **'Golden Picture'** (Benedict 1985) has golden veined leaves.

H. **'Golden Prayers'** (Aden 1970) has slightly corrugated strong, upright, good golden textured foliage, with paler undersides to the leaf. Best in some sun. Palest lavender flowers. Sometimes confused with *'Little Aurora'* in cultivation. 35x50cm (14x20"). Z3-8.

H. **'Golden Scepter'** (R.Savory 1983) makes a small quick clump of thin, golden, heart-shaped foliage. An all-gold form of *'Golden Tiara'*. Purple flowers on tall scapes in July. Fertile. 30x60cm (12x24").

Hosta 'Golden Prayers'

H. **'Golden Sculpture'** (K.Anderson 1982) at 80cm (32") tall and 1m 85cm (72") wide, this plant makes an impressive, vase-shaped mound of large, bright gold, sculptured, waxy leaves with heavy corrugation. Good sun tolerance, in fact it thrives best in hot climates. Amazing near white flowers are carried well above the foliage in July. A terrific accent plant.

H. **'Golden Spades'** (Kuk 1986) is a tiny dwarf with small, deep golden leaves. This slow grower is excellent for the rock garden where it will make a dense mound. Striped lavender flowers.

H. **'Golden Spider'** (Harshburger/Ruh 1987) makes an atttractive, dense mound of yellow leaves which are oval in shape. Fertile, lavender-pink flowers in June to July. 25x45cm (10x18").

H. **'Golden Sunburst'** (AHS 1984) has large puckered, round golden leaves making a large clump with good substance in its thick, heart-shaped leaves. Textured, deeply veined leaves which are glaucous on the underside. Palest flowers are carried on straight, long scapes in midseason. Give this all-gold *'Frances Williams'* sport a little shade as it can burn in sun. 45x90cm (18x36").

H. **'Golden Surprise'** (Simpers/Ruh 1991) has gold, veined pointed leaves.

H. **'Golden Teacup'** (Wilkins 1989) bears corrugated, deeply cupped, upright leaves suffused with bright gold. Excellent substance but is a slow grower. White flowers in July. 30cm (12") high and 45cm (18") wide.

H. **'Golden Threads'** (Benedict, NR) has slightly wavy, lance-shaped leaves of golden-yellow.

H. **'Golden Tiara'** (P.Savory 1977) has dainty leaves of differing shapes with greenish gold centres and a deeper margin. Prolific plant which rapidly spreads to 38cm (15") tall and 90cm (3ft) wide making a good edger or excellent for ground cover. Blue-lavender flowers striped purple are carried profusely on 60cm (2ft) long scapes in early July.

H. **'Golden Torch'** (R.Benedict 1984) is distinguished by upright yellow-green foliage being slightly cupped and corrugated. Lavender flowers appear in August to September. 60x50cm (24x20").

Hosta 'Hadspen Samphire'

H. 'Golden Tranquility' (Zilis, NR) has slightly cupped and veined leaves.

H. Golden Waffles' (Aden 1976) bears dense, delightfully crinkled, heart-shaped leaves. Bright golden colour intensifies as the season progresses and it is sun tolerant. White flowers. 40x60cm (16x24").

H. 'Golden Wheels' (Minks 1996) has puckered, gold-chartreuse foliage.

H. 'Golden Wiggler' (Benedict) has small, *lancifolia* type gold coloured leaves appreciating sun.

H. 'Goldene Woge' (Kohler, NR) bears lance-shaped, deeply veined small golden leaves.

H. 'Goldilocks' (Armstrong 1970) has superb, puckered and pointed golden foliage.

H. 'Good as Gold' (Aden, NR) emerging chartreuse heart-shaped foliage turns to gold. Good pest-resistance with heavy puckering on cupped leaves. A medium clump with lavender flowers. 45cm (18").

H. 'Gosan Gold Dwarf' (G.Schmid 1989) is a bright gold variety with pointed leaves which can burn.

H. 'Gosan Gold Midget' (G.Schmid 1989) is a tiny gem with narrow, pointed tiny leaves of a glossy, bright gold-green. Slightly stoloniferous and fast-growing mound reaches 7x15cm (3x6"). Fertile lavender flowers in July.

H. 'Gosan Hildegarde' (G. Schmid 1989) has lance-shaped leaves emerging green, quickly changing to yellow. Fertile whitish flowers on 20cm (10") scapes. 7cm (3").

H. 'Granary Gold' (E.Smith/BHHS 1988) has deeply veined, cupped and slightly wavy leaves with a pointed tip. A matt surface of bright gold for most of the season, head-turning bright in spring. Funnel-shaped pale lavender flowers on 90cm (36") long scapes with conspicuous bracts. Will take some sun.

H. 'Great Lakes Gold' (Ward 2000) has deeply veined, cupped rounded golden leaves.

H. 'Ground Sulphur' (O'Harra 1996) is of small stature, just 12cm (5") with a spread of almost twice the size. Small pointed sulphur-yellow leaves intensify in sun with complementary lavender flowers on 20cm (8") scapes in June to July.

H. 'Hadspen Samphire' (Smith/Eason/Ruh) has incredibly bright spring gold leaves, changing to chartreuse later in summer. Lavender flowers.

H. 'Hallie's Honor' (Maroushek 1999) The hybridizer, Lilan Maroushek, named this for her grand-daughter. Its vibrant, deeply corrugated golden leaves have rippled edges. Near white blooms in late summer.

H. 'Halo' is an upright golden-yellow with a yellow halo variegation. Bright in partial to full sun. Lavender flowers. 60cm (24").

H. 'Harvest Glow' (Walters Gardens 1988) has large, thick, heart-shaped leaves. The glow comes from lemon-chartreuse emerging leaves which progress to a rich, deep yellow. The cupped and puckered leaves sit beneath the pale lavender to white flowers on bare 60cm (24") scapes in light shade to sun. 40x50cm (16x20").

H. 'Hazel' (Stone/Ruh 1987) is cuteness in canary yellow with lavender flowers appearing in June to July on this small mound. Greens a little later in the season. 15x30cm (6x12").

H. 'Heartache' (Benedict 1985) the nearly round leaves of this bright gold cultivar have good substance and an unusual complementary deep purple flower borne on long scapes in July to August. This medium-sized clump will brighten any shade. 50x120cm (20"x4ft).

H. 'High Noon' this puckered, showy gold makes an outstanding large clump.

Hosta 'Hydon Sunset'

H. 'Hoosier Homecoming' bears round, heavily corrugated, shiny gold leaves margined in cream. A sport from *'Aspen Gold'* with pale lavender flowers.

H. 'Hydon Sunset' (BHHS 1988) bears small gold leaves subject to scorch as they are thin. Best grown in dappled shade where it will create a dense clump of various shades of yellow-green on new and old growth. Good purple flowers. Quite a dainty plant. 10x20cm (4x8").

H. 'Innisglow' bears radiant gold cupped foliage. Delightful.

H. 'Inniswood' (Inniswood Gardens 1994) a sport of *'Sun Glow'* has large quilted, rich yellow leaves with a grey-blue margin. This fast grower makes a 120cm (4ft) wide clump with medium lavender flowers in late spring. Very attractive and a favourite with many for its slug-resist foliage which is stunning when mature. Beautiful colour combination makes a perfect trio with a stronger gold and a blue variety. 60cm (24") tall. Z3-9.

H. 'Janet' (O'Harra 1981) is like a smaller version of *'Gold Standard'* with golden leaves edged in green. Pale lavender flowers top this hosta classic. 40x60cm (16x48").

H. 'Jimmy Crack Corn' (R.Sawyer,NR) think golden corn, think large pointed leaves with prominent veins and rippled, piecrust margins. Near white flowers are carried above the impressive, horizontally held foliage in June. A seedling out of *'Piedmont Gold'*. A good grower to 60cmx120cm(2x4ft).

H. 'Joshua's Banner' (Jones) emerges gold in spring, turning green-yellow later in the season. Deeply veined leaves have a white edge and are best in part sun to light shade. Lavender flowers offer lovely contrast in summer. 37cm (15") tall and 90cm (3ft) wide. Z3-9.

H. 'Judy's Surprise' (Walek 1996) small grower with upright, medium gold leaves and pale lavender flowers. 40x50cm (16x20").

H. 'Julie Morss' (Morss 1983) bears bright gold, heart-shaped spring foliage with a chartreuse-blue edging, leaves greening later. Its leaves are late to emerge and puckering only shows at maturity. This *'Frances Williams'* seedling, has *fortunei* type foliage with good substance and is best in light to full shade. Pale lavender flowers in midseason. 30x50cm (12x20").

H. 'Just So' (P.Aden 1986) has contrasting leaves of a wide gold centre and a narrow green margin best in light shade. This sport of *'Little Aurora'* is very eye-catching, having the same small, rounded and corrugated leaves. Light lavender flowers are carried in midsummer above the 45cm (18") wide clump. A fast-growing edger or good for a rock garden. 15-23cm (6-9") tall. Z3-9.

H. 'Kabitan' (Maekawa AHS 1987) is correctly *sieboldii v sieboldii f kabitan*, but rarely seen with such a long-winded tag. Iridescent, golden foliage edged in dark green. Dark striped, purple flowers are held above the low mound offering perfect contrast to the pale leaves. Makes a great edger to show off its long, pointed leaves which have a ruffled edge. Contrasts well with round or oval leaves. Stoloniferous. Needs morning sun and afternoon shade with ground kept evenly moist. 20cm (8x10").

H. 'Kasseler Gold' (Klose) is a seedling from *'Semperaurea'* selected by Klose Nursery in Germany. It bears thin, glossy, slightly puckered yellow leaves.

H. 'Katherine Lewis' is an attractive gold-leaved hosta with blue margins to the leaf, a sport of the blue-leaved *'Halcyon'*, differing from *'June'* in its brighter colouring which it retains well throughout the season. Needs a little sun and bright light.

H. 'Kinba' (Watanabe) only really displays its golden toned foliage in spring on shocking red petioles, but this colour is echoed in the red leaf stalks when it sends up its lavender flowers. Startling.

H. 'King Tut' emerges green but its wide, heavy textured leaves soon turn gold. Near white flowers are carried in summer. 30x60cm (1x2ft).

H. 'Kittyhawk' (Roy Herold 2000) has wavy, well corrugated golden leaves with good substance. Best in light shade where it will make a clump 90cm (3ft) wide topped by lavender flowers in summer on 1m (3ft+) scapes. 45cm (18"). Z3-9.

H. 'Kiwi Gold Rush' (Jury) emerges green and turns gold. Good vigour and a nice clump of veined leaves.

H. 'Kiwi Mini Gold' (Sligh 1999) has golden yellow leaves, dull on top, but shiny on the underside, having a rippled margin. Lavender flowers.

H. 'Lakeside Cha Cha' (M.Chastain 1994) the dancing hosta, cha cha cha, has deeply veined, wavy golden leaves with white edges and pale lavender flowers from dark buds. A large, upright plant to liven up any dark corner with its breeze-blown, heavy substance foliage. A real eye-catcher! 35cm (14").

Hosta 'Little Aurora'

Hosta 'Lakeside Cha Cha'

H. 'Lakeside Delight' (Chastain 1994) has fabulous spring colour of gold-yellow which will take some sun. Bears white flowers. 40x90cm (16x36").

H. 'Lakeside San Kao' (Chastain) makes a large clump emerging lime but quickly turning to yellow through to almost white in summer. Elegant, capable of making a grand display. Lavender flowers.

H. 'Lakeside Symphony' (Chastain) is a sport of *Piedmont Gold* emerging lime, but developing a good golden centre.

H. 'Lemon Chiffon' (Banyai 1988) emerges lemon-yellow with green veins and a slight wave to the leaf. Lavender flowers on this attractive hosta.

H. 'Lemon Lime' (Savory 1977) has lanceolate, wavy leaves, lemon to yellow-green, excellent at the edge of a shady border, best colour with sun. White striped, purple-lavender flowers are borne in summer. 20cm (8") with a spread of three times the height. Z3-9.

H. 'Lemon Meringue' (P.Ruh 1991) boasts gold foliage with large, thick leaves which have white backs just like the yummy pie. Topped with white flowers in summer. Slow and not too leafy. 50x65cm (20x27").

H. 'Little Aurora' (Aden 1978) bears small leaves with great texture. This rapid grower will fit the bill with puckered, cupped, thick golden metallic leaves. Glows in light shade to sun. Soft lavender flowers from late June to early July. 20cm (8") tall and 30cm (12") wide.

H. 'Little Lemon Drop' a real cutie of a gold making a fast growing clump. 20cm (10").

H. 'Little Razor' (Zilis 1988) bears small, wavy gold elliptical leaves just 15cm (6") tall and spreading to a width of 40cm (16"). Pale lavender flowers in July.

H. longipes 'Aurea' (*H. 'Ogon Iwa'*) makes a medium-sized clump of bright golden, ruffled leaves. Other attributes are reddish petioles and dark scapes. There is also a smaller version with colouring not as bright.

H. 'Lovely Loretta' (Zilis) has bright gold, wavy foliage forming a lowish, medium-sized mound 35cm (14")

high with a spread of more than double that. Tall scapes carry light purple flowers. Very attractive plant, named by the breeder for his mother.

H. 'Lucy Vitols' is a hosta with great texture and substance. Its thick, gold leaves are edged in dark green. Light lavender flowers. 30x60cm (12x24").

H. 'Lunar Eclipse' (Zilis 1985) makes a medium clump of yellow leaves with a uniform, neat white margin. Heavy textured with lavender flowers in July. Performs in hot to warm climates in light shade to sun. 60cm (24").

H. 'Made You Look' (Asch 2000) is quite an unusual colouring, emerging lime, leaves turn variegated, pale yellow in the centre with golden yellow margins. Lime petioles and leaf scapes, topped by white flowers.

H. 'Marilyn' (Zilis 1990) displays bright gold, corrugated, heart-shaped leaves with pale lavender flowers in July. Best in light shade to sun. An early riser, sometimes caught out by late frost. 30x90cm (12x36").

H. 'Maui Buttecups' (Wm Vaughn 1991) makes a small mound to 25cm (10") and a spread of 35cm (14") of heavily cupped, puckered, round gold leaves offset against violet flowers on long scapes in July. Rugged, leathery foliage on a small golden hosta respected for its colouring. Best in light shade.

H. 'May' (Hansen 1999) is an all-gold sport from *June'*. A perfect golden mound of flattish foliage, topped with lavender flowers in late summer. A vigorous grower, best in sun to light shade. 30cm (12"). Z3-9.

H. 'Maya Swingtine' (Alttara Scheer) starts out chartreuse and will stay so in shade, but with some sun, this soon turns yellow. A very attractive, deeply veined variety. A definite swinger!

Hosta 'Maya Swingtime'

H. 'Mentor Gold' (Wayside Gardens) has pointed leaves of mid gold.

H. 'Midas Touch' (Aden 1978) everything turns to gold, deeply metallic gold, deeply cupped, deeply veined, corrugated leaves. A *tokudama* type with white flowers making a clump very slowly. Pale lavender white flowers are carried on long scapes in summer. Thrives in sun or partial shade. In the U.K. it will take almost full sun. 90x90cm (30x30").

H. 'Midwest Magic' is a beauty with a wide green margin, developing a gold centre.

H. 'Montana Mountian Sunrise' is like the sun coming up, but before it gets too high in the sky, this turns green by midsummer. Fantastic early colour. Heavily veined and rippled edges with heavy substance. Slightly shiny on both leaf surfaces. Near white tubular flowers in July on tall 1m (36") scapes.

H. 'Montana On Stage' (Aden) makes quick growth even though it emerges late. Large yellow leaves have irregular green margins topped by pale lavender flowers in August. 45cm (18").

H. 'Moonbeam' chartreuse leaves turn bright gold in a large clump. A sport of *'August Moon'* with pale flowers. Needs sun and moisture.

H. 'Moonlight' this rapid grower has largish golden leaves with a cream to white edge to complement the white flowers. Best with some sunshine. 45cm (18").

H. 'Moon Lily' (Harshbarger/Trott 1993) is a heavy-substanced gold with some *tokudama* parentage. Medium sized clump of cupped golden leaves with light lavender flowers in June.

H. 'Moon Waves' (Plater-Zyberk/Solberg 1994) this *'August Moon'* hybrid differs in its lance-shaped rippled leaves. The thick, dullish yellow leaves have a rounded base and prominent veining. Good colour all season. Lavender flowers. 40x60cm (16x24").

H. 'Morning Light' (Walters) is a reverse of *'Twilight'*, a bi-coloured plant with green margins and wide gold centres. A vigorous variety with great substance.37cm.

H. 'Murphy's Gold Marge' has corrugated, golden leaves with near white flowers and looks superb in dappled light.

H. 'Old Glory' (Hansen 1999) is breathtaking with its gold, heart-shaped leaves attractively margined in green with slightly rippled edges. A sport of *'Glory'* which is quick to make a medium-sized mound.

H. 'On Stage' (Aden 1986) bears bright gold, heart-shaped leaves with striking green variegated margins, slow to make a mound. Colouring dulls in shade on the heart-shaped, puckered leaves. Funnel-shaped lavender flowers in midseason. 35cm (14").

H. 'Ophir' (Fischer) bright gold elongated leaves are wavy. Cherry red petioles on an upright clump.

H. 'Paradise Power' (Fransen) is a sport of *'Sun Power'*, golden yellow leaves surrounded by a dark green margin. Pale lavender flowers in midsummer.

H. 'Paradise Standard' is another *'Gold Standard'* sport, looking similar to *'Moonlight'* when it matures with white edges to its gold leaves.

H. 'Patriot's Fire' (Summers/Walek) is a rapid grower with heart-shaped, bright gold foliage. An attractive white margin frames each leaf. Makes a large clump, having good substance and topped by lavender flowers in summer.

H. 'Paul's Glory' (P.Hofer/P.Ruh 1987) is a gold centred, blue-edged variety with the gold bleaching out to white later in the season. Lavender flowers are borne in late spring above the distinguished foliage. Best in part sun to light shade. A personal favourite, makes my heart skip a beat. 40x60cm (16x24"). Z3-9.

H. 'Peedee Gold Flash' (Syre-Herz 1987) bright lance to spoon shaped leaves are wavy and narrow with a green margin, the base of each petal is red-violet which is conspicuous against the lighter foliage colour. A vigorous, dwarf low spreader for the front of the border. Lavender flowers are purple striped on leafy scapes. 25x45cm (10x18").

H. 'Piedmont Gold' has prominent veins on bright gold foliage, softer colouring on the underleaf. A robust form with delightful flat, cordate, ripple-edged leaves reach 25cm (10") long and 17cm (7") wide on a fine cultivar plant which is good in part shade. White to palest lavender flowers in midsummer. Has become a classic yellow which is best in light shade, with a little sun to keep the colour. 50cm (20") tall and twice in width.

H. 'Pineapple Juice' (Solberg/Zilis 1999) is an all gold sport of the one below featuring bold, bright gold, narrow, wavy leaves, quick to make a medium clump. Excellent substance but nevertheless can burn in full sun in hot climates. Lavender flowers in August.

H. 'Pineapple Upside Down Cake' (Solberg/Zilis 1999) is aptly named, a golden wavy-leaved beauty with an attractive narrow green margin which is best in part sun to light shade. Ruffled, lance-shaped leaves unfurl green in spring. Lavender flowers are carried on 65cm (26") scapes above the 120cm (4ft) wide golden clumps which make excellent ground cover. 45cm (18"). Z3-9.

H. 'Pink Flamingo' (Livingston) a tremendous, I'll say that again, tremendous, stupendous upright beauty. Warm yellow leaves sit on upright stems, prettily blushed pink at the base. Hot pink scapes bear some of the loveliest hosta flowers with pink buds. If you could paint your dream hosta, it might well look like this. A knockout, glowing star!

H. 'Pooh Bear' (Falstad 1988) is a dainty, tiny leaved bright gold form with an irregular green margin making a neat plant with lavender flowers from June to July. Slow to increase in light shade to sun. 15x25cm (6x10").

H. 'PrairieLand Memories' (Q&Z Nursery) bears slightly glossy, wavy gold leaves. Has the fragrant white flowers of its parent and makes a stunning clump to 120cm (4ft) wide.

H. 'Preconscious' (Livingston) is a mound of glowing, golden-green corrugated leaves with a tempting white reverse.

H. 'Purple and Gold' (Minks 1976) makes a smallish, wavy-leaved plant with golden foliage and the added interest of purple spotted petioles and purple flowers.

H. 'Rainforest Sunrise' (J.Anderson) this sport of *'Maui Buttercups'* has the same excellent golden colouring with the addition of a very dark green margin. Lavender flowers. Makes a clump 40cm (16") across and 25cm (10") high.

H. 'Richland Gold' (Wade 1987) displays good golden colour in early summer, turning to parchment and is a fast spreader making a vigorous large mound. An all gold sport of *'Gold Standard'* with the same finicky requirements as to placement. Lavender flowers.

H. 'Rising Sun' (Vaughn 1988) is a large golden clump with glossy, pointed leaves having good substance. Provide ample moisture in the first year. Slug resist and enjoys a sunbathe in the morning. Pale purple flowers in late July on 90cm (3ft) scapes. 60cmx135cm (2x4.5ft).

Hosta 'Sea Fire'

Hosta 'Richland Gold' on the right, the gold-edged H. 'Honeysong' on the left

H. 'Rosedale Genevieve' (Hadrava 1999) makes a large golden yellow clump to brighten shade. Leaves are dull on top and moderately corrugated, with a glaucous bloom beneath. White flowers. 90cm (36").

H. 'Roxsanne' (Gerritt Heemskerk) has golden, wavy leaves. Makes a dense clump. Lavender flowers.

H. 'Royalty' is a small variety with gold leaves and deep purple flowers. 30cm (12").

H. 'Saint Elmo's Fire' (Solberg 1995) has some of the best bright yellow emerging leaf colour with a white edge. Heart-shaped leaves then fade to green, giving a two tone effect. Light lavender flowers and showy red petioles make this one a winner. A real showstopper in spring. 40x60cm (16x24").

H. 'Sea Dream' has bright gold foliage with a white margin. Good substance. Lavender flowers. 40cm.

H. 'Sea Fire' (Seaver) makes a medium clump of intense golden yellow leaves, especially in spring. Add to that, red petioles and dark red colour scapes and deep lavender flowers and you have the perfect image of a winner. Absolutely glows in spring.

H. 'Sea Gold Star' (Seaver 1984) bears ruffled, thick, yellow leaves with a crimped texture which emerge pale green. Makes a medium mound of large, flat, round to heart-shaped, striking leaves with a slight undulation. Star-shaped pale flowers on long scapes in midseason. Heavy substance, best in light shade. 70cm (28").

H. 'Sea Peridot' bears upright, seersucker extraordinaire bright gold leaves. Heavy substance and is cupped. Bright gold in sun. 40x70cm (16x28").

H. 'Sea White Gold' holds its white-gold colour well into late autumn. Upright growth.

H. 'Sea Wiggles' radiates with narrow, bright, wavy golden leaves. A good, sun tolerant clump, perfect for the rock garden. Light lavender flowers. 15cm (6").

H. 'Sea Yellow Sunshine' (Seaver 1985) displays a sea of bright yellow, oval leaves with pale lavender flowers on green petioles. Good substance but best in half shade. 20x40cm (8x16").

H. 'Semperaurea' has emerging chartreuse foliage quickly turning to bright yellow.

H. 'September Sun' (Solberg 1985) is a green-edged sport of *'August Moon'* with fair substance to the leaves. A rapid grower making a clump to 60cm (2ft) tall and 120cm (4ft) wide. Performs well right across the U.S. and U.K. with some morning sun. Lavender to white flowers in July on 70cm (28") scapes.

H. 'Shade Master' bears yellow leaves in spring, turning green. A large mound with pale flowers.

H. 'Sharmon' ('Phyllis Campbell') is a bright yellow medio-variegated *fortunei* type with impact. A U.K. introduction.

Hosta 'Stand Up'

H. 'Shiny Penny' (Solberg 1997) is a tiny gem just 15cm (6") tall with shiny gold leaves and rippled margins. Leaves have the added attraction of turning coppery as the season progresses. Lavender flowers appear in August.

H. 'Small Sum' (Goodwin) a half-sized hybrid of *'Sum and Substance'*. Bright yellow, ovate, waxy large leaves to 20cm (8"). Near-white flowers are held just above the foliage. Makes a clump 50cm (20") tall.

H. 'Solar Flare' (US Patent. Ross 1981) has thick, pointed, puckered glossy yellow leaves on emergence, fading to chartreuse towards the edge with widely spaced deep green veins. Palest lavender flowers on 90cm (36") scapes. This big yellow hosta is capable of making a fine specimen plant. 70x130cm (28"x52").

H. 'Spotlight' (Wilkins 1995) makes a large, erect clump with shiny, wavy golden leaves and lavender flowers. 50x120cm (20x48").

H. 'Spring Break' (Asch 2000) emerges chartreuse and changes to golden tones depending upon the amount of sun it receives. The white edge changes to yellow-gold as the season progresses. Lavender flowers in mid July. A good grower which multiplies quickly. In Michigan, U.S. it reaches 45x90cm (18x32").

H. 'Squash Casserole' (Avent 1995) bears gold new growth, fading to chartreuse. Easy to grow in sun and makes a 120cm (4ft) wide clump in sun when kept moist, or in partial shade. Light purple flowers top the foliage in early July. 40cmx120cm (16"x4ft).

H. 'Stained Glass' (Hansen 1999) is an improved sport of *'Guacamole'* making a rapid mound with brilliant, glossy golden summer foliage with a dark green edge having prominent leaf veins. Enjoys sun when kept moist and retains its bright colouring but is slightly less sun tolerant than its parent. Lavender flowers with good fragrance are borne in August. 38x90cm (15"x3ft).

H. 'Stand Up' (Livingston) is a dayglow, iridescent yellow which takes some sun. Hard to beat colour, deeply veined and slighly puckered, upright growing leaves with a lovely white reverse. Heavy substance and white flowers round this off nicely.

H. 'Starboard Light' (C. Seaver 1994) bears dark yellow oval leaves which are lightly folded and have good substance. Near white flowers are borne in July. 60cm (24") tall with a spread of 75cm (30").

H. 'Sum and Substance' (Aden 1980) take your hat off to one of the finest large specimen gold plants with excellent substance and sun tolerance when kept moist. Heavily textured leaves are shiny above and mealy white beneath to 45cm (18") long and 35cm (14") wide and offer good slug resistance. Opening chartreuse the shiny leaves quickly develop old gold colour in good light, yellow in sun. Petioles are red streaked towards the base. Lavender to near white flowers are borne on very long scapes in July to August. An excellent choice for the southern states of the U.S. 90cm (36") tall with a spread of over double the height. Van Wade in the U.S. had a specimen that measured 1m 20cm (48") by 3m (114") wide with leaves the size of a serving plate, 45cm (18") long and 35cm (14") wide. Deservedly popular.

H. 'Summer Serenade' (Klehm 1998) makes a very wide clump to 1.5m (5ft) of large, pointed, ruffled golden foliage with a neat green border which is excellent in part sun to light shade. Near white flowers appear in early summer on this stunning hosta. 70cm (28"). Z3-9.

H. 'Sun Glow' is a little dazzler with crinkled golden leaves and white flowers. 40cm (16").

H. 'Sun Power' (Aden 1986) bears intense bright gold, pointed, oval leaves with wavy, twisted margins having an upright habit. This golden delight colours early and holds until first frosts. A sun worshipper appreciating a measure of morning sun to bring out the best leaf colour, but can burn in full overpowering sun. Will thrive in southern states of N. America. Lavender flowers on long scapes appear in July. 65cm (26") tall with a good spread of 1m 55cm (62"). Z3-8.

H. 'Sunlight' (Williams) bears flat yellow leaves that make an enormous clump. An early hybrid with large leaves. White flowers in July. 65x110cm (26x43").

H. 'Sunny Delight' (Solberg/Zilis 2000) has luminescent golden foliage with a delicately rippled margin. Bears long, pure white, tubular flowers with a delightful fragrance. This upright grower will take lots of sun and heat.

H. 'Sunny Disposition' (F. Nyikos 2001) is a sun-tolerant *ventricosa* type with good purple flowers in July above a medium clump of heart-shaped gold leaves which are very bright in sun.

H. 'Super Bowl' (Aden) bears deeply cupped and corrugated, heart shaped leaves in yellow. Lavender flowers. Light shade to sun. 45x55cm (18x22").

H. 'Sweet Sunshine' (Solberg 1997) makes a decent mound of cupped, round golden upright leaves beneath pure white fragrant flowers on 55cm (22") scapes in August. A dream! 35cm (14").

H. 'Sweet Tater Pie' (Avent 1995) is a small hosta bearing very shiny, oval, thick, waxy bright gold leaves with excellent contrasting deep purple spidery flowers in July. 25cm (10") and a spread up to three times the height.

H. 'Tequila Sunrise' (Johnson G) has attractive bright glowing golden leaves with a wavy edge. Interesting red petioles. 90cm (36").

H. 'Tortilla Chip' (Solberg 2002) a sport of *Stained Glass* which is a sun tolerant bright yellow with heart-shaped leaves and large fragrant pale lavender flowers in August. Smaller growing than *Fried Bananas* and holds its brighter colouring well. A good grower. 45cm (18") tall and 1m (40") wide.

H. 'Treasure' has gold leaves with heavy substance and seersucker texture. White flowers. 65cm (26").

H. 'Ultraviolet Light' (Wilkins 1989) makes a medium clump of bright golden emerging leaves which gradually change to greenish yellow as the season progresses. Slightly undulating, pointed leaves and purple flowers are features of this hosta.

H. 'Vanilla Cream' (Aden 1986) is a small form to 20cm (8") tall and twice the width, with almost round, smooth with good substance. Emerge light lemon with a green cast, through yellow to cream. Light lavender flowers appear in July to August. This seedling of *Little Aurora* will brighten any shady area of the garden and will take a little sun.

Hosta 'Wee One'

H. 'Wee One' (Livingston) has gorgeous yellow leaves with a slight wave, deeply veined with slight puckering, and pinkish purple buds.

H. 'Whiskey Sour' (Solberg 2002) makes a medium clump of undulating, oval leaves emerging and remaining gold with red petioles and some red to the leaf tip. Lavender flowers on straight scapes in July to August

H. 'White Gold' bears white flowers in July and emerging foliage is gold turning green. A *fortunei aurea* type selected by Derek Fox.

H. 'Winfield Gold' (Zilis) is an all yellow sport of *'Sea Dream'* with pale lavender flowers. Attractive.

H. 'Wogon Gold' is a tiny clump of narrow, wavy golden leaves perfect for the rock garden. 15cm (6").

H. 'Xanadu Amora' (Skaggs) makes a medium to large upright clump with radiant yellow leaves. Deep venation and a nice wavy edge to the leaf.

H. 'Xanadu Dlanor' (Skaggs) is a sport of *'Little Aurora'* with the vigour and garden worthiness of its parent. The yellow leaf has a green watermark, deeper in the centre. Very striking.

H. 'Yellow Emperor' (R.Savoy 1987) bears upright, pointed, heart-shaped golden leaves with prominent green veins beneath lavender flowers in July. 50cm (20") tall with a spread of 75cm (30").

H. 'Yellow Ice' (Livingston) will set you afire and your garden ablaze, with pure yellow young leaves, conspicuous veining, a tantalising ripple to the leaf.

H. 'Yellow Flame' (Hawes 1999) bears big yellow leaves with a thin green edge. Lavender flowers.

H. 'Yellow Swoosh' (Livingston) bears lance shaped pointed leaves which reach up to heaven, and this is hosta heaven. Nice golden colour.

H. 'Yellow Waves' bears undulate and lanceolate leaves. A good mound 20cm (8") with pale flowers.

H. 'Zounds' (Aden 1978) has intensely puckered, oval to heart-shaped, semi-glossy metallic golden leaves. Good slug-resist foliage makes excellent ground cover. White-lavender flowers on long scapes in July. Will take sun, but holds its colour well in shade and simply glows, especially at dusk. Juvenile plants are smoother leaved and greener. 50x90cm (20x36").

Hot Partner: *Heuchera 'Velvet Night', x Heucherella 'Burnished Bronze', Rheum, Rodgersia.*

Cool companions: *Amaranthus caudatus 'Viridis', Epimedium, Hemerocallis, Heuchera.*

Above: Hosta 'Xanadu Dlanor'
Below: Hosta 'Yellow Ice'

HUMULUS

Although herbaceous, the golden hop is very vigorous and can easily clothe unsightly objects in the summer months. Grown for its bright foliage in sun. Once established it is drought resist.

HOW TO GROW
A well-drained sunny position in moist, humus-rich soil will keep the golden hop happy. Prune hard to the ground in early spring. Root softwood cuttings in spring or greenwood cuttings in summer with bottom heat. Z7-10.

Humulus lupulus 'Aureus'

H. lupulus 'Aureus', the golden hop is a superb golden, herbaceous climber, especially in spring when colour is at its best. This is a quick, vigorous climber that might need restricting owing to its running root system. Easily capable of covering a fence in one season and can scramble through evergreens. Train on a pergola. As a bonus, female green cones are fragrant, even more so when dried. Male and female golden hops are available. 5m (15ft).

Just as I went to press I heard of a new dwarf version.

Hot Partners: *Viola 'Huntercombe Purple', Geranium psilostemon, Vitis vinifera 'Purpurea', Geranium 'Khan'*

Cool Companion: *Ceanothus x delileanus cvs, Ceratostigma willmottianum.*

Golden Glory: *Lonicera x heckrotti 'Goldflame', Berberis 'Bonanza Gold'.*

HYDRANGEA

Hydrangea are superb, handsome deciduous shrubs. Fabulous flowers are fascinating owing to the tonal differences on one bush. Flowerheads can be dried for floral arrangements. Best in a light woodland setting but equally useful in a herbaceous border.

HOW TO GROW

Best grown in moderately fertile, moist but well-drained soils in part shade. Will tolerate full sun in consistently moist ground. Provide shelter from cold, drying winds. Can become chloritic in shallow chalk. Z6-9.

H. anomala ssp petiolaris 'Aurea' (*petiolaris 'Aurea'*) was found by Chuck Pavlich in the Pacific Northwest. Its chartreuse emerging foliage quickly turns to brilliant sunshine yellow. Hardy climbing hydrangea is useful for clothing a shady wall or fence.

H. 'Lemon Wave' is a variegated big leaf hydrangea. This decidous shrub enjoys part shade in moist, well-drained soil. Will take full sun in consistently moist soils. Produces lacecap blue flowers on acid soils and pink ones on alkaline. 90-180cm (3-6ft). Z6-9.

H. quercifolia 'Little Honey' is an oak-leaved type, which I normally admire for their bronzing capabilities with the onset of autumn, but this one has leaves that unfold brilliant gold, the colour being well retained until summer, becoming chartreuse then finally green, when it is complemented by huge trusses of white flowers. In autumn the leaves do turn scarlet in colder weather. Both red leaves and stems will persist in warmer climates right through winter making this a perfect, all-season shrub. A sport of *'Pee Wee'*. Plant this on your patio in sun in northern U.S. states and the U.K. and partially shaded in southern U.S. states. 120x90cm (4x3ft). Z.5-9.

H. serrata 'Golden Sunlight' PBR has bronze young leaves turning clear yellow in spring, later pale green, and finally burgundy tinted in autumn. An unusual ornamental for the garden with two tone lacecap pink flowers. Thrives in partial shade. A sport of *'Bluebird'* found in Holland in 1990. A real smasher in spring. 60-90cm (2-3ft). Z6-10.

H. 'Sun Goddess' has emerging golden foliage in late spring, keeping its colour through the heat and sun of summer. Thick leaves, vigorous growth and floriferous, deep pink blooms make this a good addition to the golden garden. 120x90cm (4x3ft). Cool Companion: *Miscanthus sinensis* and cultivars

H. anomala ssp petiolaris 'Aurea'
H. serrata 'Golden Sunlight'

HYPERICUM

Usually grown for their golden flowers, I found this gold-leaf form at the Village Green Garden, Cottage Grove, Oregon. In May, this was absolutely knock-out.

HOW TO GROW
Relatively unfussy and easy.

H. 'Summer Gold' is a fabulous shrubby form with wonderful coloration. Absolutely aglow in spring. I think this looks absolutely fantastic with H. androsaemum 'Albury Purple'. Use it in a shrubby or mixed border or in the rock garden. Shelter from cold, drying winds.
Most definitely a sunshine plant.

Hypericum 'Summer Gold'

IBERIS

Normally seen at the edge of a front garden or a rock garden, this golden leaved variety will break the mould. Makes good bright ground cover in sunny areas. Can be grown in wall crevices too.

HOW TO GROW
Best in full sun and well-drained soil. Give a light prune if it becomes leggy. Remove spent flowerheads. Easy to grow and easy maintenance. Hardy. Z3-9.

I. 'Golden Candy' PBR is a gold-foliaged perennial candytuft with white flowers in spring to summer. Best in full sun at the front of a sunny border or in containers. To keep this looking handsome, deadhead and shear over lightly when it has finished flowering. Found at a nursery in Kent, England. An excellent rock plant or tub plant. 25x30cm (10x12").Z3.

ILEX

Golden holly is usually variegated. Handsome shrubs and trees grown for their usually glossy leaves and berries. Male and female flowers are usually borne on separate plants, both sexes are needed for berries to form. Excellent in the woodland garden or as specimen trees.

HOW TO GROW

Moist but well-drained, moderately fertile soil in full sun especially for variegated holly, or in partial shade. Transplant in late winter to early spring. Clip in summer. Trim hedges in early spring.

Ilex crenata 'Golden Gem' is a dwarf, compact shrub with soft yellow foliage turning yellow-green in summer. A female form which is very shy of flowering, but looks particularly good in winter and spring. Japanese holly resembles *Buxus* more than typical, prickly holly. Best colour in full sun. 60cm (2ft). Z6-10.

Ilex attenuata 'Samuel Foster' bears narrow leaves which are yellow when young, turning green.

I. 'Sunny Foster' is flushed golden with narrow, shiny foliage which is very attractive especially in winter. A sport which occurred in the U.S. National Arboretum in Washington.

There are many fine variegated forms with either a central splash of gold or a gold margin such as *I. x altaclerensis 'Belgica Aurea', I. x altaclerensis 'Lawsoniana'* and the very attractive *I. aquifolium 'Golden Milkboy'* amongst others. Z6-10.

Hot Partner: *Parthenocissus tricuspidata 'Veitchii', Potentilla atrosanguinea.*

Cool Companion: *Ceanothus, Clematis 'Violacea'.*

Golden Glory: *Clematis 'Bill Mackenzie, Potentilla recta 'Pallida'.*

JASMINUM

Winter jasmine is one of the most beautiful shrubs at this time of year, with its clear yellow flowers on naked branches from November to February. Its strong, angular form is much to be appreciated and valued for covering unsightly walls with its floral show. Cut back if needed immediately after flowering. It makes an attractive subject for fan-training on a wall and is always worth training low so that it can happily interact with smaller, early-flowering plants such as *Iris unguicularis.* Common white jasmine is a strong growing, scandent or twining climber with deliciously scented flowers. Appreciate the intoxicating scent on any pergola or arch and by the main door to the house. Personally I prefer it to have green leaves. A sheltered spot is needed to grow this in cold northern districts in well-drained soil and full sun.

HOW TO GROW

Winter jasmine does well in any aspect except an east-facing wall. Does best in sun, in fertilised, well-drained soil, well-watered if at the base of a wall. Take semi-ripe cuttings in summer or layer in autumn. Unpruned to 4.5m (15ft). Z6-9.

J. nudiflorum 'Aureum' has leaves almost entirely yellow or yellow-blotched, looking good right into summer. As usual with winter jasmine, the yellow flowers, heralders of warmer weather to come, are unscented. 3m (10ft).

J. officinale 'Aureum' (*'Aureovariegatum'*) has variegated leaves suffused yellow, with the usual white deliciously scented flowers.

J. officinale 'Fiona Sunrise' (*'Frojas'*) PBR (Dave West.) This form was found as a seedling in 1989 and launched in 1995, it bears yellow-flushed leaves with white fragant flowers in summer. 6m (20ft).

Hot Partner: *Hedera 'Glymii', Helleborus black*

Cool Companion: *Hedera 'Sulphur Heart'.*

JUNCUS

Designer rushes, this is truly amazingly golden and very desirable. Unusual twisted stems make these rushes instantly noticeable. Suitable for a bog garden or by water. Hardy. Wow!

HOW TO GROW
Grow in permanently moist, acid soil. Best in light shade. Can be grown in up to 8cm (3") water. Divide in mid-spring to early summer. Z4-9.

J. effusus f spiralis 'Blonde Ambition' is the golden plant to grow by the pond or in moist soil. It will amaze and be admired and coveted by all. Each leaf looks like it has been tightly wound around a circular object, no wonder it is known as corkscrew rush. Ten times better than the green version. Tangled, leafless stems are one of the wonders of the plant world. Suppliers will never be able to keep up with the demand this plant is going to create. If you see it, grab it. The ultimate in cool!!! Designer gold rush! Found by Bill Jansen of Collector's Nursery, Washington State, USA. 20x45cm (8x18").

J. effusus 'Gold Strike' is a rare striped Japanese rush with stiff leaves having a gold stripe. New growth is pink flushed. Excellent in boggy ground but will also perform in average garden soil that does not dry out. 30x30cm (12x12"). Z3-11.

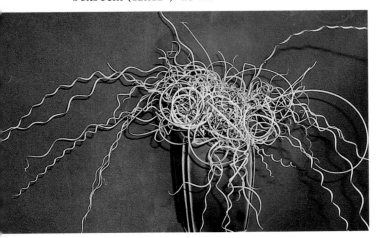

JUNIPERUS

Junipers range from prostrate or creeping alpines to dense shrubs and tall trees. They usually bear distinct juvenile and adult foliage. Evergreens do not have to be green, create a more interesting landscape with varied colourful foliage. Male and female strobili are borne on the same or on separate plants. Rounded fruits become fleshy and berry-like. Prostrate forms make excellent ground cover and columnar forms are excellent accents in the rock garden or border. Superb, low maintenance plants.

HOW TO GROW
Junipers are suited to many soils and situations and are the best conifer for chalk soils. Enjoy dryish, sandy soil and are tolerant of hot, dry conditions. Best in full sun or light, dappled shade. Root ripewood cuttings in early autumn. Z3-9 depending on species.

J. chinensis 'Aurea' is known as Young's golden juniper. It makes a tall, slender tree with green young foliage turning gold when mature. A male, conical form, it is slow to establish, but grows quickly once settled in. Foliage can scorch in full sun, especially when young, but it does appreciate a dry, sunny aspect. This very old cultivar dates from 1855. 2m (6ft) in 10 years, ultimately 10m (30ft).

J. chinensis 'Expansa Aureospicata' on little branches above ground level, this spreading juniper is cloaked in green foliage with butter yellow patches. Full sun to shade, making a good undercover story for other plants, to brighten darker areas. Slow to start. Not as attractive as *'Plumosa Aurea'*. 50cmx1.5m (20"x4ft).

J. chinensis 'Mac's Golden' has yellow outer foliage with a white stomatal band on an upright grower which is best in full sun. 1-1.5m (3-5ft).

J. chinensis 'Plumosa Aurea' (x media, x pfitzeriana *'Plumosa Aurea'*) was introduced in England before 1855 with good gold foliage and slow growth, forming a broad, bushy shape. This highly ornamental form has ascending branches which arch at the tips. Colour is enhanced in full sun. Turns bronze-gold in winter. Superb. 60cmx1.8m (24"x6ft spread).

J. communis 'Brynhyfryd Gold' has new foliage flushed yellow and steely grey winter foliage once established. Best in full sun.

J. communis 'Depressa Aurea' is a dwarf, spreading shrub with semi-erect branches but essentially procumbent growth. Its golden leaves become bronze later in the season and green up in winter. An excellent carpeting ground cover in sun, spreading its rays of sunshine even in inhospitable soils, it appreciates a very dry root run. Very hardy but prone to sun scorch in warmer climates. 60cm (24") tall with a spread to 1m (3ft). Z2.

J. communis 'Gold Cone' is grown for its golden foliage which is best in spring and summer, holding well into winter when it becomes bluish-green. Formal, compact pyramidal habit. Best in full sun. Makes a good, low-maintenance hedge in a dry climate. Successful in the Midwest U.S. Slow growing, makes a nice focal point on a rockery and is an equally good patio plant. Introduced into commerce by Kordes of Bilsen, Germany in 1980. 1.5m (5ft). Z2.

J. communis 'Hibernica Aurea' is another gold pyramidal form, elegant and slender. 3m (10ft).

J. communis 'Schneverdingen Goldmachangel' (*'Golden Showers'*, *'Golden Schnapp'*, *'Gelb'*) discovered by Gunther Horstmann in West Germany, is a fountain like form with lush gold foliage which is very bright in spring and summer and yellow-bronze in winter in full sun. 1.2mx 30cm (4x1ft).

J. horizontalis 'Golden Carpet' is a dwarf, low growing yellow-green variety making slow groundcover in semi-shade. Displays a pinkish hue in autumn and winter. A sport of the glaucous blue *'Wiltonii'*. 10cm x 1.5m (4" x 5ft).

J. horizontalis 'Kaniere Gold' makes very flat ground cover with yellow foliage turning gold in winter. Very slow growing. 8x70cm (3x28").

J. horizontalis 'Limeglow' (Vergeer) is a dwarf mutant of *J. horizontalis 'Andorra Compact'* with dark yellow needles, being less vigorous. Orange-tinted in winter.

Top: Juniperus horizontalis 'Limeglow'
Above: Juniperus horizontalis 'Mother Lode'

J. horizontalis 'Mother Lode' is a creeping, golden leaved, evergreen shrub needing full sun to maintain its colour. Attractive ground cover turns pinkish bronze in winter. Soft, feathery, scale-like foliage makes an excellent golden carpet. Fleshy seed cones are produced infrequently. Superb in a rock garden especially at the edge, or in a shrubbery as a low colour splash. Discovered in 1982 at Iseli Nursery as a sport on *'Wiltoni'*. 1mx3m (3x10ft). Z3-9.

J. x pfitzeriana 'Aorangi Gold' PVR was found in south Canterbury, New Zealand and released to the market

Top: J. x pfitzeriana 'Carbery Gold'
Above: J. x pfitzeriana 'Gold Coast'

in 1992. This sport from *'Mint Julep'* offers bright yellow foliage in full sun with rich gold colouring in winter. 2x2m (6x6ft).

J. x pfitzeriana 'Carbery Gold' (*'Old Gold Carbery'*) is bright gold for the biggest part of the year. Makes a neat, compact plant in sun. 30x75cm (12x30").

J. x pfitzeriana 'Dandelight' makes small, spreading ground cover with its golden foliage ageing to a lighter colour in winter. Very hardy, attractive juniper with soft juvenile foliage. Tolerant of coastal winds. 60cm (24") with a 1.5m (5ft) spread.

J. x pfitzeriana 'Gold Coast' spreads its wonderful chrome-yellow foliage in an irregular, compact, flat topped mound. Colouring is best in cold weather. This fine cultivar makes excellent groundcover and is best in sun. A branch sport of *'Old Gold'* found at Sakiyama Nursery, California in 1965. More open and flatter growing than its parent. 1mx1.5m (3x5ft). Hardy to -30°F. Z 4-9.

J x pfitzeriana 'Gold Sovereign' (*'Blound'*) PBR is a sport of *'Old Gold'*, having slower growth and more persistent brilliant golden foliage on a semi-prostrate form. 60cmx1.5m (2x5ft).

J. x pfitzeriana 'Gold Star' is a compact spreader which is very hardy and holds its colour well in sun or semi-shade. 70cmx1.2m (28x48").

J. x pfitzeriana 'Golden Saucer' bears bright yellow-gold leaves especially in winter. 1.5m (5ft) with a spread of just 30cm (12").

J. x pfitzeriana 'Kuriwao Gold' (*chinensis*) is a large, dense rounded shrub whose bright gold foliage is best in full sun. Takes off quite quickly to reach 1m, then growth slows down. Withstands drought and can be clipped to make a neat hedge. Has the added extra of an orange tint in winter. Raised in New Zealand before 1975. Height and spread 2m (6ft).

J. x pfitzeriana 'Mordigan Gold' is a sport of *x pfitzeriana 'Aurea'* and very similar, only differing in its more compact form. Golden foliage is brightest in summer.

J. x pfitzeriana 'Old Gold' a sport, of *'Pfitzeriana Aurea'* makes a neat, compact, semi-prostrate golden plant for a large rock garden or as taller ground cover. Bronze-gold, layered foliage retains its colour in winter. 70cmx1m (30x36").

J. x pfitzeriana 'Pfitzeriana Aurea' has gold arching leaves in summer which become bronzey green in winter. This vigorous variety is drought resistant. 1m (3ft) with a spread of at least twice the height. Z4-9.

J. x pfitzeriana 'Saybrook Gold' is a low compact spreader with intense yellow colouring in full sun, turning bronze in winter. Introduced by Girard Nurseries in the U.S. who claim that it retains its

122

colouring better than any other juniper. 1mx60cm (3x2ft). Z4.

J. x pfitzeriana 'Sulphur Spray' (*virginiana*) is a sport of *'Hetzii'* with soft yellow-green new growth which ages to grey-green. 2m (6ft) height and width. Z. 2-9.

J. x pfitzeriana 'Tiverton' was found in New Plymouth and developed by Cedar Lodge, New Zealand. A very adaptable sport of *'Pfitzeriana Glauca'* with bright lemon-yellow foliage in all seasons in full sun or partial shade. Its compact, low-spreading ground cover is ideal for a small garden. Very hardy. 40cmx1m (16x36").

J. x pfitzeriana 'Winter Gold' is similar to *'Gold Coast'* but has slightly brighter winter colouring.

Hot Partner: *Cotinus coggygria 'Royal Velvet'*, *Helianthemum red*, *Parthenocissus quinquefolia* (must be kept in check).

Cool Companion: *Aceana caesiiglauca*, *Festuca glauca*.

Golden Glory: *Anthemis 'Sauce Hollandaise'*, *Erica arborea 'Albert's Gold'*.

LABURNUM

Small, easily cultivated and highly ornamental trees are suited to most soils. The yellow pea flowers which droop admirably are the main attraction of this hardy, decorative tree. A laburnum walk with the racemes hanging from a pergola is a sight to behold in late spring and early summer. These are not plants for gardens with young children, all parts, especially seeds are poisonous.

HOW TO GROW

Grow in moderately fertile, well-drained soil in full sun. Graft in late winter or bud in summer. Z5-7.

L. anagyroides 'Aureum' although sometimes liable to revert, the rare golden laburnum has soft yellow leaves in summer to accompany the golden rain of pea flowers. Colour is retained better in cooler climates.

J. x pfitzeriana 'Old Gold'

LAMIUM

Herbaceous perennials with creeping stems forming wide mats of colour in loose, leafy soil. Radiant from early spring to autumn, what more could one ask of ground cover, but dead nettles can also be used to advantage in hanging baskets and containers. Pruned hard after flowering, *Lamium* double their usefulness with a second flush of flowers. Extremely tolerant of varied conditions, even under deciduous trees such as *Betula*. Can overpower smaller plants, although yellow-leaved varieties seem to be less vigorous.

HOW TO GROW
A little shade in hot climates, will take sun in cooler climates in consistently moist soil. Leaf scorch will occur in full sun in a dry site. Divide in autumn or early spring. Take stem cuttings of non-flowering shoots in early summer. Easy to grow, low maintenance. Hardy to -40°F (-40°C). Z. 3-8.

L. maculatum 'Aureum' (*'Gold Leaf'*, *'Golden Nuggets'*) has foliage of bright chartreuse-yellow to wholly yellow with a vivid silver central stripe. Purple-pink flowers. Pale green stems sometimes have a bronze tinge. The bright colouring is best in a little shade. I saw an exceptional patch of this at Bloom River Nursery in Oregon. Some consider *'Golden Nuggets'* to be brighter, the RHS deem them to be the same. The best of the yellow dead nettles. 20cm (8").
L. maculatum 'Beedham's White' is similar to *'Aureum'* but has the perfect complement of white flowers. Must be in shade. 20cm (8").
L. maculatum 'Cannon's Gold' prefers shade as it will scorch in full sun, produces purple flowers. Similar to *'Aureum'* but without the silver slash. Topped by purple flowers. Best in shade. 15-25cm (6-10").
L. maculatum 'Elisabeth de Haas' has leaves wholly yellow or blotched yellow on stems with a reddish brown tinge. Attractive variegation topped by lavender pink blooms.

L. maculatum 'Forncett Lustre' has silver leaves with a gold dusting.
L. maculatum 'Golden Anniversary' ('Dellam') PBR makes moderate growth on stoloniferous stems. Purplish hooded flowers held above the foliage in late spring to summer. A sport of *'Golden Nuggets'* raised by Wayne Eady of Ardelamore, Wisbech, England in 1966. Its dark green leaves are edged in gold and have a silver splash, a very unusual tricolour variegation. Vigorous in ideal conditions. 20-25cm (8-10"). L. *'Anne Greenaway'* looks the same to me.
L. maculatum 'Ickwell Beauty' has green leaves splashed with yellow and a narrow white stripe. Easy, but does revert. White flowers have a faint pink tinge. Found by Danae Johnston.
Hot Partner: *Ajuga 'Braunherz' or 'Ebony', Anthriscus sylvestris 'Ravenswing', Ophiopogon planiscapus 'Nigrescens'.*
Cool Companion: *Muscari neglectum, Muscari botryoides 'Album'.*
Golden Glory: *Origanum vulgare 'Aureum', Stachys byzantina 'Primrose Heron', Hosta 'Elvis On Stage'.*

Lamium maculatum 'Golden Nuggets'

LAURUS

A large evergreen which is very effective as a specimen. The bay laurel is grown for its aromatic foliage. This Mediterranean native makes a dense, shrub, pyramidal in shape. Foliage may be damaged by strong winds. Responds well to clipping.

HOW TO GROW
Best in sun to partial shade in well-drained, fertile soil. As a young plant provide protection in cold winters and grow in containers where prolonged frosts occur, moving into a cool greenhouse when necessary. Take semi-ripe cuttings in summer. Z8-10.

L. nobilis 'Aurea' is a golden form of the bay laurel, with the culinary uses of the green form. It looks particularly attractive in winter and spring. Some leaves are flushed more lime than others. Slightly hardier than the type. 3m (10ft).
L. nobilis 'Sunspot' is very unusual. Attractive dark green bay leaves are marked with creamy yellow variegation. Makes a very handsome shrub. Protected moist area in partial shade. Introduced by Brookside Gardens, U.S. 1-3m (3-10ft).

LEYCESTERIA

I have been promoting, for the past five years, the pheasant berry in my book on dark plants, for its wonderful deep maroon bracts which hang from branch tips. Here is a wonderful golden foliaged form.

HOW TO GROW
Moderately fertile, well-drained soil in full sun or partial shade. Protect from cold, drying winds and mulch deeply in autumn where frosts are severe. Take softwood cuttings in summer. Z7-8, or possibly as low as 6.

L. formosa 'Golden Lanterns' ('Notbruce') PBR was discovered by Bruce Barber in the U.K. Its golden foliage colours bronze in autumn and looks good even in late September in England with attractive purple bracts surrounding the white flowers in summer and red berries following in autumn. Resistant to sun scorch and is best in full sun or part shade. Behaves as a perennial shrub in hot climates, in cooler areas it will die back to the ground each winter. Makes an interesting patio container plant. Adaptable as to soil. 90-120cm (3-4ft).
L. 'Golden Pheasant' is a variegated form.
Hot Partner: Rosa 'Robin Hood', Hypericum androsaemum 'Albury Purple'.

Leycesteria formosa 'Golden Lanterns'

LIGUSTRUM

Golden privet is so much more interesting than the usual green. A golden hedge adds a lot to a garden and it can be clipped into pyramids or other interesting shapes. Hard pruning in the first year creates sweeping branches and a welcome bushy habit from the base. Keep neat for edging beds and borders.

HOW TO GROW
Fast-growing, shade-tolerant and not fussy as to soil. Full sun brings out the best colour in golden and variegated forms. Take semi-ripe cuttings in summer or hardwood cuttings in winter. Z5-8.

L. japonicum 'Howard' has young yellow leaves becoming green when mature on an adaptable shrub. Leathery, glossy foliage, white flowers and black berries if unpruned.
L. lucidum 'Excelsum Superbum' is a variegated cultivar with yellow-edged, green leaves. Flowers have a strong, overpowering odour. This species is found on hillsides in China and Korea. 15m (50ft).
L. ovalifolium 'Aureum' (*'Aureomarginatum'*) the Californian golden privet has bright leaves of rich yellow with green centres, often wholly yellow. A tough plant, tolerant of sites, loses its leaves in the coldest areas. Often reverts. 4m (12ft). Z7.
L. 'Vicaryi' is a bushy, semi-evergreen, rounded shrub with bright gold leaves in full sun. In winter, foliage turns bronze-purple. Deciduous but leaves can persist. Does not give its best if sheared often. Capable of reaching 3m (10ft or more). Z 5-8.
L. vulgare 'Aureum' performs well on chalk. This form has dull yellow leaves. Shear for hedging, or allow it to make a free standing specimen, which is often much more pleasing. Cut back hard each spring. Useful for floral arrangements. 3m (10ft).
L. vulgare 'Chlorocarpum' has green foliage, with mature yellow-green fruits, conspicuous in autumn when left unpruned. *L. vulgare 'Xanthocarpum'* is similar with yellow fruits. 2m (6ft).

LIRIODENDRON

These handsome, large, deciduous trees possess distinctive leaves which turn clear yellow in autumn, usually looking at their best in October to November. If they have one fault it is that their flowers are too high up to see, but it is for the foliage alone that these have been selected.

HOW TO GROW
Fast growing hardy tulip trees succeed in fertile soil, preferring deep, moist, slightly acidic soil in full sun to partial shade, but not in extreme heat. Z5.

L. tulipifera 'Aureomarginatum' is a striking tree with leaves broadly edged in bright yellow, turning greenish yellow by late summer. Butter-yellow autumn tints and green-yellow fruits occur on mature specimens. Handsome. 24m (80ft).
L. tulipifera 'Glen Gold' was raised in Australia and has pure soft yellow leaves all summer long.
L. tulipifera 'Mediopictum' (*'Aureopictum'*) bears foliage with a large irregular yellow blotch which is variable in size but has the advantage over *'Aureomarginatum'* in that the colour does not fade. Broadly columnar habit.

LIRIOPE

Once in awhile there comes a dream plant. **L. muscari 'Peedee Ingot'** is such a plant.
Golden leaves on an *Ophiopogon* look alike. Makes nice clumps of golden foliage in sun to shade, and is a must for every garden. From Ursula Herz in South Carolina, this neat 'grass' will lighten up woodland and look just as spectacular at the front of a border, kept moist, not wet. Brightest colour is found with new growth. A great perennial for a golden accent topped by 30cm (12") stems of lilac-lavender flowers in late summer. 25cm (10"). Z6-10.
Hot partner: *Ophiopogon planiscapus 'Nigrescens'*

LONICERA

Dense evergreen with small leaves is used for hedging where it responds well to clipping and is quick to grow. Can be left unpruned. Suitable for shade, but these golden cultivars are best in sun and cope well on chalk soils. Dislikes wet and windy sites. Easy and quick growing.

HOW TO GROW
Well-drained soil in full sun. Trim in April and September. Take semi-ripe cuttings in summer. Z6 or 7-9.

L. japonica 'Aureoreticulata' is a twining climber of the type of honeysuckle usually grown for its flowers, but this one has green leaves, intricately netted with yellow veins. 10m (30ft).

L. nitida 'Baggesens' Gold' is a beautiful, small, evergreen shrub with the tendency to turn green in shade. This bushy shrub can be clipped like *Buxus*, box, but unlike this slow grower, *Lonicera* will assume a positive shape in a year. When left unclipped it produces arching stems. Also makes a good standard and is then excellent surrounded by golden thyme or a golden ivy. An interesting, striking evergreen in winter, and in cold areas foliage can turn plum-purple, mine is thus suffused from October on. Insignificant yellowish green flowers are followed by mauve fruits. 1.5m (5ft).

L. nitida 'Edmee Gold' (*'Briloni'*) TM has excellent gold foliage for groundcover. A sport of *'Maigrun'*.

L. 'Lemon Beauty' (*'Lemon Spreader'*) an attractive new plant with tiny green leaves having a golden-yellow border. Responds well to clipping. Spring growth has a purplish tinge. Not as gold as *'Baggesen's'* but bright in winter and makes useful ground cover. 1m (3ft).

L. nitida 'Twiggy' is a sport of *'Baggesen's Gold'*, a dwarf shrub with leaves margined or entirely yellow, bronzing in winter. Bright gold leaves, best in full sun. 1.5m (5ft).

Hot Partner: when not clipped to shape will support a *viticella type Clematis, Geranium 'Khan'.*
Cool Companion: *Geranium 'Orion', Ipomoea 'Heavenly Blue'. Golden Glory: Stipa tenuissima, Yucca flaccida 'Golden Sword'.*

Lonicera nitida 'Baggesen's Gold' close-up and as a hedge

LUZULA

Woodrushes are found mainly in moist woodland, fens and bogs and are closely related to true rushes (*Juncus*) but having broader leaves. These perennial grasses make good groundcover and are excellent in containers too making a superb winter accent of glowing foliage. Easy.

HOW TO GROW
Grow in moderately fertile, moist but well-drained soil in partial shade. Will take full sun in reliably moist soil. Divide between mid-spring and early summer. Z5

L. sylvatica 'Aurea' (*L. maxima 'Aurea'*) has yellow-green leaves turning bright yellow in winter. Hardy, drought tolerant and quite adaptable to soil types. Broad grassy leaves with arching flower spikes. Evergreen groundcover for the moist, woodland floor looking like a ray of sunshine in the depths of winter. 70cm (28").
L. sylvatica 'Hohe Tatra' has light green leaves with outstanding gold colour in winter with persistent brown flowers. Compact. 50cm (20").
Hot Partner: *Miscanthus sinensis v purpurascens.*
Cool Companion: *Hosta 'Bressingham Blue', 'Devon Blue', 'Halcyon'.*
Golden Glory: *Hosta 'Elvis On Stage', 'Pink Flamingo', 'August Moon', Rhododendron luteum, Symphytum 'Belsay Gold'.*

Below: Lysimachia 'Outback Sunset'
Right: Lysimachia nummularia 'Aurea'

LYSIMACHIA

Moneywort or creeping jenny has creeping rootstocks which spread with ease wherever leaf nodes come into contact with the soil. It therefore has an indefinite spread in need of a harness. Semi-shade will limit its spread but this golden cultivar will display its yellow colouring better in sun. Thrives in damp soils that would kill many ground covers. Easy to naturalise a bank or woodland. Tolerant of limited foot traffic, but usually too invasive as an edger or in the border.

HOW TO GROW
Prefers humus-rich, moist soil which never dries out in summer in full sun to partial shade. Divide in spring or autumn. Hardy to -12°F (-25°C). Z.3-11.

L. congestiflora 'Outback Sunset' PBR bears incredibly sunshine-like yellow flowers in spring and all summer nestling over bright variegated green foliage, striped yellow. Afternoon shade is appreciated in warm climates. A variegated form of a Chinese species. This tender perennial needs a good mulch, but is much better behaved than its cousin the creep. 8x40cm (3x16").
L. nummularia 'Goldilocks' (*'Aurea'*) has a lovely trailing habit with appealing shiny, round, greenish gold leaves which turn bright lemon-yellow in sun. Small yellow flowers are borne profusely in June. Useful as groundcover in sites where it will not take over other plantings. Excellent in hanging baskets which highlight its most attractive feature, its trailing foliage. Not one to let loose in the garden in moist soil in mild areas. 10cm (4") x infinite spread to the moon and back. Z3-11.
Hot Partner: *Angelica gigas, Heuchera 'Stormy Seas', Viola 'Huntercombe Purple', Ajuga reptans 'Scallop Black', Tradescantia pallida 'Purple Heart'.*
Cool Companion: *Acaena microphylla 'Blue Haze'.*

MELISSA

Bee balm or lemon balm is a hardy herb or ornamental for almost any soil in sun or shade. Spreading by a creeping woody rootstock, this is a tough, drought tolerant little number for the edge of a path, but bear in mind that it can become invasive. Attractive to bees and beneficial insects.

HOW TO GROW
Tolerant of many sites, will grow in poor, well-drained soils. Dislikes excessive winter wet. Cut back variegated forms in early summer to encourage fresh, strong growth. Divide as new growth starts in spring or in autumn. Z6-9.

M. officinalis 'All Gold' is golden lemon balm needing some protection from full sun. Brightens any damp shady corner but needs good light. 45cm (18").
M. officinalis 'Aurea' (*'Variegata'*) is a perennial, native to S. Europe but naturalised in Britain and parts of N. America. Its bright golden leaves become green, then speckled later. Small whitish yellow flowers are borne in summer and autumn. The delicate lemon-scented leaves can be dried and used as tea. 60cm (2ft).
Hot Partner: *Dianthus barbatus 'Sooty'*.
Golden Glory: *Spiraea japonica 'Goldmound'*, *Tanacetum parthenium 'Isla Gold'*.

METASEQUOIA

Chinese Dawn Redwood was first described from fossil records. In 1941 a specimen was found by Mr T Kan in a Chinese village. In 1944 further trees were found in Sichuan province, seed collected and sent to the Arnold Arboretum in the U.S. Now there is an absolutely, must have golden variety. Lakeside or streamside plantings are superb. Unusual amongst conifers being a deciduous tree. Male and female strobili growing on the same plant. The species itself is known for autumn colour.

HOW TO GROW
Enjoys fertile, preferably acid, moist but well-drained soil in a sunny site. It prefers growing in areas with plenty of rain and a long growing season, avoid dry sites. Also dislikes high pH soils. Can be grown on chalk soil, but expect its growth to be slower. Owing to its long growing season, can be damaged by early frosts. Needs little pruning as it forms a neat shape. Propagate by hardwood cuttings in winter or semi-ripe cuttings with bottom heat in midsummer. Grafting is also succesful. Z4-8.

M. glyptostroboides 'Gold Rush' (*'Ogon'*, *'Golden Ogi'*, *'Golden Mantle'*) is a new golden variety that will cause a stir in the garden, originating from Japan. It has all the excellent attributes of its parents, tall pyramidal form and superb foliage colour as a bonus. The gold rush starts in spring when golden needles are especially bright when young, colour is retained throughout summer. Golden deciduous foliage turns orange bronze before falling. This makes a graceful, pyramidal tree with a feathery appearance, a stunning and outstanding ornamental. Best in sun with partial or afternoon shade. Easy and trouble free, provided regular watering is given. If you only choose one conifer, make it this one. Introduced by Peter Zweinberg of Boskoop, Holland in 1993. 3-5m (10-15ft). Z5-9.

Above: Metasequoia glyptostroboides 'Gold Rush'

MILIUM

Partial shade and moist soil, rich in humus are best for growing wood millet. Excellent in containers, perennial borders, water gardens or as golden ground cover. Brightens shade especially in spring.

HOW TO GROW
Grow in humus-rich, moist but well-drained soil in partial shade. *'Aureum'* comes true from seed. Divide in early spring and summer. To -20°C or less. Z6-10.

M. effusum 'Aureum' is one of the best known golden plants, Bowles' golden grass, highlights dark corners in the garden as everything about it, including the flowerheads is bright. Rich, ribbon-like leaves always seem to catch the least ray of sun. Brightest in spring, foliage becomes more green as the season progresses. Slow spreading evergreen, but does self-sow gently, spreading rays of sunshine around the garden. 40-60cm (16-24").
M. effusum 'Yaffle' has a central gold line running down each green blade. Slightly more upright and dense. For shade or part shade, will scorch in full sun. 75cm (30").
Hot Partner: *Berberis thunbergii 'Atropurpurea Nana', Helleborus orientalis black.*
Cool Companion: *Potentilla anserina* subdues, but needs to be kept in check, *Helleborus viridis.*

Milium effusum 'Aureum'

MUKDENIA

A member of the Saxifragaceae family, this deciduous perennial has attractive foliage. These slowly spreading woodlanders enjoy cool, damp summers.

HOW TO GROW
Grow in leafy, moist but well-drained soil in light, dappled or part shade. Divide in spring.
M. rossii 'Ogon' (*Aceriphyllum*) from Japan has stunning palmate, glossy leaves which emerge bright pink, slowly changing to yellow. White flowers ageing to pink. Well drained spot out of cold winds with protection from late frosts. 20cm (8"). Z4.

MYOSOTIS

Forget-me-not in forever gold. Plant a group of this under your tulips in spring and enjoy the glow.
M. Gold n' Sapphires was spotted by Oregon nurseryman, Dan Heims and introduced in 1999 by Terra Nova Nurseries. Enjoys rich, moist soil in full sun with protection from strong winds. Intense butter yellow foliage combines with blue flowers like tiny sapphires on a bed of pure gold. 10cm (4x20").
Hot Partner: *Iris 'Grapesicle', Heuchera 'Obsidion'.*
Cool Companion: *Libertia peregrinans 'Gold Leaf'.*
Golden Glory: *Acorus 'Ogon', Iris 'Curlew'.*

Myosotis 'Gold n' Sapphires'

NEPHROLEPIS

Easy to grow, but hard to find, ultimately worth seeking, the golden boston fern is a King amongst ferns with delectable golden-green fronds. Will be coveted if seen. This golden cultivar is rare.

HOW TO GROW
Grow under cover in cooler areas and in moderately fertile, humus, moist but well-drained soil in partial shade outdoors and bright light indoors. Tolerant of drier soils in very high humidity. Killed to the ground by frost but re-emerges from rhizomes in spring. Separate rooted runners in late winter or early spring. Min temperature 7-10°C (45-50°F). Z9-11.

N. exaltata 'Golden Boston' (*'Aurea'*) has broad, lance shaped, well divided, golden fronds, erect at first, then arching in an attractive habit. Superb in a hanging basket in the conservatory. 90x60cm (3x2ft), fronds arch to 2m (7ft).

ORIGANUM

A new lease of life for wild marjoram and oregano, golden leaved varieties spread sunshine in the herb garden or border. These herbaceous perennials provide good golden colouring in spring and small clusters of flowers which are attractive to bees.

HOW TO GROW
Grow in sun in poor to moderately fertile, well-drained soil, preferably alkaline with added horticultural sand. Trim back to a compact mound. Divide in spring or take basal cuttings in late spring. Hardy to -30°F (-35°C). Z.5-9.

O. 'Norton Gold' produces gold, aromatic foliage forming low mounds with pink flowers. Excellent at the front of the border in sun and well-drained soil. Looks at its best in spring. 20cm (8").

O. vulgare 'Acorn Bank' has very pointed leaves 2.5cm (1") long with distinctive curled margins. White flowers have pink stamens. 50cm (20").

O. vulgare 'Aureum' has golden foliage, especially from spring to summer. Excellent along a path or in a rock garden, or the herb basket. Leaves turn greener as the season progresses and it can scorch in full sun. This woody-based perennial produces sprays of pale purple-pink flowers in summer. It spreads less vigorously than the species to 30cm (12").

O. vulgare 'Crispum' (*'Curly Gold'*) has curly gold leaves making upright growth. This variety is known for its strong flavour. 30-60cm (12-24").

O. vulgare 'Gold Splash' bears green leaves with a splash of gold. 30cm (12").

O. vulgare 'Gold Tip' is just what it says, gold-tipped green leaves.

O. vulgare 'Pink Mist' PVR claims to have the best brilliant golden foliage yet, intensifying in summer. Topped by pink-purple flowers in summer. A seed variation of *'Aureum'* discovered by Barbara Molesworth. 30cm (12").

O. vulgare 'Thumble's Variety' from France, bears yellow leaves and refreshing white flowers in a compact, low mounding form with quite aromatic foliage. A pleasant addition to a rock garden, container or trough. 30x40cm (12x16").

Hot Partner: *Allium schoenoprasum* (chives), *Ajuga reptans 'Braunherz'* (*'Mahogany'*).

Cool Companion: *Ruta graveolens.*

Origanum vulgare 'Gold Tip'

PARTHENOCISSUS

Boston ivy has wide-spreading fame for its wide-spreading growth, faster than the speed of light ability to climb, cover and clothe. An easy, attractive climber.

HOW TO GROW

Grow in any fertile soil. Young plants may initially require support. Take softwood cuttings in early summer, greenwood cuttings in midsummer or hardwood cuttings in winter. Z4-8.

P. tricuspidata 'Fenway Park' is a glorious golden version. Found as a sport of *'Green Monster'* at a sports stadium, Fenway Park ball stadium, USA. This is a super vine, emerging golden and retaining its colour in sun. Red tones bleed into the gold foliage with the onset of colder weather. Although not quite as vigorous as the green variety, it will just keep on growing and growing and growing! Shears at the ready Hot Partner: *Parthenocissus tricuspidata 'Veitchii'*.

PELARGONIUM

Perfect summer border and container plants which can be in flower much of the winter indoors. Still so often referred to as tender *Geranium*. Fancy-leaved ones are grown more for their foliage.

HOW TO GROW

These frost tender perennials are often grown as annuals, bring them under cover in frost-prone areas for continued colour. Grow in fertile, well-drained soil. Take softwood cuttings in spring, late summer or early autumn. Min temperature 7°C (45°C).

P. 'Ashfield Jubilee' bears single salmon flowers having deeper salmon veining from the centre of each bloom over rich gold foliage with a pale zone.
P. 'Bridesmaid' (Stringer) has delicious double peach flowers on gold foliage.

P. Charmay Hybrids. There are over a dozen 'Charmay' hybrids, all raised in Australia by Ken Attfield, bearing golden foliage.
P. 'Dovedale' bears gold leaves with white flowers blushed pink.
P. 'Elmsett' (Bidwell) has double blush flowers with red spots and splashes. A golden leaved dwarf variety.
P. 'Fenton Farm' contrasts bright purple flowers with a white eye over gold foliage.
P. 'Fir Trees Jack' bears pale single pink flowers on this gold-leaved dwarf.
P. 'Fir Trees Ruby Wedding' has the striking contrast of gold foliage and rich, single ruby-red flowers forming large heads.
P. 'Fir Trees Sparkler' is a miniature variety with single white flowers, speckled red over golden foliage.
P. 'Golden Wedding' (Ken Lea) bears bright gold foliage and double, soft red flowers.
P. 'Holbrook' (Bidwell) Well-shaped double salmon flowers sit over sumptuous golden foliage.
P. 'Hope Valley' (Portas) bears bright gold leaves and bright pink flowers on a dwarf variety.
P. 'Hunters Moon' has vivid orange flowers which glow just as much as the golden leaves.
P. 'Occold Embers' (Stringer) has dwarf golden leaves and peach flowers, makes a good exhibition plant.
P. 'Star Wright' (Wright) has pale pink flowers with a reddish star-shaped centre above a pure gold leaf.
P. 'Sunridge Moonlight' bears large single white flowers over glowing golden foliage.
P. 'Swainham Spring' has golden leaves with salmon pink flowers flushed white.

PETASITES

Ideal large-leaved perennial for ground cover by a pool or stream and a great addition to a moist, wild garden. Big, palmate leaves are guaranteed to get me going and this plant has those attributes like no other. Nectar will attract bees.

HOW TO GROW
Grow in deep, humus-rich soil in moist woodland. Divide in spring or autumn. Z6.

P. 'Golden Palms' is a wild sport found by Chuck Pavlich in the Pacific Northwest, a golden leaved butterbur, excellent in moist woodland where it will provide ground cover and eventually make colonies. Needs sun for best colour when the large, striking, palmate leaves will shimmer. Provide shade in hotter climates. Pinkish male flower spikes appear in February to April. Chuck has had this grow to 1m (3ft) in ideal conditions and with amazingly large leaves to 1m (3ft) across! It is capable of eclipsing the sun. If you are looking for a large golden plant, put this on the list.

P. japonicus 'Variegatus' is handsome too in its creamy splashes on green leaves. Forms large colonies. Hot Partner: Chuck likes to grow this with *Lobelia 'Bees Flame'*.

PHILADELPHUS

The hardy golden mock orange is suitable for a shrub border or as a specimen. Wonderful in the spring garden and that scent in summer! Easy.

HOW TO GROW
Grow this deciduous shrub in moderately fertile, well-drained soil in full sun to partial shade. Prune in July to August. Tough and drought resistant. Needs protectiom from late frosts and overpowering sun. Take softwood cuttings in summer or hardwood cuttings in autumn or winter. Z6-10.

P. coronarius 'Aureus' is a popular, yellow-foliaged form of the European mock orange. A handsome shrub with admirable, oval foliage and white flowers with a heavenly perfume borne on dark stems. A little overhead shade at midday will protect against sun scorch, although leaves turn greenish gold in summer. A very handsome shrub and a lovely addition to the gold border. 2.5m (8ft) with a 1.5m (5ft) spread.
Hot Partner: *Berberis thunbergii 'Atropurpurea'*, *Cotinus coggygria 'Grace'*.
Cool Companion: *Eryngium, Anchusa 'Dropmore'*.

Petasites 'Golden Palms'

PHILODENDRON

Easy to grow houseplants with fabulous leaves, often large and glossy. Treat them fair and they will reward you for years. Will withstand a degree of neglect and are tolerant of low light. See them, want them plants for me. The glossy, usually large leaves grab me.

HOW TO GROW
Loamless potting soil in bright or filtered light is best. Keep evenly moist but never soggy. High humidity is perfect but not absolutely essential. Night temperatures above 16°C (65°F) and day temperatures above 21°C (70°F) are ideal. Prune if necessary. Take stem tip or leaf bud cuttings in summer. Layer or air layer in spring. Z10.

P. bipennifolium 'Splash Gordon' (Dave Gordon) has fiddle-shaped leaves splashed with cream, looks a bit like an ivy on steroids. Very large leaves.
P. 'Calkin's Gold' is a *P. domesticum* hybrid, the elephant's ear philodendron, with rich golden-toned foliage striated green. Young leaves appear more golden. Scandent habit and large growing. Waxy, thick leaves will resist changes in humidity. The narrow, arrow-shaped leaves of this climber are 45-60cm (18-24") long.
P. erubescens golden form has fabulous elongated leaves. A fast grower and sturdy climber.
P. 'Hansoti's Gold' bears elongated golden leaves and is quite fast growing. Similar to the above, excellent in pots or baskets.
P. 'Jose Buono' has large waxy leaves shimmering with lime gold. Huge hybrid with individual leaves dusted in gold reaching 30-60cm (1-2ft).
P. 'Lemonade' has smallish bright shiny leaves.
P. 'Moonlight' is a bird's nest type with thick stems, moonlight toned new leaves fading to lime green.
P. oxycardium 'Aureum' just look at that! Tempted?
P. scandens 'Aureum' has delicate pale lemon colouring and is a very attractive smaller leaved type. Will cascade from a basket.

Above: P. bipennifolium 'Splash Gordon'
Below: P. oxycardium 'Aureum'

PHORMIUM

Excellent, handsome, architectural foliage plants for use as specimens or added interest to the border with spiky, sword-like foliage. Superb for floral work and a good choice for coastal gardens. Golden variegated forms are particularly bright against darker greens to blacks. Provide a good focal point at the edge of a border.

HOW TO GROW
Best in moist, well-drained soil in full sun. Ideal coastal plants. In frost prone areas provide a dry, deep mulch. Divide in spring.

P. 'Alison Blackman' is an unusual deep olive green with a bright gold band.

P. 'Apricot Queen' (Margaret Jones) has pale yellow-green foliage which arches very attractively. New growth is flushed apricot, this can also occur in autumn. Intriguing variegation which varies from leaf to leaf. Will grow happily in water. If you really want a stunning hanging basket, this is the plant, combine it with golden *Supertunia and Nemesia Sunsatia.* Can be smaller or larger depending on conditions amount of sun or shade. 1.2m (4ft).

P. cookianum ssp hookeri 'Creamy Delight' (Margaret Jones 1978) with broad, gorgeous clotted cream leaves with green stripes at the edge and a dark red margin. Grows well in light shade. 1m (3ft).

P. 'Gold Spike' rigid green leaves with a bright gold margin. 2m (6ft).

P. 'Gold Sword' (Duncan & Davies) has creamy yellow leaves shading to gold margined with green, occasionally showing a faint pink stripe in the centre. 1m (3ft).

P. 'Golden Ray' (*'Gold Ray'*) has a narrow green centre surrounded by wide gold bands and a bronze edge.

Phygelius x rectus 'Sunshine'

P. 'Yellow Wave' (F. Jury) has clear yellow, arching broad leaves, developing green variegation as they mature. Narrow brown margins. A striking variety, more gold than *'Cream Delight'* which is especially attractive in evening light. Admire its arching foliage at its best on the edge of a large border. In autumn its tones are predominently chartreuse. Raised in New Zealand in 1967. 90-120cm (3-4 ft).

P. 'Wings of Gold' is a small variety with spiky, narrow green leaves edged in gold.

Hot Partner: *Bergenia cordifolia 'Purpurascens', Verbena bonariensis, Penstemon, Pittosporum tenuifolium 'Purpureum'* or *'Tom Thumb'*.

Cool Companion: *Lavandula angustifolia, Nicotiana 'Lime Green', Ipomoea batatas 'Margarita' .*

Golden Glory: *Rosa 'Happenstance', Canna 'Striata', Caesalpinia gillesii.*

PHYGELIUS

Handsome shrubby plants for the border from South Africa. Grow in fertile, moist but well-drained soil. Usually grown for their flowers, but this one is a surprise.

P. x rectus 'Sunshine' certainly emerges with sunshine tones to brighten the spring garden. Frost tender, act as herbaceous perennials where temperatures regularly fall below 0°C (32°F).

Phygelius x rectus 'Sunshine'

Picea orientalis 'Skylands'
Pinus radiata Aurea Group

A group of conifers and Hebe ochracea at Barnsdale
Platycladus orientalis 'Morgan'

PHYSOCARPUS

Excellent, vigorous medium-sized gold shrubs with dense clusters of flowers and fruit as a bonus to extend the season of interest. Exfoliating orange bark is just an added bonus. White flowers are followed by fruits. Hardy, deciduous shrubs grown for foliage and flower, look wonderful in the shrub border.

HOW TO GROW
Grow in preferably acid soil, fertile, moist and well-drained in full sun or partial shade, but this is a very adaptable shrub. Young foliage may burn in full sun, whilst mature specimens will take the sun. Thrive best in open, moist situations. Can become chloritic on dry, shallow chalk. Take greenwood cuttings in summer. Remove rooted suckers in autumn or spring. Z2-8.

P. opulifolius 'Dart's Gold' has fabulous gold leaf colour with white flowers, often flushed pink, appearing in spring and reddish fruit in autumn. A hardy and adaptable compact shrub, growing well in difficult sites, introduced in 1969. Having long lasting bright foliage, this is a big improvement over *'Luteus'*. Cut back for larger foliage the following year at the expense of blooms. 150cm (5 ft).
P. opulifolius 'Luteus' (*ribesifolius*) has young growths of a clear yellow in full sun and is effective with purple shrubs, but the golden colouring fades.
P. opulifolius 'Nugget' was found by N. Evers and introduced by South Dakota State University. A branch sport from McCrory gardens has claims to being an improvement on *'Dart's Gold'* with finer texture and form. Deep gold leaves emerge in spring, turning lime-green in summer. Appears to deteriorate in many areas as the season progresses. Possesses orange to yellow fall colour. Needs a little shade to avoid leaf scorch. 2m (6ft). Z3.
Hot Partner: *Corylus maxima 'Purpurea', Clematis viticella, Penstemon 'Raven'*.
Cool Companion: *Clematis alpina 'Frances Rivis'*.

PICEA

Spruce make superb evergreen plants. *P. orientalis* and its cultivars are hardy. They are conical when young, becoming broadly columnar as they mature. Male and female strobili are found on the same plant. The often colourful females are terminal. Cones ripen in the autumn of the first year and usually remain on the plant until falling in the second year.

HOW TO GROW
Grow in deep, moist but well-drained, neutral to acid soil in full sun. They are not suited to chalk or dry soils and dislike strong coastal winds, a little shelter brings out the best in these graceful trees. Graft cultivars in winter. Take ripewood cuttings of dwarf cultivars in late summer. Z3-5 depending on species.

P. abies 'Aurea' is a Norway spruce with glossy gold foliage, most apparent when young and ageing to yellow-green. Best in full sun. Unsuitable for coastal areas. 3m (10ft).
P. abies 'Aurea Jacobsen' has even brighter foliage, which will burn when young if exposed to full sun.
P. abies 'Effusa' is a rare variegated variety.
P. abies 'Gold Drift' is a weeping, gold sport from *P. abies 'Reflexa'* with colour turning to frosty gold in winter and finally to green as the new growth flushes gold in spring.
P. abies 'Gold Dust' is a very upright dwarf with small leaves with a gold dusting. Very slow growing.
P. abies 'Gold Strike' is a Collector's Nursery introduction with striking golden-tipped needles shining against a darker green interior. Holds its colour right through winter. 3m (10ft).
P. abies 'Mountian Dew' possesses compact form with bright yellow needles mellowing in summer.
P. abies 'Perry's Gold' bears bright spring gold foliage on a broad based conical shape. Turns green. Suitable in full sun for cooler climates.
P. abies 'Repens Gold' is a lovely dwarf golden form, looking especially bright against blue foliage. A

prostrate form suitable for a rock garden, needs a little shade from full sun.

P. abies 'Vermont Gold' is a prostrate golden form which hugs the ground, especially bright in summer. Found by Greg Williams. This very attractive form is best in partial shade. 30x120cm (1x4ft).

P. breweriana 'Fruhling's Gold' is the only form of Brewer's weeping spruce that I have found with a gold hue to the leaves. Finely textured foliage. Best in sun.

P. glauca 'Goldilocks' makes an upright oval bush with golden yellow colour. Best in a little shelter.

P. jezoensis 'Aurea' has bright gold foliage, especially in spring and needs some shade to prevent scorching. Gold needles contrast with the blue and green of older foliage. This upright conical needs some shade. A rare selection from the 1890's. 3m (10ft). Z5.

P. mariana 'Aurea' bears yellow foliage when young, maturing to glaucous green. Will lose its colour in shade. An incredibly graceful, open habit. Will tolerate more moisture than other spruce. 3m (10ft).

P. omorika 'Aurea' is a golden, slow growing form, with foliage colour showing best in spring and summer in full sun. Shows good sunburn resist. Blue needles are overlaid with gold on a slightly weeping habit on an upright form with ascending branches.

P. omorika 'Tijn' is a golden dwarf suffused with green, with a cushion habit for the smaller garden best in sun. Z5.

P. orientalis 'Aurea' (*'Aureospicata'*) has bright, creamy yellow foliage in spring, for six weeks only, contrasting with older green foliage. Makes a spectacular small tree. Z5.

P. orientalis 'Early Gold' is similar, but the new gold growth is earlier in the season.

P. orientalis 'Skylands' (*'Aurea Compacta'*) is similar to *'Aurea'*, but the creamy gold glow is retained all year. Although it may burn when young in full sun, the foliage is strikingly bright gold. In too much shade it will green up, but is faster growing. Midwest U.S. growers will find this suffers sunburn. When cones come, they are red, making quite a conspicuous feature. Short needles on stiff, horizontal branches on

a narrowly conical habit make a fine lawn specimen tree which maintains its lovely dense habit. One of the best golden conifers. 2m (6ft). Z5.

P. orientalis 'Tom Thumb Gold' (Spingarn) is a witches broom from the above, exhibiting bright gold foliage in a dense, miniature mound with slow growth. A very rare miniature suitable for a trough.

P. pungens 'Aurea' produces gold new growth in sun which is retained throughout the year, more sulphur in summer, very golden in winter. Z3.

P. pungens 'Gold Find' makes a conical upright plant with golden leaves all season in full sun.

P. pungens 'Lutea' has green foliage which turns light yellow on the surface in summer, richer colouring than *'Aurea'* and not as susceptible to burn as *'Walnut Glen'*. Withstands full sun.

P. pungens 'Stanley's Gold' is a golden Colorado spruce found at Stanley & Sons Nursery, Oregon in 1978. A light yellow that withstands sun and retains its colour well. A dwarf conical tree. 120cm (4x3ft).

P. pungens 'Summer Gold' has gold colouring right into summer.

P. pungens 'Sunshine' flushes bright gold in sun and keeps its colour in winter. Lower branches become blue-green in summer. Susceptible to sunburn. 1.2m

P. pungens 'Walnut Glen' (*'Goldie'*) is a blue-leaved spruce which turns golden in spring. An intermediate size having a fabulous spring show of creamy-yellow growth, best in a little shade. Can suffer foliage burn until well established. Works well with other golden or green conifers. 1.2m (4ft). Z.3.

P. sitchensis 'Aurea' some call it chloritic, its colouring is pale gold. Bob Fincham of Coenesium gardens, an avid and knowledgable collector, describes this as one of the brightest golden conifers. Needs shade, where it will glow. Z5.

P. sitchensis 'Bentham's Sunlight' originated along a river in British Columbia. Site in shade where golden colouring will still look good as this is very susceptible to burn. In winter the foliage turns green and blue. Originally sold as *'Aurea'*, Bentham was the first to successfully propagate and distribute this plant.

PINUS

Pines are some of my favourite conifers. I love running my fingers along those with long needles. It is the bark of pines that is used as a mulch in many gardens. Highly ornamental specimen trees, useful for providing shelter. Although many pines are large, smaller cultivars can be used in a rock garden. Male and female strobili are borne on the same tree. Cones ripen at the end of the second year and in most species release their seed on ripening. *P radiata* retains its cones for many years, seed of this species is released in forest fires.

HOW TO GROW

Grow in well-drained soil in full sun. Some species will thrive on poor soils. They resent disturbance and dislike shade and pollution. Graft cultivars in late winter. Tolerance of heat and cold varies from species to species. Z2-9 depending on species.

P. contorta 'Frisian Gold' has long golden needles which display their colouring in the second year. Like golden bottlebrushes of an outstanding brilliance. A dwarf mound, twice as wide as high. Z7-9.

P. contorta 'Taylor's Sunburst' produces very bright gold growth for two months in spring, turning yellow-green as growth hardens. Eye-catching in spring making upright, broad growth. Found by Alan Taylor in the Colorado Rockies in 1984. Best in full sun. 2-2.5m (6-8ft). Z3.

P. contorta v latifolia 'Chief Joseph' makes a dramatic accent of dazzling yellow in winter, turning yellow-green in summer. Very slow growing, but a real sparkling gem all year round. Can be chief of my garden any day. Named after the leader of the Nez Perce nation who lived where it was found in the mountains of northeastern Oregon. Z5.

P. densiflora 'Aurea' golden Japanese red pine is distinguished by bright light yellow new growth and orange bark. Colouring is good in winter and best in sun. A fast-growing cultivar with good branching and long golden pine needles. Use this to best effect as a specimen to appreciate its silhouette. Z3b-8.

P. densiflora 'Gold Ghost' is an introduction by Bill Devine. An improved dragon eye type with golden banded needles. 30-45cm per year (12-18").

P. densiflora 'Oculus-draconis' has soft green needles marked with two yellow bands, giving the appearance of having been dusted liberally with gold. Best in full sun. 3m (10ft).

P. halepensis 'Cedar's Lemon' has a lemon stripe on needles, retaining its golden colouring throughout the year in cooler climates. Found in a batch of seedlings at Cedar Nursery in 1983. Makes a round to oval bush 3x1.5m (10x5ft).

P. jeffreyi 'Gold' has golden new growth on long needles and added interest in winter when the colouring is orange-yellow. Z6-9.

P. mugo 'Amber Gold' has almost fluorescent, outstanding gold colouring in winter, but is greener in summer. A form from Australia. Z2-9.

P. mugo 'Aurea' shows its dazzling, golden colouring when young in winter, older plants are yellow-green. Best colour in sun. 1-1.5m (3-5ft).

P. mugo 'Carsten' (*'Carsten's Wintergold'*) is brilliantly bright in winter, and very dwarf and dense, much wider than high. Intense orange-gold winter colour. Mr. Haddow who owns one of the NCCPG collections of dwarf conifer cultivars in Devon, England, says this is the best golden conifer for outstanding winter colour. 25x50 (10x20").

P. mugo 'Gold Spire' emerging golden spires of needles fade to yellow-green. The surprise is that it has the same growth rate as the species, unusual in a yellow form. Best in full sun. 1.5m (5ft).

P. mugo 'Honeycomb' is warm gold in winter, bringing a little sunshine in the depth of winter even in cold areas. Globose, spreads with time. 1m (3-4ft).

P. mugo 'Kokarde' is a dragon eye type with bright gold banding on needles. A striking rapid growing small plant. 60cm (2ft).

P. mugo 'Marand' has bright variegation in the yellow banding on needles which looks best in winter. This dragon-eye type grows exceptionally well at Trompemberg Arboretum. It was raised by A. van Nijnatten in Holland in 1984.

P. mugo 'Northern Lights' wears many cloaks, emerging creamy-yellow in spring, in summer it changes to a dragon eye banding and in winter it is lime green. Selected by Horace Jackson, Washington State, U.S. 30x30cm (12x12").

P. mugo 'Per Golden' is a gold-tipped variety. Its upright form looks like it is sprinkled with golden fairy dust.

P. mugo 'Pot o' Gold' is a delightful dwarf that simply glows in winter. The clear yellow fades to green in spring. Best in full sun. 1-1.2m (3-4ft).

P. mugo 'Winter Gold' is a dwarf, spreading bush with an open habit. Golden-yellow foliage is best in winter. Makes an attractive small focal point with its rounded form. 1m (3ft)

P. mugo 'Yellow Tip' (*'Yellow Point'*) has longer than usual needles, tipped yellow. Z2.

P. mugo 'Zundert' is bright gold in winter on a dwarf, compact form with long needles.

P. nigra 'Aurea' is rare, discovered in 1909 in Hungary, its yellow candles are quite amazing, standing erect on the tips of branches against the darker green interior foliage. 10m (30ft). Z4-9.

P. parviflora 'Dr. Landis Gold' is a low growing, spreading golden-leaved form originally from the U.S.

P. parviflora 'Goldylocks' grows into a small, dense cushion with bright golden variegated needles. It needs a little shade, but in full shade it will only appear frosted. Introduced by Billy Schwartz.

P. parviflora 'Ogon-Janome' grows about 30cm (12") each year, displaying its sulphur yellow needles on an open-branched plant. Intense colour in winter. Z3-9.

P. parviflora 'Tenysu-kazu' is a very slow upright growing form with good golden colour on recurved leaves. Full sun for best effect. Mr. Haddow of Kenwith Nursery rates this as the best golden *parviflora* he has seen.

P. radiata Aurea Group exhibits good golden foliage especially with plenty of sun worthy of a place in any garden that has the room. Long cones remain intact for many years on this attractive tree with deep, fissured bark. Good for mild inland and coastal areas but out of severe salt laden winds. Needs very free draining soil so avoid low lying areas. Originally found in New Zealand. 5x3m (16x10ft). Z8-10.

P. radiata 'Marshwood' retains its creamy golden variegated colouring all year round in cooler climates, but does not look as good as a fine specimen from the *'Aurea'* group. Better colouring in high altitude gardens. 14x10m (45x30ft), Z8.

P. resinosa 'Aurea' is a quick grower with bright gold colouring with long twisted needles. Not easy to find.

P. strobus 'Bennet OD' has bright gold new spring growth on bark and needles. Eventually needles green up, and two golden bands are left, hence the OD for *Oculis-Draconis*. Grow in partial shade. A small, open tree making 15cm (6") growth a year. Z3-9.

P. strobus 'Gold Candles' has tips of bright gold in late summer and autumn.

P. strobus 'Hillside Winter Gold' has light yellow needles and turns completely gold in winter. A broadly upright form with bluish green foliage, offering much needed spectacular colouring in winter. 4m (12ft).

P. strobus 'Louie' is golden all year with soft foliage, intense in winter. Does not have winter burn.

P. strobus 'Pacific Sunrise' has intense bright gold foliage fading to lime green at the base of each needle. A good grower keeping its colouring throughout the year, not as bright as *'Louie'*. Introduced by Collector's Nursery. Z3.

P. strobus 'Winter Gold' is bright gold in winter, giving a spectacular colouring much needed in the winter garden. 1.5m (5ft). Z3.

P. sylvestris, the Scot's pine, the only pine native to Britain, has a number of gold leaved cultivars. Z4-9.

P. sylvestris Aurea Group bears bright golden foliage developing in summer in sun, but at its best in winter. By the time this slow-growing plant matures, it has lost some of its brightness. Rarely seen, even though it has been in cultivation since 1876. There is a mature specimen at Castlewellan, Co. Down which has reached 16.5m (54ft) tall. 10-15m (30-50ft).

P. sylvestris 'Gold Coin' is a slow-growing shrub with light golden foliage, much smaller than the species. It is similar to the *Aurea Group* but shorter and slower growing. This striking conifer is worthy of a prominent place in the garden. 2m (6ft).

P. sylvestris 'Gold Medal' is a slow-growing dwarf with bright yellow foliage which looks good in winter right through to spring.

P. sylvestris 'Moseri' (*nigra*) is a small pyramidal cultivar with dense, yellow foliage in winter. Very slow growing.

P. sylvestris 'Nisbet's Gold' is bright with longer needles and a fairly fast growth rate. Colouring is similar to *P. sylvestris 'Aurea'*.

P. sylvestris 'Wolf Gold' is a wolf in gold lamé. A dwarf, conical form which is golden in summer and even brighter in winter. Found on a Baltic island off Sweden.

P. thunbergii 'Aocha Matsu' makes a bushy plant with small branches some of which are entirely golden and others have a touch of yellow leaves.

P. thunbergii 'Ogon' (*thunbergeriana*) has golden foliage most of the year and is at its best in winter, with the brightest gold at the needle tip. Slow growing. 5m (15ft). Z5-9.

P. thunbergii 'Shirone' has gold-tipped foliage on a large open-branching specimen tree. 5m (15ft). Z5-9.

P. virginiana 'Wate's Golden' turns from the normal green to vivid, bright gold in winter, especially where it is cold. As the gold fades in spring, female red cones appear on mature trees. Also has interesting bark. An open branching habit on a rapidly developing, hardy tree with outstanding winter colour. Tolerant of poor soils and heavy clay, it is easy in moist, well-drained soil and best in full sun. Can suffer winter burn in the Midwest U.S. 2-4.5m (6-15ft). Z4.

Cool Companion: *Lithodora diffusa 'Grace Ward'*, *Juniper 'Skyrocket'*.

PITTOSPORUM

Handsome shrubs or trees chiefly grown for their foliage, needing protection where temperatures fall below 0°C (32°F), although *tenuifolium* is one of the hardier species. In warm climates they make attractive specimens in fertile, moist but well-drained soil in full sun. They thrive especially well in coastal sites, and are a useful hedging plant. Small, chocolate-purple, honey-scented flowers appear in spring. Can clip to a small hedge.

HOW TO GROW
Hardier if the wood is well ripened in summer. Grow in fertile, moist but well-drained soil in full sun for best leaf effect. Prune lightly as desired. Take semi-ripe cuttings in summer. Layer or air layer in spring.

P. tenuifolium 'Abbotsbury Gold' has yellow leaves with irregular green margins, the variegation being most apparent on young foliage. Appeared as a sport at Abbotsbury Gardens, Dorset around 1970. 3m (10ft) with a spread of 1.5m (5ft).

P. tenuifolium 'Aureum' attractive light green leaves which develop a golden tone over time. Useful as a hedge or windbreak. 3m (10ft).

P. tenuifolium 'Eila Keightley' (*Sunburst*) bears leaves which are conspicuously veined bright greenish-yellow in the centre, in this case it is most marked in older foliage. Easy to grow with black stems. 3m (10ft).

P. tenuifolium 'Gold Star' has young yellow-green leaves with a narrow dark green margin on red branchlets, a stunning wavy-leaved variegated form. This compact, evergreen shrub is best in sun to part shade. Attractive colour as a patio pot. 1.5x1m (5x3ft).

P. tenuifolium 'Golden Cut' (Hardizjer) is a sport of *'Silver Queen'* making a compact shrub with gold-green leaves with pale venation.

P. tenuifolium 'Golden King' is erect, with light gold-green leaves. 3m (10ft) with a spread of just 1m (3ft).

P. tenuifolium 'Golden Sheen' (2001) golden wavy

leaves are edged in ivory white against blackish stems. Vibrant colour in sun or part shade. Excellent in the border or as a container plant. 3m (10ft) can be trimmed shorter.

P. tenuifolium 'Loxhill Gold' has new leaves emerging gold, edged green.

P. tenuifolium 'Stirling Gold' is a sport of *'James Stirling'* raised in New Zealand with tiny golden-edged leaves against blackish-grey stems. Compact habit. 2-3m (6-10ft).

P. 'Tandarra Gold' is a neat and compact bushy shrub with smooth, black branches covered in small, rounded leaves prominently splashed with gold in the centre. Makes a great screen or hedge. 2m (6ft).

P. 'Warnham Gold' is an attractive form raised in England at Warnham Court, Sussex with golden green young leaves maturing to golden yellow. Foliage is wavy which adds to its attraction and it looks particularly good in autumn and winter. 6m(20ft).

Hot Partner: *Phormium 'Platt's Black', P. 'Evening Glow', Dodonaea viscosa 'Purpurea', Dahlia 'Bishop of Llandaff'.*

Cool Companion: *Agapanthus 'Storm Cloud'.*

PLATYCLADUS

These evergreen conifers from China and Korea feature flat, fan-like sprays of aromatic foliage. They are closely related to *Thuja*, and were once included in this genus, often still seen listed as *Thuja orientalis*. Known as Oriental Arborvitae, and not as hardy as American Arborvitae. Often suitable for rock gardens and golden forms are best in full sun to part shade. Long lived conifers offering year round interest and easy maintenance.

HOW TO GROW

Appreciate deeply dug ground before planting and a position in well-drained, reasonably fertile soil in sun to part shade. Keep well watered in dry spells. Z6a-11.

P. orientalis 'Aurea Nana' (*Thuja orientalis 'Millard's Gold'*) is a dwarf golden-green variety which keeps its juvenile, fuzzy foliage held in flattened sprays. Colour intensifies in winter. A neat, slow-growing, low rounded to pyramidal bush up to 1m (3ft).

P. orientalis 'Beverleyensis' is a golden glowing dome in spring giving perfect contrast in the garden. Colours orange in winter. 2mx1m (6x3ft).

P. orientalis 'Collen's Gold' makes a quick, glowing orange-yellow dome, very narrow. 3.5x1m (12x3ft).

P. orientalis 'Elegantissima' is taller with a broad, columnar habit having foliage sprays tipped yellow, and developing an old gold colouring, being golden-green in winter. 2.4m (8ft).

P. orientalis 'Gold Pygmy' is a golden form, much smaller than *'Aurea Nana'* with finer foliage which has a reddish cast in autumn. Needs shelter from frost. 40x30cm (16x12").

P. orientalis 'Golden Ball' is an improvement on *'Aurea Nana'*, a neat dwarf. 1mx80cm (3ftx32").

P. orientalis 'Golden Rocket' bears bright yellow foliage against the lime green of older foliage. A spectacular glow which turns bronze in winter. Versatile, its narrow habit lends itself to screening or a golden avenue by a path. 4mx80cm (13ftx32").

P. orientalis 'Kaitake' has bright yellow foliage in sun, lime green in shade, discovered at Cedar Lodge. 1.6mx75cm (5ftx30").

P. orientalis 'Morgan' displays bright gold foliage in summer in a neat, tight ball. A real cutie.

P. orientalis 'Semperaurea' is a dense, medium shrub with yellow foliage throughout summer, becoming bronzed later. A multi-stemmed form which has open branching with age and needs snow and ice clearing from its branches. A specimen is planted at Longwood Gardens, Pennsylvania, USA. 3m (10ft).

P. orientalis 'Southport' is an oval, slow growing golden bush with tight foliage, turning red in winter.

P. orientalis 'Westmont' in full sun new growth on this form will dazzle. A slow growing globe with coarse, variegated foliage making an upright conical with time. 65x45cm (26x18").

PODOCARPUS

Quite unusual, attractive evergreen conifers. They make specimen plants which are also useful in a woodland garden. Capable of making a neat hedge with their Taxus-like (yew) foliage. Male and female plants are needed to produce fruits.

HOW TO GROW

These conifers are reliable in most soils in full sun to partial shade, depending on the species. They succeed in acid or alkaline soil in humid or high rainfall areas. Intolerant of frost but can be grown under glass. Take semi-ripe cuttings from upright leading shoots in late summer. Z9.

P. totara 'Albany Gold' has new pale green growth and golden colouring in winter. More intense in its winter coat than *'Aureus'*. 4mx2m (13x6ft).

P. totara 'Aureus' from New Zealand is much smaller than the species. Its pyramidal form and rich, golden foliage which is at its best in winter, coupled with graceful branches make this a supreme choice for warmer climates. Prune to suit small gardens. In the Home Counties of England, if sited amongst sheltering evergreens, this species proves hardy. Dislikes wet. 5m (15ft). Z9-10.

POPULUS

Fast growing, hardy trees, capable of forming a quick, attractive tall screen. Their rapid growth and surface rooting means they should be given plenty of room, away from buildings. Some are good shade trees, others withstand pruning.

HOW TO GROW

Need to be planted into their permanent positions by the time they are 3-4 years old. Moist, free draining loam suits them best, though they are very tolerant of anything but waterlogged soils. Remove lower branches while trees are still young in summer or autumn. Best grown 40m (130ft) away from buildings. Take hardwood cuttings in winter. Remove suckers in autumn or late winter.

P. alba 'Richardii' makes a smaller than the type, suckering tree and an excellent choice for exposed sites, especially on the coast. Can be cut severely to keep smaller stature as a shrub. Leaves are bright yellow above with the typical white woolly undersurface which makes these trees look so attractive, especially when wind blown. Excellent for stooling.

P. x canadensis 'Serotina Aurea' (*'Aurea'*, *'Van Geertii'*) the golden poplar has clear golden-yellow leaves in spring and early summer, becoming green but ending the season in a delicious golden yellow. Originated as a sport in Van Geert's nursery in Ghent in 1871. Colour is best in sun, and moist soil. 15m (50ft).

P. nigra 'Lombardy Gold' is a striking tree bearing yellow-gold foliage. Discovered in 1974 as a sport on a mature Lombardy poplar near the village of Normandy in Surrey by John Whitehead. There is a mature specimen at Wisley. 12m (40ft).

PSEUDOTSUGA

Tall, hardy evergreen conifers develop scaly buds unique to this genus. Make imposing specimen trees.

HOW TO GROW

Grow in any well-drained soil except chalk. Best in full sun. Graft cultivars in late winter. Z5.

P. menziesii 'Aureovariegata' is a Douglas Fir with bright gold spring colouring, turning green in late summer.
P. menziesii 'Hillside Gold' is better in a little shade.
P. menziesii 'Seattle Mountain' is a bushy, yellow-needled form of Douglas Fir which is slow growing. How could I not like this? I have come to love Seattle, sleepless though I am when I am there!

RANUNCULUS

Ideal for damp shady places, these creeping buttercups are wildflowers gone really wild.
R. repens 'In Vein' has leaf veins effectively picked out in pale yellow in winter and spring.
R. repens 'Joe's Golden' is a yellow leaved buttercup which is greener in shade. Yellow flowers. Found by Joe Sharman of Monksilver Nursery, U.K.
R. repens 'Little Creep' has small leaves which are very pale yellow when young. Not vigorous, needs a bit of coddling.
Hot Partner: *Ophiopogon planiscapus 'Nigrescens'.*

Robinia pseudoacacia 'Frisia' in autumn

ROBINIA

Fast growing, hardy deciduous trees, admired for their loose open habit and attractive, pinnate foliage and pendent racemes of flowers. The rugged bark and deeply furrowed twigs are another attraction. Best as a specimen tree, never goes unnoticed.

HOW TO GROW

Suitable for any soil, but good in dry, sunny well-drained soil. Common false acacia make large, picturesque, suckering trees which are tolerant of atmospheric pollution. Prefer a sheltered position out of strong winds. Prune in late summer or early autumn. Suckers can be a problem, remove them in autumn. Take root cuttings or graft in winter. Hardy to -20°F (-29°C). Z.4-9.

R. pseudoacacia 'Aurea' the soft yellow leaves which become greenish have been superseded by the better known cultivar 'Frisia'.
R. pseudoacacia 'Frisia' was raised at the nursery of W. Jansen in Holland in 1935 and is named after Friesland. This is a fast growing, conspicuous tree often seen in parks. There are more subdued yellows to be had, but perhaps it is so often chosen for the almost delicate effect of the leaves which are very attractive and its rather brittle stems which wave in the breeze. Its brightness makes it a definite focal point, and it undoubtedly adds a brilliant splash of colour wherever it is grown. Colour deepens as summer progresses. Drooping clusters of scented, white pea-like flowers are borne in summer. Can be stooled each spring and kept as a shrub. Best in sun where it makes one of the brightest landscaping trees. 15m (50ft) with a spread of 8m (25ft).
Hot Partner: *Allium rosenbachianum, Clematis viticella 'Etoile Violette', Geranium 'Ann Folkard'.*
Cool Companion: *Allium 'Globemaster', Myosotis sylvatica.*

144

Above: Rubus laciniatus gold
Centre: Rubus spectabilis 'Golden Ruby'
Bottom: Rubus cockburnianus 'Goldenvale'

RUBUS

A plant lovers delight, ornamental Rubus are desirable for many reasons, flower, handsome foliage and sometimes their attractive winter shoots. Cut old stems back in autumn for best stem effect. Prostrate species make good ground cover. Vigorous species are good in a wild or woodland garden.

HOW TO GROW
Well-drained, moderately fertile soil. Deciduous species grown for winter shoots are best in full sun. Evergreen or semi-evergreen species are good in sun to part shade. Root greenwood cuttings of deciduous species and cultivars in summer or hardwood cuttings in winter. Evergreens can be propagated by semi-ripe cuttings in summer. For prostrate evergreens detach rooted pieces between autumn and spring. Hardy to - 10°F (-23°C). Z. 6-9.

R. cockburnianus 'Goldenvale' ('Wyego') PBR is a deciduous shrub valued for its golden foliage all summer long and for its dazzling white, thorny winter canes. Best in sun. It is low growing and not as vigorous nor invasive as the species and admirable when planted in groups. In the border, it will still occasionally be necessary to keep it in check. Season long interest with ferny foliage in spring with striking, golden colouring perhaps at its best until June, small purplish flowers and white canes which make it an excellent choice for a winter garden. 1.8-2.5m (6-8ft).
R. fruticosus 'Pant Gwyn' from Martin Cragg-Barber who specialises in mutations, plant ones that is. Bright yellow variegation fades to cream. Slow and difficult but sought after.
R. idaeus 'Aureus' is an excellent golden counterpart for the woodland garden. Will ramble. Deciduous shrub suitable for ground cover in dry shade under trees, a situation most plants would not welcome. Smaller growing than the species. 40cm (16").
R. idaeus 'Fallgold' ('Allgold') you might be forgiven for thinking I am jesting, if you have never come

145

across this everbearing raspberry, which has golden fruits draped around its thorny canes. Two crops on each biennial cane. 1.5m (5ft). **'Kiwigold'** is more peachy. For the biggest crops mulch annually with well-rotted manure.

R. laciniatus the evergreen blackberry comes in a startling yellow leaved form.

R. parviflorus 'Aurea' has fabulous, rough-textured, maple-like leaves of greenish yellow providing textural contrast in the woodland garden or border. Keeps its bright gold colouring in sun. Found by Chuck Pavlich in the Pacific Northwest. Happy with wet feet.

R. parviflorus 'Sunshine Spreader' bears golden foliage on a prostrate shrub with white flowers followed by red fruits. 40cm (16").

R. spectabilis 'Golden Ruby' was also found by Chuck Pavlich. An amazing find. This spectacular plant has young foliage startlingly bright yellow which is retained when grown in sun. This form also possesses unusually large pinkish flowers. Will tolerate wet feet.
Hot Partner: *Bergenia cordifolia 'Purpurascens'*, *Ranunculus 'Brazen Hussy'*.
Cool Companion: *Hosta sieboldiana, Muscari 'Valerie Finnis', Gentiana asclepiadea, Helleborus.*

SALVIA

Enjoying moist but well-drained soil, golden sage will cheer the herb bed or border, but there is also a new tender sage with the usual flower power and late summer interest associated with these fabulous plants.

HOW TO GROW
Light, moderately fertile soil. Well-drained in full sun to partial shade. Divide perennials in spring. Root basal or softwood cuttings in spring or early summer.

S. x jamensis 'Moonlight over Ashwood' (Ashwood Nurseries) is a sport from *'Moonlight Serenade'* with creamy-white flowers, pink flushed over golden foliage, some leaves having a feint green mark. Free flowering from summer to first frosts in the U.K. Enhance hardiness by planting in a well-drained, sunny position. In cold areas, take cuttings or bring under cover. Keep plants on the dry side. 90cm (3ft).

S. officinalis 'Icterina' is a splendid variegated form with green and gold splashes and a low spreading habit, sometimes seen sold as *'Aurea'*.

S. officinalis 'Kew Gold' bears oblong, aromatic leaves of flushed gold. Best in sun or part shade. A choice cultivar, very attractive. 30cm (12"). Z5.
Hot Partner: foliage types, *Salvia officinalis Purpurascens Group.*

Rubus parviflorus 'Aurea'

Salvia officinalis 'Icterina'

SAMBUCUS

Cultivars of elder are extremely handsome in foliage. They can be kept small by pruning, giving even greater foliage effect. Tremendous, should be in every golden garden. These handsome forms are suitable for a shrub garden as well as specimen trees or shrubs.

HOW TO GROW
Tolerant of a wide range of conditions, but preferring moist soil in a cool position, with rich organic matter incorporated. Give dappled shade and cut down to within 30cm (1ft) of ground level in early spring for lush growth, thereby sacrificing berries. Z3-10.

S. canadensis 'Aurea' bears yellow leaves and red berries. Excellent and trouble free in full sun and moist soil. Will green up in shade. 3m (10ft).
S. nigra 'Ardwall' is a little-known golden elder collected by Michael Wickenden, found on Ardwall Island. The yellow and green leaves make a handsome shrubby bush if pruned.
S. nigra 'Aurea' is a golden form of the common elder with rugged, fissured bark and golden-yellow leaves which deepen with age. This resilient form withstands hard frosts and full sun. 6m (20ft).
S. nigra 'Aureomarginata' has leaves with an irregular golden margin. 6m (20ft).
S. nigra 'Fructuluteo' is unusual for its yellow fruits.
S. nigra 'Madonna' has a gold edged leaf marbled with green, and occasionally with yellow blotches. Not a vigorous grower, reaching around 1.2m (4ft) without coppicing. It is similar to *'Aureomarginata'*.
S. racemosa 'Aurea' has iridescent young golden-green shoots coming to life in spring. White flowers.
S. racemosa 'Goldenlocks' has golden-yellow leaves, which are bronze-tinted and very divided. Scented clusters of white flowers, sweetly fragrant in June followed by scarlet berries. 2-3m (6-10ft).
S. racemosa 'Plumosa Aurea' is a deciduous shrub grown for its superbly gold-green foliage with heavily dissected margins. Strike a happy balance in the right light for best colour. It scorches in full sun and looks dowdy in shade. Slow growing with rich yellow flowers. Hard prune each winter for the best leaves. New growths are coppery and the plant is a blaze of scarlet and gold when covered in red berries in August. Annual pruning to ground level in spring ensures brightest colour. 1.5m (5ft). Hardy to -25°C.
S. racemosa 'Sutherland Gold' bears bright yellow deeply cut, feathery leaves and spring growth of copper-red. Its graceful habit is very appealing. More scorch-resist than *'Plumosa Aurea'*, but still best in a little shade in moist soil where it holds its colour better than other cultivars. Fragrant white flowers are borne in April and May, occasionally followed by glossy red berries in autumn. 1.5-3m (5-10ft).
Hot Partner: *Clematis 'Jackmannii Superba'*.
Cool Companion: *Rosa glauca, Digitalis purpurea*.
Golden glory: *Ligularia, Gunnera manicata, Lysichiton americanus*.

Sambucus racemosa 'Sutherland Gold'

SCIADOPYTIS

Quite unlike any other conifer and golden cultivars are fairly rare but they are becoming available, largely thanks to Mr. Wittboldt-Muller. Attractive, hardy small trees for the garden, similar to Bald Cypress. Worthy of a place in the garden, like Ginkgo, these plants have a real history, they go way back in time. They are found in forests in Japan. *S. verticillata* is slow-growing and very hardy. Bark peels to reveal reddish-brown new bark. Foliage is borne in lush clusters, like the spokes of an umbrella and is highly attractive. The green form reaches 36m (over 100ft) but these golden forms will be much less vigorous. Slow growing like many conifers for the first 10 years.

HOW TO GROW
Thrive in lime-free soil and do well in partial shade. Moderately fertile, moist, well-drained soil in sun with midday shade. Take semi-ripe cuttings in late summer. Z3-6.

S. verticillata 'Aurea Trompenberg' although even this does not seem to be propagated, there is a mature specimen in the Arboretum at Trompenburg.

S. verticillata 'Firework' (Wittboldt-Muller) is an outstanding variety with golden tipped leaves which just look like the sparks from a firework. Like catherine wheels as described to me by Gordon Haddow of Kenwith Nursery, Devon.

S. verticillata 'Gold Rush' a dwarf golden form developing quicker than *'Ossorio's Gold'* but with more of a green underlay, best in full sun. This upright, bushy tree with stiff golden needles looks really golden in summer. 1m (3ft) Z6.

S. verticillata 'Gold Star' not as small as the above with golden leaves. Really shines like summer parasols.

S. verticillata 'Ossorio Gold' makes a golden tree. Good gold colour and form from the Ossorio collection on Long Island. Best in partial shade. 120x90cm. (4x3ft). Z6.

S. verticillata 'Ruslyn's Gold Parasol' is an excellent golden leaved variety with leaf whorls simply glowing.

S. verticillata 'Starburst' is 24 carat gold, it makes a fabulous statement with its golden growth. Has real impact in full sun. This form was found at Stanley & Sons Nursery, Oregon. 180x120cm (6x4ft). Z3.

Top: Sedum 'Angelina'
Bottom: Sedum 'Ogon'

148

SEDUM

Sun lovers eminently useful in the garden, providing a long season of interest. Often planted with bulbs coming through, but the effect of these small golden plants is ruined by the fading bulb leaves. Allow these to creep around and through perennials. Small-leaved varieties are useful in the rock garden.

HOW TO GROW
Enjoy moist, well-drained soil in sun to part shade. Drought tolerant. Divide in spring.

S. acre 'Aureum' is a lovely bright, golden gem of a plant with both leaves and flowers in yellow. Flowers are borne in May to June. This mat-forming, evergreen is useful for underplanting in the dark garden. Best in sun and well-drained, alkaline soil. 5cm (2"). Z4.

S. rupestre 'Angelina' PPAF is a superb gold leaved form with bright gold needle-like foliage, greener at the base. Excellent for containers or edging where its trailing habit is seen at its best. Prefers well-drained soil on the dry side in full sun. Developed in a private garden in Croatia. Absolutely fabulous. 15cm (6") Z3.

S. 'Ogon' (makinoi) is superb, use it to make a glowing, golden carpet beneath darker plants. The tiny succulent leaves on this little Japanese beauty will really shine in the garden. Foliage glows golden. The best little Sedum I have ever laid my eyes on. I love this. Use this everywhere, springy mats of carpeting at the edge of a border or rock garden, between pavings and cracks (will not take foot traffic), in stone walls, containers. Hardy and easy. 5cm (2") with a spread 30cm (12"). Z5-9.

Hot Partner: *Ophiopogon planiscapus 'Nigrescens'*, *Ranunculus ficaria 'Brazen Hussy'*.

Cool Companion: *Ruta graveolens 'Jackman's Blue'*.

Top : Sedum 'Aureovariagatum'
Bottom: Selaginella pallescens 'Aurea'

SELAGINELLA

S. pallescens 'Aurea' is a little known fern with pale golden tips to the end of its feathery foliage. This deciduous perennial will keep going until really cold weather sends it to sleep. Its attractive flattened sprays of foliage look conifer-like.

An unusual plant for shade. 60cm (2ft). Will survive to Z6 with a protective mulch.

SOLENOSTEMON

Formerly known as *Coleus*, these plants, by whatever name, are an essential part of the foliage garden. Once known as shade plants, some are sun and heat lovers ready to take over your baskets, containers and border. For best foliage effect never let these flower.

HOW TO GROW

Outdoors in summer in full sun to part shade, in humus rich, fertile well-drained soil enriched with organic matter for lush growth. Best in a sheltered position. Water freely in dry weather. Pinch out shoots to promote bushiness. Use indoors as a houseplant in cooler areas. Frost tender.

S. 'Butter Kutter' is a yellow and ochre selection by Doug Lohman. Fasciated stems resemble twisting ribbons.

S. 'Diane's Golden' is an all gold-ochre with pinked, furled leaves reminiscent of an *Acalypha*. Will need some shade in intense heat.

S. 'Freckles' bears creamy yellow foliage with a scalloped edge with bronze and orange splotches to lift a planting.

S. 'Gay's Delight' has bright golden ochre cupped foliage of good substance with radiating maroon veins. Excellent heat and sun tolerance.

S. 'Germann's Yellow' has soft, cream-yellow leaves with intriguing faint lavender pencilling. Makes well-branched plants with light-green stems. 60cm (2ft).

S. 'Golda' is a favourite for its elegance and good rich colouring, introduced by Color Farm in the U.S. 45-60cm (18-24").

S. 'Goldspun' makes a graceful plant with elongated, ruffled leaves, slightly puckered in the pale green centre, surrounded with a golden halo, spotted red.

S. 'Gold Giant' has superb large leaves making a real sunshine splash.

S. 'Gold Storm' is a sport of *'Stormy Weather'* with golden-ochre, slightly puckered leaves with a bold, whitish margin, edged with crenulations and having a vigorous, erect habit.

S. 'Golden Bedder' has slimmish, pointed leaves golden to chartreuse.

S. 'Golden Wizard' holds its soft yellow all season long.

S. 'Greening's Yellow' is a neat coleus with new leaves of bright yellow and older leaves being mottled attractively in green. Semi-trailing. 45cm (18").

S. 'Lemon Giant' large leaves with yellow stems having red bands at the nodes. 45cm (18").

S. 'Life Lime' is solid yellow with ochre undertones and excellent substance. Parents *S. 'Amazon Ochre' x 'Pineapple Queen'*. Durable on stout stems.

S. 'Old Gold' is really stunning with leaves mottled in gold and green towards the edge and a vibrant red line to the centre of the leaf. There is also **'Pale Gold'** which has the same colouring in paler tones.

S. 'Pineapple' has brilliant contrasting colours of yellow and bronze which spreads beautifully into the veins.

S. 'Pineapple Prince' has light metallic bronzy gold leaves, tinged pink or purple with stems and undersides deep, rich purple. Tall, upright growth. A Frieling hybrid.

S. 'Pineapple Queen' an excellent cultivar with gold leaves and maroon stems, rarely flowers. Can have large blotches of maroon. Vigorous and self-branching. 45-60 (18-24").

S. 'Sunshine' has new leaves almost pure yellow ageing to green splashed and veined foliage. Light lavender stems. 40-45cm (16-18").

S. 'The Line' often used by Martha Stewart this golden-ochre, elongated leaved selection was made by Doug Ruhren. The central magenta vein jumps out of the paler leaf colouring making this a very attractive selection with instant appeal. Compact, well-branched plants.

Hot Partner: Grow with *Canna, Phormium* and other *Solenostemon* in hot colours of purple, bronze, red and copper or in chartreuse and orange shades.

Golden Glory: Heuchera 'Amber Waves', Dahlia 'Yellow Hammer'.

Above: Solenostemon 'Roy Pedley'
Below : S. 'Buttercup', Right: S. 'Pineapple'

SORBUS

This genus of deciduous shrubs and trees is normally grown for its attractive foliage and for the berry-like fruits. Easily cultivated in any well-drained, fertile soil. Many end the season in a blaze of golden and red tones. Tolerant of atmospheric pollution.

HOW TO GROW
Moderately fertile, humus-rich, moist but well-drained soil in full sun or light, dappled shade. Pinnate leaved varietes are best in acid to neutral soil. *S. aria* also thrives on chalk. Take greenwood cuttings in early summer, they do not always root well. Bud in summer. Graft in winter.

S. aria 'Aurea' whitebeam makes a small to medium tree with deep crimson fruits in autumn. Deeply veined, and slightly toothed leaves are tinted yellowish
S. aria 'Chrysophylla' has yellow foliage with red berries in autumn. 7m (22ft), spread 5m (15ft).
S. aria 'Lutescens' the effect of the upper tomentum is creamy-white. 8m (26ft).
S. aucuparia 'Beissneri' bears yellow-green, fern-like leaves especially when young. Dark coral-red young shoots. Winter stems are an attractive bright orange-red. Bears flat heads of white flowers. 8m (26ft).
S. aucuparia 'Fructo Luteo' has amber-yellow fruits which last well into winter.
S. 'Carpet of Gold' bears gold fruit on a small tree.
S. 'Covert Gold' is a fine golden rowan tree.
S. esserteauana 'Flava' is worthy of growing for its yellow fruits, an excellent clone.
S. 'Ethel's Gold' (aucuparia section) bears bunches of amber-gold fruits which persist into the New Year.
S. folgneri 'Lemon Drop' is a graceful tree with an attractive pendulous habit, bearing bright yellow fruits in autumn. Narrow leaves are silvery beneath.
S. 'Golden Wonder' (aucuparia section) makes a small tree with sharply toothed blue-green leaflets which turn yellow and red in autumn with golden fruits in large clusters.

SPIRAEA

Valuable, hardy, deciduous foliage shrubs, offering season long interest. Repeat blooming can be had by removing spent blooms. Many cultivars are very similar, recent breeding has concentrated on improving scorch-resist foliage. Attractive to butterflies. Light shear after flowering to encourage additional bloom. Excellent for borders, smaller varieties can be used as low ground cover en masse and taller varieties can make an informal hedge.

HOW TO GROW
Easy to grow, best in full sun, in well-drained soil. New growth may be damaged by frosts. May become chloritic on very shallow chalk. Prune in late winter. Tolerant of many soil types. Take greenwood cuttings in summer. Z4-10.

S. japonica 'Allgold' bears golden yellow leaves and pink flowers. 45cm (18").
S. japonica 'Alpine Gold' is a dwarf shrub, with dense deciduous foliage which is gold when young, turning pale green. Small pink flowers are borne all summer. Best in full sun. 45cm (18"), spread of 60cm (2ft).
S. japonica 'Candlelight' (Peter Catt) is a good recent cultivar, holding its soft yellow colour well. If you are looking for subdued colouring, this is not as bright and glaring as others. Foliage emerges rich orange-red to end the season in a blaze of fiery tints. Pink flowers in summer in full sun. 60-90cm (2-3ft) tall and wide.
S. japonica 'Dakota Goldcharm' (*'Mertyann'*) is a dwarf spirea with gold leaves, tipped bronze with pink flowers, making a good choice for smaller gardens. It is also useful in containers and needs little or no pruning. Best in full sun. Dwarf version of *'Gold Mound'*. 30-60cm (12-24"). Z4.
S. japonica 'Firelight' (Peter Catt) is an improvement on *'Goldflame'* with deeper orange spring growth and fiery autumn colour. Unlike *'Goldflame'* it does not revert. Deep pink flowers appear in summer on a compact mound of golden foliage. 60-90cm (2-3ft).

S. japonica 'Flaming Mound' (W.H.Perron) is a low spreading mound with rich red and gold foliage and dark pink blooms in full sun. 30-50cm (12-20"). Z4.

S. japonica 'Gold Mound' (W.H.Perron) is a low mounding shrub with gold foliage and pink flowers in May to June. Leaf colour is held well even in the southern states of N. America. Fiery orange-red colouring completes the season. Can be subject to mildew. Raised in Canada before 1984. 60-90cm (2-3ft), with a wider spread of 90-120cm (3-4ft).

S. japonica 'Golden Dome' this compact dwarf shrub has golden-yellow foliage in spring and early summer and pink, flattened flowerheads. 40-50cm (16-20").

S. japonica 'Golden Elf' TM makes a small, shrubby, low mound, useful as golden ground cover. Oval leaves retain their colouring quite well into autumn. Tiny pink flowers appear in spring, with sporadic reblooming. 15-30cm (6-12") tall.

S. japonica 'Golden Princess' (Lisp PBR) has bronze-red new growth turning bright yellow then red in autumn. Makes a dense, upright mound. Bright purplish pink flowers in spring and summer. Useful as a short, informal hedge. Found as a seedling by Peter Catt before 1985. 60-90cm (2-3ft).

S. japonica 'Golden Thumbelina' (Klm Fourteen) is a dwarf, compact mounded shrub selected by Roy Klehm and is ideal for small gardens. In early summer numerous pink flowers stand out against the non-burning green-yellow foliage turning golden yellow in autumn. 60cm (2ft) tall.

S. japonica 'Goldflame' (W.H.Perron) spring foliage is aflame with colours of red, copper and orange, changing to a soft yellow-green, then green by summer, finishing in a fiery burst of copper-orange. Dark pink flowers appear in summer, but are not always formed. Shoots can revert to green and this cultivar, a sport of 'Anthony Waterer', has been superseded by newer cultivars but remains a good choice for southern U.S. gardens. 60-90cm (2-3ft).

S. japonica 'Lemon Princess' makes a mound of very bright golden foliage, holding its colour extremely well in full sun. Sharply toothed, oval leaves retain their yellow colouring into summer. Tiny pink flowers are produced from spring to early summer. Foliage sometimes displays attractive autumn tints of red and orange. 60cm (2ft).

Spiraea japonica 'Candlelight'

Spiraea japonica 'Lemon Princess'

S. japonica 'Limemound' is similar to *'Gold Mound'* looking good as low hedging or ground cover. Leaves are lemon-yellow in spring, and lime-green when mature. It has a much more chartreuse appearance overall. Attractive autumn colouring of red and orange. Numerous pink flowers appear in late spring to mid-summer. 60cm (2ft) and 90cm (3ft) wide.

S. japonica 'Magic Carpet' PBR was bred by David Tristam as an improvement on *'Goldflame'*. Young growth is fiery red, intense on new shoots produced early in spring, turning gold with pink flowers in summer. Colour is lost, fading greenish in full sun in the heat of summer. Compact, spreading habit. 25-45cm (10-18").

S. 'Queen of Golds' (Peter Moore) offers rich golden foliage throughout summer. 60cm (2ft).

S. japonica 'White Gold' (Peter Catt) has white flowers and pointed, golden foliage. Foliage becomes green, then gold again.

S. thunbergii 'Ogon' (*'Mellow Yellow'*) is a Japanese selection introduced into the U.S. by Barry Yinger, with bright yellow, small, willow-like leaves. This fine-textured shrub shines all season long like a shaft of light with white flowers in early spring and bronze autumn colour giving a final flourish. 90-120cm (3-4ft). Z4.

S. x vanhouttei 'Gold Fountain' has arching stems of orange-gold leaves accompanied by white flowers in May. Makes a small, attractive hedge. 90cm (3ft).

Top: Spiraea japonica 'Magic Carpet'
Centre: Spiraea japonica 'White Gold'
Bottom left: Spiraea thunbergii 'Ogon'

Hot Partner: *Acer palmatum v dissectum 'Atropurpureum'*, *Verbena bonariensis*, *Dicentra eximia*.

Cool Companion: *Baptisia australis*, *Polemonium caeruleum*, *Geranium 'Johnson's Blue'*.

STACHYS

Evergreen, herbaceous perennials, better known for their silver forms. The yellow-leaved lamb's ears makes dense mats of foliage with erect stems. Ground cover effect can be enhanced by removing flowering stems. A tactile, front of the border perennial.

HOW TO GROW
Grow in any good, well-drained soil in sun. Appreciates light shade in hot climates and although it is drought tolerant, it does not perform well in humid summers. Can be mildly invasive in very rich soils as it spreads by creeping stems. Avoid overhead watering. Divide in spring as new growth begins. Hardy to -10°F (-23°C). Z. 4-9.

S. byzantina 'Primrose Heron' PBR bears pale yellow-green leaves covered in soft white hairs which give it the feely touch. Very strokable, felted leaves of great value in a tactile gaden. New growth can look grey and older leaves are apt to look sickly, but it is particularly good in spring and autumn. Whorls of purplish pink flowers are carried on long stems. Best in full sun and well-drained soil. An effective edger, providing good contrast colouring and interesting texture. 45cm (18"), 15cm (6") without flowers.
Hot Partner: *Ajuga , Viola 'Bowles' Black'*.
Cool Companion: *Veronica 'Georgia Blue'*.
Golden Glory: *Origanum vulgare 'Crispum', Allium flavum, Lysimachia congestiflora 'Outback Sunset'*.

SYMPHYTUM

Variegated and golden varieties tend to be better behaved than the invasive comfrey, but be aware that once planted they are hard to get rid of. They will regenerate from any small rhizome left in the soil, their tap roots go down a long, long way. Excellent in light woodland and shade gardens where they will brighten any space as robust groundcover. Also suitable for borders and cottage gardens.

HOW TO GROW
Excellent hardy, herbaceous perennials in sun or half shade in moist, fertile soil, needing little care and attention. Easy in average, moist, well-drained soil. Capable of doing well in dryish shade. Suitable for clay soils. Divide as necessary in spring. Trim foliage to shape. Z4-8.

S. 'Belsay Gold' bears good, arrow-shaped gold foliage, and glows anew after being cut back. A golden arrow that goes straight to the heart. Greens up in summer but delightful nevertheless. 60cm (2ft). Z3.
S. ibericum 'All Gold' (*S. grandiflorum 'All Gold'*) bears narrowish, pointed golden foliage. Exceptional colour. Electric yellow sparks of light emerge in late February in the U.K., simmering down to green in summer, leaves can reach 60cm (2ft). This handsome woodlander is best in moisture retentive soil. Topped with lilac flowers. 40x60cm (16x24").
S. 'Goldsmith' (*S. ibericum 'Jubilee'*) has variegated green leaves marked with cream and gold, making an attractive, well-behaved mound. Lovely in shade, even dryish shade, where its light green, crinkled leaves to 10cm (4"), irregularly edged in yellow will get noticed. Drooping clusters of pale blue, pink or white flowers are attractive in mid-spring to early summer. A second flush of growth occurs in autumn and leaves can persist into winter. 60cm (24").

Stachys byzantina 'Primrose Heron'

S. 'Lambrook Sunrise' is a non-invasive form of comfrey with acid lemon leaves showing a little green in spring and fading by summer. Blue flowers in May to July. Very well behaved and worth growing for the bright spring colour. 55cm (22"), spread 30cm (12"). Z5.

S. x uplandicum 'Axminster Gold' is an outstanding gold-leaved comfrey edged in chartreuse. Leaves are large to 30 cm (12") and have impact, stand back and admire. Elegant, narrow leaves are accompanied by blue flowers in summer. Can be cut back before flowering to rejuvenate the foliage effect. Has vigour and a definite presence. A great plant for a large pot. Bold and dashing. I know many who rate this very highly. Unlike the white variegated type, this has much more oomph and sun power. Found at RD Plants, Devon and named by nursery owner Lynda Windsor. 60cmx1m (24x36").

Hot Partner: *Viola 'Bowles' Black'*.
Cool Companion: *Corydalis flexuosa 'China Blue'*.
Golden Glory: *Verbascum 'Letitia', Corydalis flexuosa 'Golden Panda', Milium effusum 'Aureum'*.

Top: Symphytum
Bottom left: S. 'Belsay Gold'

156

SYRINGA

Well known deciduous suckering shrubs with wonderful perfume to please the senses in spring. Hardy to -20°F (-29°C). Z.5-9.
S. vulgaris 'Aurea' bears clusters of very fragrant, small, pinkish-purple flowers in spring. Distinguished by its yellow-green leaves. Rather rare.

TALINUM

T. paniculatum 'Kingwood Gold' has golden leaves and carmine flowers. Will make a bright splash on the windowsill or in a sunny border. Has the bonus of persistent red seed pods. Golden form of a Caribbean native, known as golden flame flower or jewels of Opar, selected at Kingwood Center, U.S. A tender perennial which can be grown as a half hardy annual.

Tanacetum vulgare 'Isla Gold'

TANACETUM

Medicinal uses of feverfew abound, but this is also a decorative ornamental, especially in its golden forms. Still often found under *Chrysanthem parthenium*. One of the few daisy types I can put up with for sake of the golden leaves. Usually self-seed prolifically.

HOW TO GROW
This short-lived, herbaceous perennial will grow well in any soil, well-drained in sun or shade, prefers sandy soil but must not dry out, neither must it be over-wet. Divide in spring. Z5-9.

T. parthenium 'Aureum' is a golden feverfew which looks cheerful even in the dowdy days of winter. Its bright yellow, pinnate leaves are best in sun, but perform their task of emitting a ray of sunshine even in shade. Clusters of daisy like flowers in summer. Comes true from seed.15x30cm (6x12").
T. parthenium 'Golden Moss' is a dwarf cultivar with golden, moss-like foliage, useful as edging, white button daisies. Normally seen in seed catalogues. 15cm (6").
T. parthenium 'Minety' is a feathery yellow foliage form discovered at Lower Minety, England.
T. vulgare 'Golden Feather' as the name suggests bears gold-leaved, feathery foliage. Fresh acid fronds provide perfect contrast with more solid leaves. Distinct in that its foliage is more deeply divided than the above. Yellow flowers are borne in June and can be cut down for a second flush of foliage instead.
T. vulgare 'Isla Gold' has deeply dissected, feathery leaves, in variegated golden tones which is very effective, especially in sun in the dry garden. Easy, giving gold colouring from early spring to the first frosts. Very close to *'Golden Feather'* with deeply cut leaves, but this one has yellow button daisies. This highly ornamental form appeared as a sport at West Acre Gardens, Norfolk, U.K. 40cm (16"). Z4-8.
Hot Partner: *Nepeta, Sisyrinchium striatum, Parahebe perfoliata., Foeniculum vulgare 'Bronze'.*

157

TAXUS

Useful as an evergreen, evergold backdrop and perfect for topiary. Tolerant of urban pollution and exposure. Dry soils are not a problem. Male and female strobili are borne in spring, usually on separate plants. *T. baccata* is one of only three conifers native to Britain.

HOW TO GROW

Yews tolerate a wide range of conditions, provided the soil is well-drained and fertile, including chalk and acid soils. Green forms are suitable for shade, but golden forms prefer some sun. Trim in summer or early autumn, can be pruned and clipped as required. Poisonous to cattle. Z4-6 depending on species.

T. baccata 'Adpressa Aurea' has shortened needles of gold. The bright gold shoots of this male form turn yellow in spring, then variegated. The variety commonly offered is usually *'Adpressa Variegata'*. Best in sun or semi-shade, bearing in mind more sun, more colour. Easily trimmed. 60 x60cm (2x 2ft).

T. baccta 'Aldenham Gold' is a slow grower making a mound which given plenty of time will become conical. Short leaves have a small green centre and wide pale yellow margins.

T. baccata Aurea Group has yellow-green foliage making an attractive backdrop for golden flowers. Its colouring is lost in its second year. 1.5x1.5m (5x5ft).

T. baccata 'Dovastonii Aurea' is an excellent male gold form with an upright, slender habit and spreading branches, holding its colour all year in sun or semi-shade. Slower than the green form. Stays golden even in shade. 2m x 2m (6ft x 6ft).

T. baccata 'Elegantissima' makes a good hedge maturing from rich gold to light green. This most popular female form makes a dense, large bush. 4.5m (15ft) height and spread.

T. baccata Fastigiata Aurea Group is very similar to *'Fastigiata'*, a columnar female, but has variegated leaves with deep gold. Withstands hard pruning. Makes a superb vertical accent. 6m (20ft) with a spread of 3m (10ft). *Photograph opposite.*

T. baccata 'Itsy Bitsy' makes an extremely narrow column with deep yellow summer foliage becoming variegated in autumn. Orange tints in winter.

T. baccata 'Ivory Tower' makes a slender column with pale gold-yellow foliage.

T. baccata 'Repandens Aureomarginata' is a small spreader, with rich golden colouring in summer, remaining until winter in sun or shade. 60cm (2ft) tall and up to 120cm (4ft) across.

T. baccata 'Repens Aurea' is very similar to *'Dovastonii Aurea'* but propagated from side shoots only to form ground cover. It loses its colour in deep shade. Spread of 1-1.5m (3-5ft).

T. baccata 'Semperaurea' is a slow growing male with short ascending branches. Leaves are gold, turning rusty yellow with age and retaining colouring in winter even in semi-shade. Makes a good hardy evergreen hedge which is tolerant of most soils. Best in full sun. 1.5 x 1.5m (5 x 5ft).

T. baccata 'Standishii' slowly makes a narrow, golden column, excellent for adding height. Forms a very slender column with a diameter of just 30cm (12"). An old female cultivar from 1908 with perhaps the best golden colouring of the genus and with red berries in autumn. Ideal in a patio planter. 1.5m (5ft) tall in 10 years. Z5-6.

T. baccata 'Summergold' is gold all year through but brighter in summer. This semi-prostrate form is best in full sun or semi-shade. Does not scorch in full sun. 40x90m (16x36").

T. baccata 'Watnong Gold' is similar to *T. baccata 'Repens Aurea'* with brighter gold colouring. Broader than high.

T. cuspidata 'Aurea Low Boy' is a compact form, growing wider than tall.

T. cuspidata 'Aurescens' is an attractive cultivar with brilliant orange-gold colouring even in shade, turning green in the second season. A low-growing, compact form. 1-1.5m (3-5ft).

T. cuspidata 'Bright Gold' this slow growing form with a spreading habit is much brighter gold than *T. baccata 'Aurea'*, having yellow and green striations. Light shade is appreciated as this form can burn, especially in hot climates. 2-4.5m (6-15ft).

Hot Partner: *Cotinus coggygria 'Royal Velvet'*, *Tropaeolum speciosum*.

Cool Companion: *Chamaecyparis lawsoniana 'Pembury Blue'*.

Previous page: Taxus baccata Fastigiata Aurea Group
Below: Taxus baccata 'Repens Aurea'

THUJA

Dense foliage to ground level in attractive conical shapes on hardy, evergreen trees and shrubs is eminently desirable. Male and female strobili are borne on the same tree in early spring. An excellent substitute for *Chamaecyparis* in colder areas. Make fine specimen trees and are suitable for hedging.

HOW TO GROW
Provide a sheltered position in bright sun and deep, moist, well-drained soil. They dislike dry conditions. Protect young plants from cold winds even though they are cold tolerant. Trim in late spring or early autumn. Take semi-ripe cuttings in late summer. Z3.

T. occidentalis 'Amber Glow' makes a small, globular bush with good deep gold colour.

T. occidentalis Aurea Group (*'Mastersii Aurea'*) makes a medium sized tree or large bush with golden-yellow foliage on a broadly conical habit.

T. occidentalis 'Aureospicata' is an erect form with young shoots becoming yellow, more intense in winter when they are burnished old gold.

T. occidentalis 'Elegantissima' has heavily textured foliage with better colouring in summer, mainly creamy yellow. A broad pyramidal habit. 3m (10ft).

T. occidentalis 'Europa Gold' is a narrowly conical large shrub or small tree with golden-yellow foliage.

Thuja occidentalis 'Amber Glow'

T. occidentalis 'George Peabody' is a golden upright, narrowly pyramidal form, which is sun tolerant and retains its colouring for most of the year. Nice orange-gold glow in winter. 3m (10ft).

T. occidentalis 'Gold Drop' is a very nice globose plant with deep gold foliage. Outer tints are orange.

T. occidentalis 'Golden Globe' is a dense, globe shaped shrub without shearing with bright yellow foliage which retains its colouring year-round and which does not burn. Excellent for sun or part-shade in well-drained soil. A mutation of *'Woodwardii'* introduced in 1946. 90-120cm (3-4 ft). Z3.

T. occidentalis 'Holmstrup's Yellow' is a golden-leaved sport raised in Denmark before 1951.

T. occidentalis 'Lutea' becomes rich, golden bronze in winter, orange-yellow in summer. Straggly when young, but becomes pyramidal. 2.4x1m (8x3ft).

T. occidentalis 'Lutea Nana' is a small, conical bush of dense habit with deep golden-yellow foliage. Best in winter, but retains some colouring in summer too.

T. occidentalis 'Pumila Sudsworth' is a golden upright form which does not scorch in sun.

T. occidentalis 'Rheingold' (*'Ellwangeriana Aurea'*) is a radiant, slow growing conical shrub with deep gold, feathery foliage, pink tinged when young and turning copper to bronze in winter. Full sun gives outstanding colour. Responds well to regular shearing. Prefers well-drained soil in sun or part shade. One of the most popular golden conifers. 1.2m (4ft).

Thuja occidentalis 'Rheingold'

T. occidentalis 'Sunkist' forms an upright, dense bright golden pyramid which is scorch-resist in summer. Shows some purplish tints in winter. Enhanced by a summer trim each year. Vigorous and useful as a hedge, screen or focal point. Introduced in 1986, one of the best yellow conifers.1.2m (4x3ft). Z3.

T. occidentalis 'Techny Gold' (Walter Brown, USA) is a golden sport of *'Techny'* long considered the earliest Arborvitae. Tested for winter burn and discoloration for 7 years, this golden form passed with flying colours. Colour is retained year round. Use as a specimen or hedge in full sun or partial shade. 1.8-3.6mx90-150cm wide (6-12ftx3-5ft).

T. occidentalis 'Wareana Lutescens' (*'Wareana Aurea'*) is a compact form with pale butter yellow foliage. Displays a bronze cast in winter. A slow-growing bush, useful as a screen, hedge or a specimen plant, eventually making a broad, pyramid. Very effective contrast colour. 1.5x1m (5x3ft).

T. occidentalis 'Yellow Ribbon' bears narrow, upright golden yellow foliage in summer, fading to bronze in winter in sun or part shade. Makes a tall, narrow focal point. 2.5 x 60cm (9x2ft). Z3.

Thuja occidentalis 'Techny Gold'

Thuja plicata 'Irish Gold'

T. plicata 'Aurea' has rich golden antique yellow leaves on an outstanding ornamental.

T. plicata 'Brooks Gold' makes a small, squat plant with bright gold foliage. Its conical shape is useful in the border, rock garden or trough.

T. plicata 'Collyer's Gold' is slow-growing and similar to *'Stoneham Gold'* with brighter coloured foliage. A showy plant with an upright habit. 2m (6ft).

T. plicata 'Irish Gold' is a handsome shrubby conifer with a definite gold effect to the edges of its leaves.

T. plicata 'Old Gold' has yellow foliage early in the season changing to old gold in winter, colouring is deeper in colder weather. A reliable grower in most areas, tolerates light frost with moderate toleration of salt winds, better than the species. Tall, upright conical habit is easily pruned. 5x3m (16x10ft).

T. plicata 'Rogersii' slowly makes a compact cone with gold summer leaves and bronze foliage darkening in winter. Retains its colour well in shade. Its dense, upright growth can be pruned to size if required making it ideal for small gardens. Just slightly faster growing than a tortoise moves! 90-60cm (3-2ft).

T. plicata 'Stolwijk's Gold' has fine foliage, dusted handsomely with gold, especially at the tips. 150cm (5ft).

T. plicata 'Stoneham Gold' is an attractive, medium grower in sun to shade, with new growth having a golden edge to contrast with the dense, darker green interior. Best colour is in sun. Its fragrant, upright, bushy foliage makes a good screen. 1.5m (5ft) . Z7.

T. plicata 'Sunshine' stands out in a crowd with its golden colour which withstands full sun. A good choice where hot summers are the norm. Graceful, pendulous new growth on a semi-dwarf which forms a wide cone. 3m (10ft).

T. plicata 'Zebrina' makes a broadly conical tree with a mahogany trunk. Striped yellow-green fragrant foliage like a golden zebra for sun or part shade. Makes a beautiful specimen. 10mx3m(30x10ft).

Thuja plicata 'Stolwijk's Gold'

THUJOPSIS

Related to *Thuja*, this slow-growing conifer has broader, flatter branchlets and larger leaves and is known as deer horn cedar, you will know why if you have seen the foliage, like a deer's antler. Thrives in any type of well-drained soil, including shallow chalk in full sun. Male and female strobili are borne on the same tree. Z6.

T. dolobrata 'Aurea' makes a distinctive, attractive golden conifer, deserving to be planted more frequently. In winter the tips of leaves turn rich orange-gold. It makes a small tree of dense, conical habit with thick, scale-like leaves. 2x1.2m (6x4ft).

TRACHELOSPERMUM

I have long admired this slow growing evergreen with its pure white windmill sail-like flowers. The usual species grown with green leaves is *T. jasminoides,* known as star jasmine. Stems contain a milky latex. Not a beginner's plant, but an interesting woody climber for the gold garden.

HOW TO GROW
In milder areas, grow against a sunny wall or in a conservatory. For well-drained soil in sun or a little shade with protection from cold winds. Take semi-ripe cuttings with bottom heat in summer. Layer in autumn. Z7-11.

T. asiaticum 'Golden Memories' has an air of purity. Its beautiful white flowers with a yellow centre echo the yellow of the leaves. Flowers appear in May to July and they have one of the most delightful flower fragrances. Position where you can enjoy the wafting scent around a sheltered arbour with a seat where you can dream of warmer climates. 90cm (3ft).

TRADESCANTIA

Creeping, mat-forming perennials are suitable for a mixed or herbaceous border. They are also great container plants. Lax leaves and startling flowers make a striking contrast.

T. 'Blue and Gold' from Aubrey Barker of Hopley's Nursery, UK., produces vigorous mounds of golden foliage, perfectly complemented by the blue flowers. Best in full sun or partial shade. Z5.
T. 'Chedglow' from the same stable has similar coloured foliage but with mauve-purple flowers.
T. 'Sweet Kate' is a brilliant gold form to dispel the clouds and turn grey skies blue. I cannot see much difference, if any between this and *T. 'Blue and Gold'*.
Hot Partner: *Iris chrysographes black.*

Tradescantia 'Blue and Gold'

TRICYRTIS

Toad lily is an unattractive name for these attractive flowers and foliage which are good in shade. Hardy, rhizomatous, herbaceous perennials occur in moist woodland. Will take full sun in Maine and Pacific Northwest as well as England. Good in autumn when many plants are past their best. New breeding is bringing that sought after golden colouring into the leaves.

HOW TO GROW

Grow in moist, well-drained, humus-rich soil in shade. Provide a deep winter mulch in areas where there is snow cover. Divide in early spring when still dormant.

Tricyrtis 'Gilty Pleasure'

T. formosana 'Gates of Heaven' a gold sport spotted by Clarence Falsted of Walters Gardens in the U.S.

T. 'Gilty Pleasure' PVR is a sport of *'Gilt Edge'* with electric yellow foliage in spring and throughout the season, contrasting with lavender flowers in autumn. Has good vigour for a golden form. Spectacular.

T. 'Golden Gleam' introduced by Dan Heims has long upright to arching stems of gold foliage which is a superb backdrop for the purple spotted flowers in autumn. 30-45cm (12-15"). Z4-8.

T. hirta 'Gold Leaf' an upright form with narrow, hairy leaves which holds its colour well all season. White flowers are heavily speckled purple.

T. 'Lemon Lime' bears golden foliage sometimes with a green line. A Terranova introduction with some *hirta* parentage bearing lavender flowers. Z4-9

T. macrantha ssp macranthopsis and **T. ohsumiensis** have fabulous golden yellow flowers.

TSUGA

Some of the most attractive hardy, evergreen conifers, making shade tolerant specimen trees. These evergreens have a broadly conical habit and spreading branches. The leader is pendent. Male and female strobili are borne on the same plant with small, pendent cones ripening in the same year and remaining on the plant for a further year. They are suitable as a hedge out of cold winds.

HOW TO GROW

Well-drained but moist, acid to alkaline loam in full sun to partial shade. Shelter from cold winds. Trim hedges from early to late summer. Root semi-ripe cuttings in late summer or early autumn. Z4.

T. canadensis 'Arnold Gold Weeper' is quite robust and excellent growing down a bank.
T. canadensis 'Aurea' is slow growing and compact. Its young yellow foliage turns green with age. 8m.
T. canadensis 'Everitt's Golden' (*T. canadensis 'Aurea Compacta'*) found by Sam Everitt in 1918. A desirable, stiff-textured and fairly upright, compact plant with gold colouring in full sun in spring, but can burn. Performs well in light shade. 90cm(3ft).
T. canadensis 'Golden Beacon' possesses a graceful, upright habit with arching branches which keep their golden foliage colouring even in a little shade.
T. canadensis 'Golden Splendour' is a fast-growing plant, broadly upright, pyramidal coniferous tree tolerating full sun fairly well. Needs shearing to produce graceful, dense branching. 4.5m (15').
T. canadensis 'Lutea' is a slow growing tree whose golden foliage is at its best in winter.
T. canadensis 'New Gold' is upright with bright gold new growth in spring giving a two-tone effect against the dark green foliage of the previous year. 4.5m (15').
Tsuga heterophylla 'Aurea' is a golden dwarf form of western hemlock, native to NW America, and found by Chuck Pavlich in the Pacific Northwest. At 20 years old, this will still only be around 1m (3ft) tall.

ULMUS

Suitable for sun or light shade and for most soils as long as it is kept moist, especially in dry periods. Elms have suffered greatly over the years with Dutch elm disease which has led to a downturn in plantings. Many have superb autumn colouring and make attractive, hardy specimen trees.

HOW TO GROW

Any well-drained soil in full sun or partial shade. Take greenwood cuttings in summer or remove rooted suckers in autumn.

U. glabra 'Lutescens' has soft cream-yellow leaves in spring, becoming green-yellow. An attractive and fast growing tree.
U. minor 'Dampieri Aurea' (*x hollandica or glabra 'Wredii'*) makes a narrow columnar tree with golden foliage all summer which seems to swirl around the columnar form. A quick trim may be necessary to achieve the desired cylindrical shape. A spectacular golden elm and a superb specimen tree for restricted spaces in sun. 3.5m (12ft).
U. minor 'Dicksonii' is a very slow growing tree with beautiful bright golden foliage. Its graceful habit is enhanced by the yellow leaves.
U. procera 'Louis van Houtte' (Vanhouttei) makes a handsome tree with golden-yellow foliage throughout summer. The species, often seen in the English landscape, has exceptional yellow autumn colour too.
U. 'Sapporo Autumn Gold' PBR is greenish-yellow in autumn.
U. x viminalis 'Aurea' is an extremely graceful, medium growing tree with leaves of golden-yellow when young becoming yellowish-green.
Hot Partner: *Clematis viticella*.

URTICA

Gardening with a sting might not be to everyone's taste, but several nettle cultivars have golden foliage. Important ecological plants, they do support a wide variety of insect species. Young shoots are edible. Grow amongst trees and shrubs, in containers if well-watered or in the wild garden.

U. dioica 'Chedglow' shows little vigour with its outstanding clear yellow foliage, a subtle green mottling appearing in May gives a spurt to growth. Delicate.

U. dioica 'Good as Gold' was found by the banks of the River Ouse in Cambridgeshire with excellent gold foliage in spring, accentuated by a reddish tint in the juvenile foliage and stems. On flowering, the colour is a more subdued yellow-green. Revive the golden tones by cutting back. Leaves are interestingly but minutely speckled and splashed in green and cream. Pull out any all-green shoots. A well-behaved nettle.

U. dioica 'Spring Fever' bears leaves suffused with bright, acid yellow dazzling in early spring with just a recurring hint on new shoots in autumn.

U. dioica 'Worn Gilding' has leaves unfolding green, then developing the gold dust effect, a soft marbling in two tone yellow.

Below: Veronica 'Aztec Gold'
Right: Veronica 'Gold Halo'

VERONICA

Small golden mats of colour are very useful in the garden. These hardy, golden cushions are at their best in the rock garden.

HOW TO GROW

Easily grown, herbaceous perennials in any moist, well-drained soil in full sun to part shade. Get the best from these mat-forming ground covers by avoiding poorly drained, wet soils. Shear after flowering to encourage new growth and sparse, intermittent rebloom. Spreads indefinitely by sterile, prostrate stems. Divide in autumn or spring. Z4-8.

V. 'Aztec Gold' PVR (Dan Heims) is sunproof, where the best colour will be obtained, grown in shade it will green up. Golden mats make a statement no-one can deny, especially when teamed with violet blue flowers in May. Z3-9.

V. prostrata 'Buttercup' bears sunproof, brilliant gold foliage spreading mats of gold with blue flowers in May. Foliage turns chartreuse in shade.

V. repens 'Sunshine' is a prostrate golden variety making vigorous mats of groundcover with occasional small, purple flowers in May to June. 5cm (2"). Z6.

V. 'Trehane' is a diminutive, golden foliaged, blue flowered variety, blooming in early summer. 15-20cm (6-8").

VIBURNUM

Handsome deciduous shrubs, interesting in flower, leaf and fruit. Suitable for a shrub border or woodland garden. Fruiting is often at its best when several of the same species are grown together.

HOW TO GROW
Easy to cultivate given reasonable soil and sun to light shade. Fairly drought tolerant when well established, but require ample water to begin with. Take greenwood cuttings in summer. Z3b.

V. lantana 'Aureum' is a neglected hardy, native shrub. Heavily textured foliage and creamy-white flowers in May and June. Dense habit, clothed in leaves almost to the ground. Tolerant of shallow, chalky soil but prefers rich loam and will appreciate a little shade. Some reddish autumn colouring, deep maroon when early frosts occur, accompanies red berries which turn black. A fabulous addition with interest almost year round. 2.5-3m (8-10ft).
V. opulus 'Aureum' bears butter yellow foliage all summer and white flowers in spring. A medium shrub, best in light shade. Ornamental red fruits from late summer onwards, persist into winter. 3.5m (12ft). Hot Partner: *Euphorbia dulcis 'Chameleon'*.

WEIGELA

The National Collection is held in my home town at the Sheffield Botanic Garden, and they are one of my favourite hardy, deciduous shrubs, highly ornamental in both foliage and in flower too given plenty of sun. Suitable for a mixed or shrub border or for open woodland. Easy.

HOW TO GROW
Any fertile, well-drained soil in full sun or partial shade. Root greenwood cuttings with bottom heat in midsummer, hardwood cuttings from autumn to winter. Hardy to -10°F (-23°C). Z4-9.

W. 'Briant Rubidor' (*'Olympiade'*) has bright yellow leaves against ruby red flowers. Leaves can occasionally be margined yellow or green. Best in partial shade where it will grab all the attention. A branch sport of *'Bristol Ruby'* introduced by Andre Briant nursery, France. Tim Wood of Spring Meadow Nursery, U.S. has had this growing in a shaded spot under an oak tree. Season long colour in shade, may burn in the hot south of the U.S. in sun, but should do well in a sunny position in the U.K and cooler parts of the U.S. 120-150cm (4-5ft).
W. 'French Lace' (*'Brigela'*) PPAF has dramatic variegation with bright yellow leaf margins and astonishing dark red flowers. From Andre Briant.120-150cm (4-5ft).
W. 'Gold Rush' is a consistent variegated form with gold and green leaves and light pink flowers. 120-150cm (4-5ft).
W. 'Jean's Gold' (Paul Zako 1988) PPAF is a sport of *'Bristol Ruby'* with golden-green foliage. Has scorch resist leaves.
W. 'Looymansii Aurea' two-tone pink flowers are borne in early summer against the golden backdrop of the leaves. Foliage colour is best on emergence when it is sulphur-yellow, but remains a soft lime-yellow all summer. Best in part shade to sun. Found as a seedling in 1873. 1.5m (5ft).

W. 'Sunny Princess' is a variegated form with narrow yellow bands to each leaf, having improved hardiness. Best in full sun. 12-150cm (4-5ft).

W. florida 'Variegata' seems to have been superseded in so many ways now by the above variegated cultivars, but I always found the variegation extremely pleasing on this, and that is a compliment from me. Suffers from tip die back in cold areas. Pink flowers fade to white. 120-180cm (4-6ft).

Hot Partner: *Berberis thunbergii 'Atropururea Nana'*. Cool Companion: *Euphorbia x martinii, Geranium pratense 'Wisley Blue'*.

XANTHOCYPARIS

X. vietnamensis is a new species of conifer found in Vietnam and has given rise to the third new genus since 1948. The golden cypress is very attractive. It was found in a heavily wooded area in 1999 by an international team of botanists. In the thin soil where the new species was found, plants reached 15m (50ft) but it is suspected that it may attain a greater height. It displays two types of foliage on mature plats, some branches have foliage similar to *Chamaecyparis*, others have linear leaves with pointed tips. No other plants were found, but the specimen is producing viable seed.

The discovery has led to plant name changes within the conifers.

Top and Centre: Weigela 'Briant Rubidor'
Bottom: Xanthosoma maffafa 'Aurea'

XANTHOSOMA

X maffafa 'Aurea' ('Golden Delicious') in the deep south of the U.S. you could release this golden beauty into a moist spot in the garden, but it will perform elsewhere outdoors in a container in the garden in summer or under glass. Full sun and moist soil will see it reach impressive stature and retain its golden tones. Often found labelled incorrectly as *Alocasia* or *Colocasia*.

Aquilegia vulgaris Vervaeneana Group

Below left: Abutilon pictum 'Thompsonii'
Below: Sanchezia nobilis

GOLD DUST
BEST VARIEGATED PLANTS

Bergenia 'Tubby Andrews'

I am not a big lover of variegated plants, the variegation has to be extremely elegant and quite dapper to please my eye. Variegation comes in the form of splashes, dots, stripes or, the type I prefer, a margin. There are far more yellow variegated plants than white, so the list is still quite a long one. They make excellent link plants between green and yellow.

Abutilon megapotamicum 'Variegatum' and **A. pictum 'Thompsonii'** are highly attractive in both leaf and flower. Suitable for a conservatory in cold areas.
Aciphylla aurea, speargrass, so named for their spiky, stiff foliage, are not actually related to grasses. These perennials of the carrot family are from New Zealand and Australia and are often found in alpine areas. *A. aurea* is found in dry regions and forms a large clump of grey-green margined golden fan-shaped leaves. Large specimens are subject to collapse outside their natural habitat. 1m x1.5m (3x5ft). Z8-11.
Aechmea 'Aztec Gold' has to be a remarkable feat of breeding, a superb cultivar.
Agapanthus africanus 'Aureovariegata' has attractive bright new growth with fine green stripes, later turns more chartreuse.
Agave americana 'Marginata' for its brilliant yellow leaf margins. Blooms after about 10 years, but produces offsets quite freely. Living sculpture, these architectural plants deserve a place where they serve as a focal point. Not by the edge of a path, they are armed with spines! 1.8m (6ft).

Agave americana 'Marginata'

Aralia elata 'Aureovariegata'

Alopecurus pratensis 'Aureus' is a fabulous gold and green foxtail grass, giving a glow to the garden. 30cm in flower (12").
Ananas comosus 'Variegatus' is a comely terrestrial bromeliad forming dense rosettes of spiny-margined leaves which are dark green striped yellow.
Aralia elata 'Aureovariegata' is a superb large shrub or small hardy tree with excellent variegation, green leaves are edged in gold. Deservedly popular for its wonderful habit.
Artemisia vulgaris 'Cragg-Barber Eye' has strong yellow foliage flecked green.
A. 'Oriental Limelight' is a little vigorous, but very attractive with leaves of gold splashed green.
Astrantia major 'Sunningdale Variegated' has foliage elegantly marked with yellow and green.

Below: Artemisia 'Oriental Limelight'

Aucuba japonica 'Variegata'

Aucuba japonica 'Gold Dust' or **'Crotonifolia'**, some shudder at the thought, but I have always liked the hardy variegated spotted laurels, their bold leaves splattered in yellow. Best with a little shade, in fact one of their attributes is their ability to survive where little else will flourish. Z. 7-10.

Bergenia 'Tubby Andrews' is irregularly splashed with gold. An unusual hardy perennial to lift any shady border. 15-30cm (6-12"). Z4-11. *Photograph Page 169.*

Bromus inermis 'Skinner's Gold' bears green and gold grass blades in vertical stripes, giving the appearance of a gold plant from a distance. Plumes, 60cm (2ft) long appear in July in similar tones. Z6-8. 50cm (20").

Canna 'Striata' (*'Pretoria', 'Bengal Tiger'*) the ultimate in gold striation. Imported from India into the U.S. in 1963 by Glasshosue Works. Brilliant green and yellow striped leaves are accompanied by bright orange flowers in summer. Works well as an aquatic too. 1.8m (6ft).

Carex, hardy grasses for a superb foliage effect. Best in sun to shade. Soil conditions and amount of water depends on individual species.

C. caryophylla 'Beatlemania' selected by Alan Tower, Spokane, WA, bears dark green foliage, striped gold. Making a 30cm (12") wide, slow-spreading clump, best in damp soil. 15cm (6") tall. Z 5-7, maybe colder.

C. dolichostachya 'Kaga nishiki' (*'Gold Fountains'*) has striking, finely gold variegated foliage forming a teeming fountain of evergreen, arching leaves in a dense clump. Best in sun or partial shade in moist soil. 60cm (2ft). Z7.

C. elata 'Aurea' (stricta 'Aurea', riparia 'Aurea'), Bowles' golden sedge, is a superb golden, perennial happy in shallow water. Striking, arching, bright yellow leaves, especially in spring, with a mere suggestion of green in narrow margins, becoming greener as the season progresses. Slow to settle, this deciduous grass makes a good clump in time in sun, foliage will green up in shade. A little sunshine goes a long way in containers, borders or massed plantings. Needs constant moisture and makes a superb marginal water plant. 50-70cm (20-28"). Hardy to -10°F (-23°C). Z5-9, Z4 with protection.

C. elata 'Knightshayes' is not as golden nor as hardy, but is very attractive. Z7.

Above: Canna 'Striata'

Above: Carex dolichostachya 'Gold Fountains'
Centre: Carex oshimensis 'Evergold'
Bottom: Carex siderosticha 'Shima nishiki'

Above: Carex elata 'Aurea'
Centre: Carex testacea 'Old Gold'
Bottom: Carex siderosticha 'Lemon Zest'

Carex elata 'Knightshayes'

C. flava the golden sedge has bright yellow-green leaves with orange-brown flowerheads in June to July. Cool growing. 1m (3ft). Z7.

C. morrowii 'Fisher' Form' (*'Goldband'*) makes a good sized, evergreen clump with leaves edged and striped yellow fading to creamy white, best in rich, moist but well-drained soil in sun or partial shade. Broad, stiff, shiny foliage is complemented by arching flowerheads. Striking in a light woodland setting. 45-50cm (18-20"). Z7.

C. morrowii 'Gilt' is a smaller version of the above, better marked. 25cm (10"). Z7.

C. muskingumensis 'Oehme' is a very attractive variety with yellow margins to the pale green leaves. Greenish spindle-shaped flowerheads from June to August. 50cm (20"). Z7.

C. oshimensis 'Evergold' (hachijoensisis, morrowii), Japanese weeping sedge, forms a low, cascading mound of tufted, evergreen cream-gold foliage, neatly edged in mid-green. Best in moist, rich soil but will tolerate dry sites, prefers light shade. 30cm (12"). Z5.

C. pendula 'Moonraker' bears creamy gold foliage with a weeping habit, becoming greener. These tufted perennials are erect at first, becoming pendulous with age. Fertile moist or wet soil in sun or partial shade. Best in moist soil in light shade. 1.5m (5ft).

C. pilulifera 'Tinney's Princess' is a delightful, delicate small sedge with tufts of creamy yellow foliage, margined with dark green stripes. Best in neutral to acid soil in sun or partial shade. Similar to *C. 'Evergold'* but more delicate. 15cm (6").

C. siderosticha 'Banana Boat' has vivid gold leaves with a thin green edge and appreciates warm weather to emerge. Fertile, moist or wet soil in sun to partial shade. Deciduous. 30cm (12"). Z6-9.

C. siderosticha 'Shima Nishiki' (*Island Brocade*) has lovely broad, green leaves edged in brilliant gold, forming attractive carpets of foliage. Excellent in shade. Lots of vigour, but does not spread, as it has non-rooting stems. Z5-9.

C. siderosticha 'Lemon Zest' is a Japanese selection with solid yellow variegation, making a mound of broad, lance-shaped leaves. A definite golden glow to add zest to any tired planting.

C. testacea 'Old Gold' has wonderful antique gold hints glittering amongst its foliage. I have been growing this, and I am not sure that it is at all distinct to the species, which is worthy of growing. The species itself has lovely gold tints in late summer to autumn, this cultivar is supposed to be golder all season. I have not found it to be so. This New Zealand grass is not hardy, survived outdoors in Sheffield, Yorkshire even when it went below 0°C (32°F). 30cm (12").

Cistus 'Gold Prize' has red tinted buds opening to pure white flowers against the golden foliage suffused with lime green splashes. Performs well in containers and shows no signs of scorching in full sun. Excellent for dry banks, rock gardens and with very good drainage can withstand light frosts. Good maritime plants and also perform on chalk. Pinching back after flowering encourages compact growth. 1m (3ft).

Cistus x argenteus 'Golden Treasure' (Nepond) is a variegated sport of 'Peggy Sammons' found in 1993. Its sage green leaves are irregularly margined golden-yellow in spring and summer, deepening in autumn. 1m (3ft).

Clematis now comes with netted variegated leaves. The deep green lines stand out against golden foliage.

Clematis 'Gold'

Euonymus 'Blondy'

Codiaeum are superbly variegated with interestingly shaped leaves. Ones splattered and marked in gold include **'Banana', 'Gold Dust, 'Gold Finger', 'Golden Ring'.** Excellent houseplants in cooler areas, marvellous outdoors where temperatures allow. Z10.

Coprosma 'Beatson's Gold' has a tracery of wiry stems clothed in tiny gold and green leaves. This evergreen brightens the gloomiest days. Will reach tree like proportions in favourable conditions, but needs protection in cold areas. **C. repens 'Gold Splash'** is worthy too. Z-11.

Cortaderia selloana 'Aureolineata' (*Gold Band*) has rich yellow margined leaves ageing to dark golden yellow. This perennial grass needs room to develop. Creates vertical drama. Too often squeezed into sites that are far too small. Give these big grasses plenty of room. 2.2m (7ft).

Disporum are woodland gems with variegated leaves worthy of inclusion. **D. cantoniense 'Aureovariegatum'** bears glossy, evergreen foliage, flushed golden. Sturdy upright stems carry white flowers in late spring. Evergreen in the Pacific Northwest, may prove hardy elsewhere, though it may become deciduous in colder regions. Worth giving a good mulch as protection. Z7.

Disporum smilacinum 'Aureovariegatum' makes a low mound of spreading ground cover with leaves striped yellow. Z5.

Duranta erecta 'Gold Edge' has dark green leaves surrounded by a gold edge, best in sun or part shade. Can be pruned. Hardy to 27°F. 2.4m-3m (8-10ft). Z10.

Eleagnus are ideal for a shrub border or as a specimen, these hardy evergreens also make a good hedge. Grow preferably in full sun, although partial shade is tolerated, as is dry soil and coastal winds.

Eleagnus pungens 'Frederici' has small pale yellow leaves with variegated dark green margins. A slow grower to 2m (6ft).

Eleagnus pungens 'Maculata' (*'Aureovariegata'*) has bold, glossy yellow leaves with a green margin. 2m (6ft). Create Golden Glory by underplanting with *Narcissus* cultivars.

Erythrina variegata is a fabulous coral tree with leaves marked yellow along the veins. Terminal racemes of those fabulous flowers look wonderful against such a backdrop. 18-25m (60-80ft) Min. 7°C(45°F).

The sulphur yellow flowers of **Erythronium 'Pagoda'** are well worth including in the woodland garden. This hardy, vigorous perennial bears glossy, bronze-mottled, handsome leaves. 15-35cm (6-14")

Escallonia 'Gold Ellen' bears attractive gold variegated, evergreen foliage and red flowers from early to midsummer. Good in a border or against a wall or fence. Z8-10.

Euonymus 'Blondy' has to be the best *Euonymus*. A sport from *'Sunspot'* spotted by Gus Bolwijn. A neat perennial shrub, very hardy and sunburn resist. Its gold foliage is nicely edged in dark green. Full sun or

Farfugium japonicum 'Aureomaculatum'

Lavatera olbia 'Variegata'

part shade. Adaptable to many well-drained soils. Provides year round colour and interest. 45-60cm (18-24"). Z5-7.

Farfugium japonicum 'Aureomaculatum' has to be the loudest variegated plant I know. The leopard plant could equally be known as spotted dick in green and yellow. Loud spotted variegation, a fun plant which is highly attractive and a good conversation piece. Z7-10.

x Fatshedera 'Annamieke' is a beautifully variegated form of this evergreen shrub, a cross between *Hedera* and *Fatsia* with glossy green leaves and yellow markings.

Graptophyllum pictum is a glossy-leaved plant loving heat and humidity. Its green leaves are splashed with

Graptophyllum pictum

cream and gold. Z10.

Heuchera sanguinea 'Aureomaculata' is a rare coral bell with leaves splashed and speckled in yellow. A bit on the blotchy side.

Iresine herbstii 'Aureoreticulata' has mid green leaves with wonderful yellow veining. Z10-12.

Lavatera oblia 'Variegata' is one of the most subtley variegated and most useful shrubs, blending into a yellow and green scheme easily.

Libertia cranwelliae has wide yellow leaves, with golden yellow fruits after white flowers which are a perfect complement to the foliage. This is a threatened plant in its native New Zealand. 40cm (16").

L. peregrinans 'Gold Leaf' has fine, burnt gold to rusty orange striped green, rush-like foliage. 30-45cm (12-18"). Excellent over fading *Iris* or *Hemerocallis* leaves. Superb in a container with *Ophiopogon*. Z8, not reliably hardy.

Liquidamber styraciflua 'Aurea' has leaves attractively striped and marbled in yellow. Likes warm summers.

Liquidamber styraciflua 'Golden Treasure' is a hardy, slow-growing tree with mid-green leaves handsomely edged in yellow with red-purple autumn colour. 10m (30ft).

Miscanthus 'Gilded Tower' PPAF is a fabulous green, gold, chartreuse and white variegated clumping grass which reaches over 2m (6ft) tall. Z5.

Plectranthus 'Sasha'

Pleioblastus auricomus and below P. 'Chrysophyllus'

Miscanthus 'Goldfeder' was the first gold variegated form. Deciduous, slow growing and rare, but very beautiful. Graceful, arching, glossy yellow-striped and edged leaves with reddish pink plumes fading to silver. Does well in sun or part shade. Z7-9.

Miscanthus 'Gotemba' a spreader from Japan with highly attractive gold, dark green and lime leaves. Vigorous, give it plenty of room. Z5.

Miscanthus 'Little Zebra' PPAF holds its green and yellow banding all season. Reddish purple plumes in late season. Z5.

Molinia caerulea 'Carmarthen' bears pale green leaves, striped cream-yellow with buff-coloured flowerheads on 60cm (2ft) long stems. Z5.

Monstera deliciosa 'Marmorata' simply takes your breath away. Golden variegated swiss cheese plant is intolerant of low humidity.

Osmanthus are evergreen shrubs which are holly-like, but easily distinguished by their opposite leaves. Make an attractive, dense hedge. Thrive in moist soils and respond to protection from cold winds.

O. heterophyllus 'Aureomargiantus' (*Aureus*) is an extremely slow growing, yellow margined shrub with holly-like leaves. It forms a dome shaped shrub needing dappled light to avoid sun scorch.

O. heterophyllus 'Ogon' is similar with new growth all yellow. Oustanding evergreen.

Plectranthus 'Lemon Twist' (*'Sasha'*) being sold under a variety of names, is a fantastic gold-leaved form, splashed with green markings, very handsome. Excellent in containers. **P. 'Easy Gold'** is fabulous too, an all-over gold. Z9-11.

Pleioblastus auricomus (*P.viridi-striatus, Arundinaria viridistriata*) well-known, hardy Japanese bamboo with bright yellow and green stripes, useful in the border. Stays small when grown in shade and is useful in a large container. Old canes can be cut to ground level in autumn to encourage brightly coloured new foliage.

Pleioblastus auricomus 'Chrysophyllus' has yellow foliage and occasionally appears as a sport of the typical form. It can burn in full sun. Z7-10.

Potentilla anserina 'Golden Treasure' is a golden variegated-leaved form of silverweed. A low growing silky-looking, feathery foliaged native U.K. species with yellow flowers in May to June and a running habit like a strawberry. Vigorous. Hates winter wet and is only suitable for free draining soils. Found in Anglesey by Corinne Tremaine. **P. anserina 'Shine'** is

Sutera 'Gold n Pearls'

Solidago flexicaulis 'Gold Spangles'

golden yellow-lime, not variegated.

Pseuderanthem atropurpureum 'Yellow Dwarf' a fabulous golden form from Grenada raised by John Criswick. A small shrub with golden wavy leaves of buttery yellow and milky green. Needs humidity and heat.

Pseudopanax lessonii 'Gold Splash' has yellow marked green leaves on a large shrub or small tree suitable for warmer areas. To 6m (20ft) usually smaller. Minimum temperature 2°C (36°F).

Pseudosasa very hardy bamboos from east Asia are often cultivated. **P. japonica** is an adaptable species, capable of forming dense thickets. Retains its culm leaf sheaths. Usually fairly well-behaved except in warm climates. Known as arrow bamboo as this Japanese and Korean native is used to make arrow shafts. Mulched plants remain evergreen down to -10°F. If heavily mulched, underground rhizomes are capable of surviving -25°F.

P. japonica 'Akebono' has yellow leaves with green shading at the base. Variegation does not always show on young plants. 3-5m (10-16ft).

P. japonica 'Akebonosuji has leaves conspicuously streaked with creamy-yellow, and sometimes produces all yellow sports. 3-5m (10-16ft).

Rosmarinus 'Golden Rain' (*'Joyce de Baggio'*) has new foliage edged in gold, a perfect foil for the blue flowers. Best foliage colour is in spring and fall. Makes a good small edger. Long admired for its fine, aromatic foliage and blue flowers. Full sun, well-drained soil. Has the same culinary uses as any rosemary. Excellent for dry, Mediterranean gardens. Z8. 60-90cm (2-3ft).

Sansevieria trifasciata 'Golden Hahnii' is a class act.

Neat variegated leaves of gold and green vertical stripes. Bold and beautiful. 20cm (8"). Z10-12.

Silene dioica 'Clifford Moor' PBR originated at York Stock Nursery in England. Its evergreen, narrow, strap-like leaves are attractively variegated with creamy gold margins and dark green centres. Single pink flowers adorn all summer as this bears only male flowers, no seed drop on 45cm (18") stems. Makes a 30cm (12") clump which prefers partial sun to light shade and moist, well-drained soil. Z5-9.

Solidago flexicaulis 'Gold Spangles' is a new variegated plant. The solid gold leaves are attractive, but I do not go for the spotty ones.

Sutera, (*Bacopa*), are superb and versatile plants, excellent as fillers and in container plantings. Good in shade. New varieties such as **S. 'Gold n' Pearls'** are self-cleaning, flowers drop as they finish, so no deadheading. Bears gold and green variegated foliage with white flowers. Z9-11.

Sutera 'Olympic Gold' (Francis Muzuro) is a vigorous clone with striking green and gold foliage. Sutera make ideal carpeters in summer. Perfect to cool down deep, loud yellows.

Thymus, lemon scented thyme make excellent ground cover and can withstand foot traffic, emitting the lemon scent as you walk over them. Relish sun but will do alright in partial shade. Heavenly! These attractive edgers, will bring bees and pollinators into the garden. You will spot them with other names in cultivation, they have been quite mixed up in the past, but they are umistakeable by their scent. Z5 or 6-10.

T. x citriodorus 'Aureus' has gold dappled leaves, an attractive, lemon-scented variety, known as lemon

Thymus x citriodorus 'Aureus' with Ajuga

thyme. Trim to keep neat. 30cm (10").

T. x citriodorus 'Doone Valley' has dark green, gold variegated leaves which develop red tints in autumn on a prostrate variety with a strong scent. Bears tiny pink flowers.

T. x citriodorus 'Golden King' has a lovely golden edge to each green leaf and a quite open habit. Pink flowers.

T. pulegioides 'Bertram Anderson' (*E.B.Anderson, 'Archer's Gold'*) is a good, bushy cultivar retaining its golden leaves well. Can revert. 25cm (10").

T. pulegioides 'Goldentime' (*vulgaris 'Aureus' h.*) common golden thyme ages to yellow-green. Bright in spring with a fresh lemon fragrance.

T. serpyllum 'Goldstream' creeping golden thyme is quite vigorous creating spreading mats of light green and yellow variegated leaves covered in lilac flowers in summer. 25x20cm (10x8").

Trifolium pratense 'Susan Smith' has bright yellow variegated clover leaves with pink flowers. Clumping rather than running, it is best in full sun and partial shade in any well-drained site. Z6-10.

Vinca minor 'Illumination' bears the brightest of gold foliage, edged delicately in mid green. Blue flowers appear in spring. This graceful trailer adorns pot, basket or container in sun or partial shade. 15cm (6"). Z4-11.

Yucca filamentosa 'Bright Edge' has green centred golden leaves. Quite impressive.

Yucca filamentosa 'Colour Guard' has bright yellow-centred leaves with coral winter colour making a striking display. Z5-10.

Yucca filamentosa 'Golden Sword' bears excellent variegated foliage, golden centred, green edged sword-like leaves. Suitable for a warm, sunny, well-drained position. When mature, incredible, ivory-white flowers are borne on long stems. 60cm-48cm. (2-4ft). Z6-10.

Vinca 'Illumination'

Yucca filamentosa 'Color Guard'

BEST GOLD FLOWERS

Alstroemeria

Achillea 'Anthea'

Argyranthemum 'Butterfly'

Yellow is the flower colour I use least in my garden. Not being a daisy lover, or a lover of deep yellow, I find I can avoid it quite easily. I tend towards the softer side of yellow, which blends so nicely. These are simply personal favourites from the tints and hints that come under the colour yellow.

Achillea are always better, I think, in their paler shades. Choose **A. 'Moonwalker'** for a quieter contrast instead of the overpowering and much used **A. 'Gold Plate'**. **A. 'Anthea'** is one of the palest.
Allium are always useful, **A. flavum** has small but plentiful yellow nodding flowers, nicer than **A. moly**.
Alstroemeria are wonderful flowers that come in hot shades of yellow-orange, many possess wonderful markings for colour echoes.
Anemone multifida (*A. globosa, A. magellanica h*) is a vigorous, rhizomatous perennial with darling pale yellow flowers against equally darling palmate, finely divided foliage. This hardy anemone likes well-drained, humus-rich soil in sun to partial shade.
Anigozanthos 'Bush Gold', a hybrid of the Australian native kangaroo paw, bears golden yellow flowers. These appear like velvet covered plastic. Clump-forming perennials flowering from late spring to midsummer in sandy loam in full sun. Z9-11.
Aquilegia elegantula is certainly an elegant columbine from the Rocky Mountains and N. Mexico, similar to but smaller than *formosa* and having longer spurs. 60cm (24"). Z5-9.

Argyranthemum 'Butterfly' is a canary yellow with a deeper centre producing flowers all season long. Perfect for summer containers. **A. 'Lemon Delight'** and **A. 'Tanya'** are equally attractive. **A. 'Midas Gold'** has a rich gold-bronze eye to contrast perfectly with the butter yellow petals which fade to cream at the edge, this one is a perfect echo and linking plant. 30-45cm (12-18"). Z9-11.
Arisaema concinnum yellow spathe form from China. Incredible yellow spathe, striped purple at the base emerges at almost the same time as the finely cut leaves. Yellow threadlike tipped mousetail. A purple spadix hides inside the spathe. Z6-10. 75cm (30").
Arisaema flavum bears small but conspicuous greenish yellow to yellow spathes in summer. This handsome tuberous perennial has palmate leaves.
The hardy **Arnebia pulchra** is little seen in cultivation. A perennial with vibrant yellow flowers with a brown basal spot to each petal which fades with age. Ideal addition to a rock garden or woodland glade. Partial shade in moist, well-drained soil, happy in sun if kept constantly moist.
Arum creticum is almost hardy in part shade to sun, its strong yellow spathe often fades to chartreuse at the tip. A sweet-scented, golden spadix protrudes from the vase shaped spathe. Green, arrow-shaped

Asarina procumbens with Sedum 'Ogon'

Glorious colourful Bougainvillea

handsome foliage. Sheer delight!

Asarina procumbens (*Antirrhinum asarina*) is a perfect little evergreen trailer with pale whitish-yellow 'snapdragons' nestling amongst the attractive, grey-green, kidney-shaped foliage in summer. Tolerates partial shade.

Ascocentrum 'Thai Gold' is very deserving of its name, a golden yellow to die for epiphytic orchid hybrid, closely related to *Vanda*. Z10-11.

Banksia lehmanniana is an unusual Western Australian banksia in which the 10cm (4") yellow flower spike points downwards. Z10-11.

Asphodelus luteus is a lemon shade, very attractive.

Bougainvillea, better known in pink, come in golden tones too. I found this in Caleta de Fuste, Fuerteventura, The Canaries. It will need a conservatory in cooler climates. Very flamboyant on a

Asphodelus luteus

sunny wall where conditions allow. It is the bracts not flowers that are showy.

Brugmansia aurea has large pale yellow trumpets to adorn any summer patio or garden in warm areas. These plants make a big statement. Remember all parts are poisonous. Z10-12.

Calceolaria tenella is an interesting pouch flower in gold with tiny red spots. Hardy evergreen creeping perennials from Chile.

Calendula officinalis, humble pot marigolds can do a great job in the garden by attracting beneficial insects. **'Lemon Queen'** is the right shade for the golden garden.

Callibrachoa 'Million Bells Terra Cotta' is a warm mix of colours giving the effect of an evening glow. A perfect colour echo for *Heuchera 'Amber Waves'*. If you are looking for a purer yellow, try **'Million Bells Yellow'**. Their upright, cascading habit is perfect for hanging baskets, earlier blooming. Easy to grow, with self-cleaning flowers, no dead heading. Z9. 15cm (6").

Callistemon pallidus has cream to lemon-green bottlebrushes. Handsome Australian shrubs.

Calochortus clavatus the upright golden flowers, marked reddish brown inside of this southern Californian beauty are held on 1m (3ft) long stems. **C. luteus** is equally beautiful. Z5-9.

Caltha palustris 'Flore Pleno' makes a change from the single marsh marigold. It has a greenish centre.

Camellia nitidissima (*C. chrysantha*) is a golden beauty, its single pure yellow flowers are fragrant and borne in leaf axils in winter against dark green, deeply veined leaves. Unfortunately it requires a warm,

humid site in partial shade. 2m (6ft) min 7°C (45°F).
Campsis radicans 'Flava' favoured for many years for its clear yellow, 7cm (3") long trumpet flowers. An excellent climber against a hot sunny wall or fence. Z4-10.

Cananga odorata might not be the most beautiful flower, but I find its twisted petals attractive and most would succumb to its scent, it is the source of ylang-ylang. Z11-12.

Canna 'King Midas' for its golden-yellow sunshine flowers carried over dark green leaves. 1.5m (5ft).

Caragana arborescens 'Walker' must be obtained for the most fantastic ornamental cascading shrub, excellent in a smallish space. Finely textured foliage and yellow pea-like flowers in spring. 6m (20ft). **C. brevispina** is equally desirable. 3m (10ft).

Cassia fistula is rightly known as golden shower tree, raining drooping clusters of golden flowers. Z10-12.

Both plumy and cristate **Celosia** come in yellow. I prefer the crinkly cristate types, they look like part of the brain in kaleidoscope colours.

Cephalaria gigantea has long been a favourite for its sulpur-yellow flowerheads, giant scabious needs room to develop. Big and airy. 2.4m (8t) tall and 1.2m (4ft) across. Z3-9. *Photograph this page.*

Cestrum parqui is actually known as green cestrum, its yellow-green flowers are night-scented. Z9-11.

Chimonanthus praecox for its sweet-scented yellow flowers in winter on mature plants. Best in a warm, well-drained position against a sunny wall or fence. Grows excellently on chalk and any reasonable soil. **'Luteus'** has buttercup coloured flowers. Z6-10.

Chlidanthus fragrans is a tender bulbous perennial with strongly scented, trumpet yellow flowers.

Chrysocephalum 'Baby Gold' has button yellow flowers making a great show in containers against the silver-green foliage. 25-30cm (10-12"). Z9-11.

Clematis 'Bill Mackenzie' for its lemon peel look-alike, lantern flowers borne over a long period. Added attraction of silky seedheads. Vigorous and showy. Z5-9. The paler **C. rehderiana** is pure delight, bearing cowslip-scented single flowers from midsummer to autumn.

Colutea arborescens bears flowers with almost haunting red markings on a strong yellow background. Bears interesting seed pods on a shrubby plant useful in poor, dry soils.

Coreopsis verticillata 'Moonbeam' is compact with neon-yellow flowers. Z6-10.

Corydalis wilsonii has blue-green foliage upon which sit loose spikes of yellow flowers. 20cm (8"). Z7-9.

Corylopsis glabrescens bears the clearest yellow flowers of the species, not a dominant shade so one can swoon to the delicious scent. Z7-9.

Crocus chrysanthus 'Gipsy Girl' bears attractive yellow flowers striped purplish brown on the outside. Z4-9. The lemon-yellow flowers of **C. 'E. A.Bowles'** are very striking too.

Crotalaria agatiflora, canary bird bush bears unusual flowers, bright yellow with a greenish tinge in spring to autumn. Z10.

Cypripedium calceolus v pubescens has large flowers with green petals and sepals and a bright yellow pouch. Z3-9.

Cytisus x praecox 'Warminster' looks like a snowstorm of yellow flowers. **C. x praecox 'Allgold'** has deep yellow flowers. **C. battandieri**, the pineapple broom has pineapple-scented yellow blossoms but is not fully hardy. Z5-9.

Dahlia 'Moonfire'

Dahlia 'Moonfire' has a real glow about it. **D. 'Yellow Hammer'** has rich yellow flowers and bronze-black foliage. **D. 'Clair de Lune'** is a collarette dahlia of a much paler tone, sumptuous. The semi-cactus blooms of **D. Hamari Katrina'** are pale also, whilst **D. 'Lady Sunshine'** is a dazzler. Z8-10.

Delphinium semibarbatum (*zalil*) is a short-lived, tuberous type from Iran and central Asia where it is used to dye silk. Bears sulphur yellow flowers from spring to midsummer. 1m (3ft). **D. 'Sungleam'** is a clump forming perennial *elatum* type with double cream pale yellow flowers, with sulphur yellow eyes. Exquisite. 1.5m (5ft). Z6-9.

Dicentra scandens 'Athens Yellow' selected by Allan Armitage for its floriferous nature. This climbing bleeding heart is smothered in yellow flowers from April to November. *Corydalis*-like grey-green foliage is an added advantage. Z7b-10. A tender perennial in colder areas. 120cm (4ft).

Dillenia alata is an evergreen tree with red, flaking bark and flat-opening yellow flowers followed by bright red seed pods. Z12.

Edgeworthia chrysantha has small, fragrant yellow flowers borne in heavy clusters on an open, rounded shrub with dark green leaves. Tender.

Epimedium x versicolor 'Sulphureum' bears sulphur yellow flowers and bronze-tinted foliage when young.

Eremurus Shelford Hybrids bear lofty spikes of densely packed flowers available in many colours including yellow. Valuable vertical accent. Z5-9.

Erodium chrysanthum is a delicate beauty, with creamy to sulphur yellow flowers throughout summer above silvery foliage. A Greek perennial for a sunny rock garden. Z6-9.

Erysimum ochroleucum is a restful yellow which does not shout as loud as many wallflowers. This short-lived perennial is best as a biennial. 30cm (12"). Z6-9.

Eschscholzia caespitosa, is a fast growing, erect annual with yellow flowers like a ray of sunshine, best as a drift. Bluish green leaves complement perfectly. Creamy **E. californica** is attractive with ferny blue-green leaves, there are named varieties available from seed in all sorts of sunset colours as well as the usual orange of the species. 15cm (6"). Z7-10.

Euphorbia characias 'Lambrook Gold' selected by Margery Fish at Lambrook Manor, Somerset, England. A superb, gold effect is had from the bracts of this lovely sun-loving, frost hardy spurge. Z8-10.

E. polychroma, a frost hardy, clump-forming perennial is equally delightful. 45cm (18"). Z 6-9.

E. shillingii has a quieter colour echo in its bracts.

E. sikkimensis is worthy of growing for the colour echo effect of its bright yellow bracts in summer. Leaves are red tinged and have ruby red veins. New shoots are pinkish.

Hedychium gardnerianum

hazel with bright yellow, fragrant flowers appearing on bare twigs in winter. **'Allgold'** bears small dark yellow flowers. So welcome in the winter garden. Z4-9.

Hedychium gardnerianum is a heart-stopping ginger with the most wonderful fragrant, lemon-flowers with bright red stamens, in dense cylindrical, terminal racemes above green leaves. The flower is incredibly beautiful, the scent divine. 2m (6ft more).

Helenium 'Butterpat' is a bright, clear yellow with a gold boss of stamens.

Heliconia caribaea has glossy dark banana like leaves and has white inconspicuous flowers within red or yellow bracts. The yellow form of this ginger is golden. Z11-12.

There are numerous **Hemerocallis** in yellow, so difficult to choose so I asked Rebecca Board of Cyberlily Gardens for her favourites. She recommends **H. 'Bill Norris', 'Omomuki'** and **'Sherry Lane Carr'** for overall quality. I also like **'America's Most Wanted'**. There are some great peachy shades too, and everything in yellow from strong to pale plus those with exciting rings and eyes.

Hemerocallis 'Now and Zen'

Fremontodendron californicum for a succession of golden flowers from mid to late spring. Z8.

Fritillaria chitralensis is a native to eastern Afghanistan with clear yellow bells flushed green at the base.

Fritillaria imperialis 'Maxima Lutea', a well-known stately crown imperial with hanging sunshine yellow flowers. Z4-9.

Grevillea robusta bears fern-like leaves, silvery on the underside which are partly shed just before the branches are all but hidden by masses of long, golden yellow blooms which appear in spring. The silky oak is moderately frost hardy once established, but does need warm, dry summers. Z8-10.

Halimium lasianthum has grey-green foliage to complement the bright yellow flowers with maroon markings, similar to a rock rose. Well suited to coastal gardens. 1m (3ft) tall with a spread of 1.5m (5ft). Z8.

Hamamelis x intermedia 'Arnold Promise' is a witch

Hemerocallis 'Omomuki'

Lilium 'Green Magic'

Hibbertia scandens is a shrubby twiner with beautiful bright yellow flowers. Tender.

Hibiscus calyphyllus is a tropical African species producing large sulphur yellow flowers 8-10cm (3-4") with a purple-brown eye. 1-1.8m (3-6ft). Z10-11.

Hibiscus rosa-sinensis 'Butterfly' is yet another lovely golden form of these fabulous flowers.

Hibiscus tiliaceus is deeper yellow with crimson centres, in warm tropical areas this will flower most of the year. An evergreen tree. Z10-11.

Hibiscus trionum is one annual everyone should grow, cream flowers with contrasting dark centres.

Hyoscyamus gyoerffyi is a lovely shade of yellow, a handsome relative of henbane.

Iris 'Saltwood' is a dwarf bearded Iris with lime-yellow petals having a pale yellow edging in April to May.

Iris 'Tut's Gold' (Schreiner 1979) this tall bearded Iris bears large gold flowers. Superb. 1m (3ft).

Kniphofia 'Little Maid' has butter yellow blooms suffused orange, fertilise well. 30-45cm (12-18") K. **'Wrexham Buttercup'** has clear yellow pokers. Z6-11.

Koelreutia paniculata is aptly named as the golden rain tree. Brilliant yellow flowers.

Laburnum x watereri 'Vossii' bears rich buttercup yellow flowers on racemes up to 60cm (24") long. Z3.

Lathyrus chloranthus is a sweet pea of an unusual sulphur, green-yellow shade. I doubt that **'Lemonade'** differs from the species.

Leucadendron eucalyptifolium is a vigorous species from the coastal ranges of the Cape Province, found growing in deep, sandy soil. Small flowerheads have yellow bracts surrounding yellow-cream flowers. Easy shrub. 4.5m (15ft). Z9-10.

Leucospermum cuneiforme is one of those fabulous flowers which deserve a closer look, in fact, you'll find it hard to take your eyes away. Yellow pincushions change through orange to red in full sun. Drought tolerant.

Lilium have to be a favourite with just about everyone. I adore them. **L. 'Green Magic'** is definitely more yellow than green. Its large trumpets are fab!

Limnanthes douglasii is a humble little plant, valuable in the garden as its wide open yellow flowers edged in white attract beneficial insects. Z8-10.

Hyoscyamus gyoerffyi

Lonicera 'Graham Thomas'

Nemesia 'Sunsatia Banana'

Lonicera periclymenum 'Graham Thomas' has pale scented flowers which turn yellow from late spring to early autumn. 6-8m (20-26ft).

Lupinus 'Chandelier' is a bright yellow adding spires of gold to the border. For newer and better cultivars take a look at Sarah Conibear's breeding work at West Country Nurseries, Devon.

Lysichiton americanus is the perfect water perennial with bright yellow spathes in early spring protecting a green spadix. Makes colonies of lush leaves to 1m (3ft) in adequate moisture. Full sun or shade.

Macfadyena unguis-cati is a frost tender climber with showy yellow trumpet flowers. Grows best in full sun and a moist site with protection from cold. Z9-12.

Magnolia 'Yellow Bird' has beautiful, cup-shaped, pale yellow flowers.

Mecardonia 'Gold Flake' PPAF is a new cross, bred by Garry Grueber of Kientzler, Germany. Use as groundcover, or in containers, where its golden flowers will be much appreciated.

Meconopsis pseudointegrifolia bears downward facing blooms of a soft yellow in late spring and summer. The plant is covered in fine golden-brown hairs. Z7-9. **M. regia** is a monocarpic evergreen perennial with densely silver or gold-hairy leaves and cup-shaped, soft yellow flowers in midsummer. 2m (6ft). Hardy.

Mimulus sp often bear yellow flowers, usually spotted with a different colour, such as the red spotted M. moschatus. Z7-10.

Narcissus 'Tahiti' bears soft yellow double blooms with orange corona. **N. cyclamineus** is favoured for its down-turned tubes. **N. 'Cassata'** has ice-cream pale lemon flowers which turn white. **N. 'Golden Ducat'** is a double flowered frilly affair. **N. 'Rip van Winkle'** is unusual in its narrow petals. Z4-10.

Nemesia 'Sunsatia Lemon' is bright yellow and daring, use it to cascade from containers. **'Sunsatia Banana'** is equally eye-catching. 15-25cm (6-10"). Z9.

Nymphaea 'Marliacea Chromatella' is an extremely elegant waterlily, a free-flowering, reliable hybrid with creamy yellow blooms and foliage marked with bronze. Z5-10. You might also like to try **N. 'St. Louis'** and **'St. Louis Gold'**.

Nemesia 'Sunsatia Lemon'

Osteospermum 'Lemon Symphony'

Rosa 'Golden Showers'

Osteopsermum 'Lemon Symphony' is one of a new range of Osteos, covered in blooms all season, bred by Masayuki Sekuguchi. Great for colour echoes.

Oxalis citrina is a more restrained *Oxalis* with the brightest yellow flowers of the bunch, sought after by collectors of rare bulbs. Z8-10.

Paeonia mlokosewitschii bears big, open pale yellow to brighter flowers. This herbaceous perennial enjoys semi-shade and is frost hardy. 75cm (30"). Z6-9. **P. witmanniana** is perhaps hardier with deeply cupped, primrose yellow flowers and yellow anthers. 1m (36").

Papaver radicatum, or at least that is what I found it labelled as, is a lovely pale poppy.

Phygelius 'Moonraker' has pale creamy lemon flowers. Z8-11.

Plumeria rubra 'Golden Kiss' has large heads of golden yellow flowers with a soft flush of apricot to each petal. Frangipani is much favoured for its delicious perfume. Z10-12.

Potentilla recta 'Pallida' for its delicate shade of palest yellow. **P. recta 'Warrenii'** is equally desirable, a stronger colour. **P. fruticosa 'Primrose Beauty'** is a delicate shade.

Primula vulgaris 'Val Horncastle' has to be one of the best primula around in clear yellow. **P. vulgaris 'Double Sulphur'** is a vigorous primrose with lovely pale flowers, excellent in the spring garden.

Rhododendron luteum is a deciduous azalea preferring partial shade to partial sun in moist, well-drained soil. Sweetly scented yellow blooms adorn this shrubby species. Z5a.

Rhododendron 'Mariloo' is a *lacteum* hybrid, admired for its pale milky yellow, bell-shaped flowers carried in large trusses. Z8-10.

Rosa 'Alchemyst' is a hybrid climbing old rose with lovely multi-petalled soft yellow flowers with hints of apricot and amber. Gorgeous. Z5-11.

Rosa 'Golden Showers' this large flowered climber has beautifully fragrant flowers of the perfect shade for an English garden. 2.5m (8ft).

Phygelius 'Moonraker'

Papaver radicatum

Santolina pinnata 'Sulphurea'

Rosa 'Golden Wings' bears flat pale yellow petals with deeper stamens.

Rosa 'Graham Thomas' is a modern English rose bred by David Austin with strongly scented yellow flowers over a long season. I could choose so many golden roses, extend the palette to include amber and peachy shades.

Santolina chamaecyparissus has lovely little buttons of pale flowers. **Santolina pinnata 'Sulphurea'** has the right pale notes to temper strong yellows. These make good link plants with their grey-green foliage and pale flowers and are excellent in the yellow-blue garden.

Sarracenia, carnivorous perennials revelling in acid conditions and nutrient-deficient bogs. These nectar-secreting, insect catching pitchers always delight those looking for something unusual, and what more than your own personal fly catcher. Never feed insects to pitcher plants, they are capable of satisfying their own diet. If temperatures fall below -5°C (23°F), grow in a cold glasshouse or on a windowsill. In warmer areas, they appreciate a damp spot in shaded peat.

Sarracenia flava

Sarracenia flava is a variable plant, often seen with yellow green trumpets and clear yellow flowers in spring. 50-100cm (20-39") with a spread of 1m (3ft). Blow those trumpets!

Scabiosa columbaria v ochroleuca blooms all year round with small, pale pincushion flowers on 45cm (18") stems. Soft grey-green foliage in full sun. I like this mini *Cephalaria gigantea*, though I have heard complaints that it does not flower freely.

Solandra maxima, no wonder this bears the common name of cup of gold, there is only one word to describe this beauty, fabulous! Large trumpet-shaped, night scented flowers with purple veins, a must from Mexico and S. America. 7-10°C (45-50°F) minimum.

Sophora microphylla bears yellow flowers in dense clusters from late winter to early summer. These small trees are noted for their wonderful flowers. Z8-10.

Stachyurus chinensis 'Celina' bears long, stiffly pendulous racemes of soft yellow flowers in March on a medium to large, hardy shrub which prefers a sheltered site to protect from late frosts and is best in light shade. Tremendous.

Strelitzia reginae 'Mandela's Gold', this bird of paradise has yellow and purplish blooms. Grow in a large pot and protect through winter. Z10-12.

Tabebuia chrysantha is a deciduous tree with palmate leaves and glorious trumpet-shaped, scented yellow flowers to 2.5-8cm (1-3") long. 8°C (46°F).

Thalictrum flavum ssp glaucum should be added to the garden not only for its pastel yellow flowers but also its steely blue leaves. 1.8m (6ft) might need staking or give it the support of other plants. Any *Thalictrum* is usually worth adding to the garden. **'Illuminator'** is noteworthy. Z5.

Above: Trillium luteum
Below: Trillium cuneatum yellow

Tropaeolum

Thunbergia mysorensis

Trillium luteum is notable for its upright, sweet-scented golden flowers. 40cm (16"). Z6-9. **T. cuneatum** is quite rare in the yellow form.

Tropaeolum are quite humble in their annual form, but more exotic in their perennial forms. Both are worthy of a place in the garden. The annual nasturtiums enjoy poor soils, feed them well and all you will see is large leaves not flowers. **T. 'Ken Aslett'** is a perennial with small, orange and yellow flowers.

Tulipa batalinii is a species from Uzbekistan that has grey-green leaves with red margins and produces bowl-shaped, pale yellow flowers. 35cm (14").

Tulipa 'Golden Baby' has gardenia-like flowers in rich yellow.

Tulipa 'Yokohama' is a bright sunshine yellow.

Verbascum 'Cotswold Queen' for its delightful yellow flowers with purple filament hairs. 1.2m (4ft). Hardy.

V. 'Gold Leaf' a Crug collection that Bob Brown has from them, and possibly not *V. bombyciferum*, possesses gold leaves and fabulous gold flowers. Takes a long time to reach flowering size and is monocarpic.

Zantedeschia pentlandii bears golden to yellow spathes marked purple inside. Hardy. **Z. ellottiana**, the golden arum lily or calla lily bears golden yellow spathes surrounding golden spadix sometimes followed by golden berries. Heart-shaped leaves are covered in white spots. 60-90cm (2-3ft).10°C (50°F) minimum.

Thunbergia mysorensis is a vigorous, woody-stemmed climber with unusual yellow and brownish maroon flowers from spring to autumn. They dangle temptingly displaying their remarkable beauty. Attractive, pointed leaves are marked and splashed with lighter green 6m (20ft). 13-15°C (55-59°F) minimum. I photographed this on a trip to Kew. I have often seen it and it always astounds. One of those incredible plants, that make you stop and stare and simply marvel at the art that is nature itself. This is the power of the plant world. Z10-11.

Tropaeolum 'Ken Aslett'

GOLDEN FRUIT

Chaenomeles japonica bears small, round yellow fruits with a pleasant fragrance. Rarely grows higher than 1m (3ft). Z4-9.

Citrus limon 'Meyer' produces small fruits and is the best choice for growing in containers. Z9-11.

Coriaria terminalis v xanthocarpa is a deciduous shrub bearing translucent yellow berries with poisonous seed. Handsome, deciduous shrub with deeply veined green leaves. Z8-10.

Corokia x virgata 'Yellow Wonder' bears golden berries. Z8-10.

Cotoneaster salicifolius 'Rothschildianus' is remarkable for its clusters of clear yellow fruit. A vigorous, large evergreen shrub with attractive, pale green leaves. Z6-9.

Crataegus flava bears greenish yellow fruit, this wild hawthorn is not one of the most ornamental. C. **frigidus 'Fructo Luteo'** is handsome in berry.

Encephalartos transvenosus has the most amazing phallic golden cones. Appreciates a sheltered position in moist soil in cultivation. Z10-12.

Ilex aquifolium 'Bacciflava' bears creamy yellow berries in abundance on a female form which can make a very fne hedge. A nearby male holly will ensure plentiful fruiting.

Malus 'Butterball' is distinguished by its orange-yellow fruit. This ornamental crab apple bears pink-flushed white flowers in spring. 8m (25ft). Z3-9.

Malus 'Golden Hornet' is a small tree with white flowers and yellow fruits in abundance.

Passiflora quadrangularis has oblong to oval fruits with a thick yellow rind to 30cm (12") long. Z10-12.

Phlomis russeliana bears butter yellow flowers. Z7-10. The leaves of **P. chrysophylla** are covered in a fine golden down when young, fading to yellow-grey with bright golden flowers in summer. Z9-11. **P. fruticosa** has very striking bright yellow flowers. Z7-10.

Viburnum sargentii 'Fructolutea' has clusters of golden fruit. Z4-9. Also try **V. opulus 'Xanthocarpum'**. Z2-10.

Verbascum chaixii in charming spires

Hemerocallis 'Ruffled Perfection'

GOLD PALMS AND EXOTICS

Amorphophallus konjac 'Gordon Gold'

Mouthwatering, what more can I say. These are simply fabulous. I just need to take over the tropical glasshouse at Kew.

Aglaonema has leaves splashed gold with red veining bleeding into the gold.

Alocasia macrorhiza 'New Guinea Gold' has mid to dark green leaves speckled and splashed with gold. The young leaves are completely green. This dramatic plant has thick, glossy leaves with crinkled edges held on upright stems. Best in sun to part shade. Known to survive 0°C (32°F). Z9-11.

Alocasia macrorhiza 'Lutea' is gold marked with almost white veining. Leaves 1m (3-4ft) long with marbling more pronounced on older plants.

Alocasia macrorhiza 'Orinoco Gold' has enormous leaves marbled in gold with yellowish stems and prominent yellow veins.

Amorphophallus konjac 'Gordon Gold' has incredible golden leaves, matched by the equally incredible variegated variety **A. konjac 'Variegata'**.

Archontophoenix cunnighamia 'Aurea' is stunning, superbly golden.

Caryota mitis 'Aureovariegata' is a real wow plant, one of the best variegated palms with attractive green-gold leaves in striped variegation.

Chamaedorea humilis 'Aurea', the most well-known palm used as a house plant, takes on a different image in gold.

Cycas revoluta 'Aurea' is a 5-star plant that just glows.

Ficus altissima 'Aureovariegata' has glossy leaves, edged in gold, ageing more limey.

Ficus 'Gold Angel' is a small leaved variety variegated green and gold.

Ficus 'Amstel Gold' has wide gold margins to the leaf.

Nolina recurvata 'Aureostriata' (*Beaucarnea*) is attractive with its 'pony tail' in green and yellow stripes.

Pereskia grandiflora 'Mediovariegata' is an interesting member of the cactus family with large blackish spines. Its green, succulent leaves have yellow centres.

Philodendron saggitifolia rubra aureo variegata, not too sure on that name, but that is how I found it labelled. Older leaves green, new leaves are blushed pinkish bronze and in between are gold flushed leaves. Big leaves.

Philodendron selloum 'Aureovariegata' has many divided, finger-like leaves of gold splashed green. See more Philodendron in the main section. These exotics make good houseplants.

Rhapis excelsa 'Lutea' is an incredible golden-leaved palm, with fans of pale gold.

Rhapis excelsa 'Zuiko-lutino' just takes your breath away. Lemon-lime palm fronds.

Sabal palmetto 'Aureovariegata' has some fans almost wholly yellow.

Schizmaglottis aurea variegata is an unusual aroid with rich, golden-green marbled leaves. Best in shade. Z10-11.

Syagrus romanzhoffia 'Aurea' is a beautiful golden palm.

Veitchia johannis x Wodyetia bifurcata 'Aureovariegata' is unevenly variegated, some leaves wholly yellow, some green, others whitish, it has a pleasing effect overall.

Veitchia merrillii 'Aureovariagata' has similar variegation.

Wodyetia bifurcata 'Aureovariegata' has whole palm fronds in shades of yellow.

Rhapis excelsa 'Zuiko-lutino'

SPRING AND AUTUMN GOLD

Abelia schummanii 'Saxon Gold' bears bright gold new shoots, fading greenish with pinkish white flowers. There are many gold sports of *Abelia x grandiflora*. Z7-10.

Aesculus flava has excellent autumn yellow colour, Two cultivars of *hippocastanum* which offer colour in spring and autumn. The horse chestnuts are champion hardy ornamentals in spring and early summer. These decidous woodlanders are easily cultivated and besides those noted here, many turn attractively yellow in autumn. They make excellent specimen trees and need plenty of room, being unsuitable for small gardens. Capable of thriving in any soil but happiest in deep, fertile moist but well-drained sites. Graft in late winter or bud in summer.

A. hippocastanum 'Hampton Court Gold' bears young leaves of a soft yellow becoming yellow-green. This slow growing tree can burn in full sun. Derived from a tree in the wilderness garden at Hampton Court. 6m (20ft).

A. hippocastanum 'Honiton Gold' is a similar mutation but faster and more vigorous growing. Found in a hedgerow before 2002 in Honiton, Devon, where the original plant still grows.

Alangium platanifolium bears autumn maple-like foliage in banana yellow with yellow anthered white flowers.

Amsonia hubrichtii is a U.S. native perennial with handsome willow-like leaves and light blue flowers, ending the season with autumnal golden tones.

Alders are deciduous shrubs and trees found in all parts of the northerm hemisphere on poor or wet soils. Male and female flowers are found on separate yellowish catkins on the same plant, the females being less conspicuous. Both **A. glutinosa** and **A. incana** are favoured for their ornamental foliage, especially when seen close to the water's edge. Fast growing, slender hardy trees are happy in most soils except shallow soil over chalk. They are tolerant of difficult sites and thrive in damp to wet conditions.

A. glutinosa 'Aurea' is a soft yellow form of the common alder with leaves becoming paler in summer and finally maturing to light green. This slender tree bears yellow-brown catkins in March. Please it with wet soil where many choice trees and shrubs would curl up their toes. Raised in around 1860. 12m (40ft).

A. incana 'Aurea', the golden elder has soft yellow leaves becoming paler and greenish in summer. In addition, orange shoots and golden-orange branches in winter plus yellow and red tinted catkins in spring make this a choice tree for a damp site. 10m (30ft).

Astrantia 'Sunningdale Gold' is brightest in spring, another shining glory from Dan Heims.

Betula costata, B. lenta, B. maximowicziana and **B. pendula** have autumn yellow leaves. **B. medwedewii 'Gold Bark'** not only has good butter yellow autumn leaf colour, but also has gold bark on mature specimens. Conditions and temperatures vary with species. **B. medwedewii** is the Transcaucasian birch, its branches spread with age and it has lovely form. 5m (15ft).

Callicarpa japonica has yellow autumn foliage contrasting with the purplish fruits, best in an open, sunny spot with moisture in summer. Z6-9.

Carya cordiformis has outstanding brilliant yellow autumn colour. The swamp hickory also has ornamental ridged grey bark. Other **Carya** such as **C. ovata** and **C. glabra** also display good colouring in autumn.

Caragana arborescens 'Spring Gold' has bright gold leaves which turn green in summer. Yellow flowers. Drought resistant. (90-180cm) 3-6ft).

Celastrus orbiculatus, the staff vine turns butter yellow in autumn. The foliage effect is further highlighted by clusters of yellow, bead-like fruits. A vigorous, woody, twining, deciduous climber which will need a substantial tree to support it. Z4-9.

Celtis occidentalis has glorious autumn colour, enjoys a streamside setting. Z3-10.

Cercis canadensis has yellow autumn colouring.

Cladrastis lutea, yellow wood has autumn yellow leaf colour and white fragrant flowers in June, with a touch of yellow. Needs a warm, sunny site to encourage flowering. 9m (30ft). Z6-10.

Clematis rehderiana is a species from western China grows slowly at first, but if left to its own devices can cover a small tree. The yellow flowers with recurved petals fade to parchment. Z7-10.

Clethra alnifolia and **C. fargesii** have excellent yellow foliage in autumn. Z4-9.

Corylus avellana is the native English hazel making a large shrub or small, many-stemmed tree. Beautifully impressive when draped with long yellow catkins in February, although the golden form is grown more for its foliage. Useful for hedging which should be trimmed in March. Suitable for moist soil and can be pruned hard as required.

C. avellana 'Aurea' has bright yellow foliage when young, greening when mature, making a large shrub. Can create a useful screen. The species has yellow leaves in autumn. Outstanding foliage. 4.6m (15ft).

Digitalis lutea 'Yellow Medley' goes for gold in spring, with new yellow foliage fading to apple green. Flowers are small and yellow in spikes up to 60cm (2ft) from May to July.

Escallonia 'Gold Brian' has fresh yellow spring growth. Compact and slow growing.

Fagus grandifolia, the American beech has superb autumn yellow colouring.

Fraxinus angustifolia, F. latifolia, F. pennsylvanica and **F. velutina** display good golden autumn colour. Z4-10, depending on species.

F. excelsior 'Aurea' has pale yellowish green summer foliage, deepening in autumn. Z4-10.

F. excelsior 'Aurea Pendula' is a slow grower, forming an umbrella shape in time.

F. excelsior 'Golden Desert' has black, fuzzy buds and bright golden foliage in spring and autumn which is green in summer. Its small, rounded habit has the added attraction of golden bark all year. 9-10m (26-30ft) tall with a spread of 3.5-3.5m (12-15ft) wide.

F. excelsior 'Jaspidea' exhibits attractive golden spring and autumn colouring, with yellowish branches too. Happy in all good soils.

F. nigra 'Fallgold' does not produce fruit but gives a wonderful autumn display of long-lasting gold.

Galega, Goat's rue makes a tall, bushy perennial in sunny but damp sites. The pinnate, soft foliage looks even better in this golden spring colouring. Cut back to prevent self-seeding.

G. x hartlandii 'Spring Light' has brilliant gold new foliage fading to green through summer. Coconut-scented white flowers in July to September. Straight from Paradise. 120cm (4ft).

G. 'Lincoln Gold' from Hall Farm in Lincolnshire, England is this amazing rich gold-leaf form. Lilac flowers in summer. 80cm (32").

Ginkgo biloba, the maidenhair tree, has glorious golden colour in autumn and is an excellent choice for town and city. **G. biloba 'Autumn Gold'** exhibits the best colouring. Z3-10.

Gymnocladus dioica, the Kentucky coffee tree bears golden foliage in autumn. Z4-10.

Hamamelis x intermedia 'Pallida', witch hazel's are renowned for their autumn colouring, and this is one of the best.

Lindera benzoin, is related to *Laurus nobilis*, its aromatic leaves turn clear yellow in autumn. Z2-10.

Molinia caerulea ssp arundinacea 'Sky Racer' has leaves which turn pure gold in autumn. 2.2m (7ft). Attractive autumn foliage and panicles of flowers on long stems are two reasons for growing these grasses which appreciate a damp site but will tolerate dry soil. They prefer acid to neutral soil in full sun or partial shade and are good in the herbaceous border or in light woodland. Z4.

Nothofagus antartica turns golden yellow in autumn. Fast growing when young, these shrubby trees have low branching making an unusual specimen tree. 7.5m (25ft).

Ostrya species usually exhibit golden autumn colouring. Z 2/3-9.

Picrasma quassioides is a little grown tree, valued for its spectacular autumn colouring. Mid-green leaves turn yellow, then orange and red. Attractive sharply toothed, ovate leaves. Hardy.

Platanus, plane trees can turn golden brown in autumn.

Poncirus trifoliata bears buttermilk yellow leaves in autumn contrasting well with green stems. Beware the thorns! **P. trifoliata 'Flying Dragon'** is superb. Z5-11. **Pseudolarix amabilis**, the golden larch is a slow growing hardy tree with golden foliage in autumn. 20m (60ft). Z3-9.

Ptelea, a deciduous north American native tree with glossy, trifoliate foliage bearing highly scented flowers in June. A broad, round canopy tops a slender grey trunk. Best in full sun to partial shade in most well-drained soils. Inconspicuous flowers are followed by interesting bitter fruit, once used in the past as a substitute for hops in brewing, giving rise to its common name of hoptree. Z4a-9a.

P. trifoliata 'Aurea' makes a large shrub or small tree suitable for any fertile soil in sun or very light shade. Showy especially in autumn, yellow spring colour fades to green in summer, then back to yellow for a finale in autumn. 1.5-4.5m (5-15ft).

Pyracantha 'Knaphill Lemon' bears a profusion of clear lemon-yellow berries in autumn. Suitable for most conditions and ideal trained against a wall.

Quercus montana (*Q.prinus*) Z3-9, and **Q. phellos** Z5-9, turn yellow in autumn, and **Q. pontica** is rich yellow. **Quercus robur 'Concordia'** Z6-10, and **Q. rubra 'Aurea'** Z3-9, have bright gold spring foliage turning green. **Q. rubra 'Sunshine'** is perhaps the best, not as prone to sun scorch as *'Aurea'*.

Ribes, at their very best in spring, the yellow leaved flowering currants are hardy and best grown in moderately fertile, well-drained soil in full sun, with a little midday shade. Easy to cultivate.

R. alpinum 'Aureum' bears bright gold foliage becoming paler as the season progresses. This small, dense shrub, usually wider than high, is suitable for full sun and well-drained soil. Small greenish flowers in spring followed by tasteless red fruits in late autumn.120x120cm (4x4ft). Z2-8.

R. sanguineum 'Brocklebankii' is a slow growing cultivar with bright yellow leaves, paler in summer, with pale pink flowers. Shade from the hottest sun as it will burn. This is highly ornamental. 1.2m (4ft).

Sagina subulata v glabrata 'Aurea' golden Scotch moss is a tiny creeping evergreen cover which hugs the ground with its moss-like foliage. Tiny white flowers are produced in summer. Most effective between paving stones. Attractive, but it does not know when to stop and creeps to the very stems and branches of plants. Any well-drained acid to neutral soil with midday shade. 2cm (1") and spreads. Z4-7.

Salix, willows are numerous and diverse, valued for their catkins and foliage. The one thing to remember with willows is to place them well away from drains. White willow is a native species of water meadows and riversides. It makes a large elegant tree.

S. alba 'Aurea' makes a less vigorous tree than the type, with elegant yellow leaves on yellowish-green branches. Suitable for moist, sandy areas by the sea.

S. alba 'Hutchinson's Yellow' vies with any yellow-stemmed Cornus (dogwood). Clear yellow stems are best when pruned severely in April.

Saxifraga exarata ssp moschata 'Cloth of Gold' is a mossy, cushion-forming saxifrage making a neat mat of golden foliage in spring which is best in shade. Star-shaped cream or yellow flowers are borne in spring. Appreciates humus rich, moist but sharply drained soil in a scree, alpine house or rock garden. I have this in a pot outside where it is fine and does not like to dry out. Turns more lime as the season progresses, but I shall always have this in the garden, it is dainty and sweet.

Sinocalycanthus sinensis bears white flowers and has yellow autumn leaves, making a medium sized shrub to 3m (10ft).

Staphylea pinnata is a tall, erect shrub with yellow tones in autumn. Z5-9.

Stipa gigantea and **S. gigantea 'Gold Fontaene'** are unsurpassed for their golden inflorescences in late summer to autumn. Tall perennials with spikes of gold waft in the breeze. these plants have immense prescence. 2.5m stems (8ft). Now there is a compact form from Roger Grounds growing to only 1.2m(4ft).

Styrax japonicus, the snowbell tree has excellent yellow autumn tints. It is a most handsome, choice tree which is best shaded from the hottest sun. Bell-shaped white flowers are borne in June. Plant where it can be appreciated from below. Z6-9.

Valeriana phu 'Aurea' bears soft golden foliage which is outstanding in early spring. Turns lime-green with insignificant white flowers in summer. Leaves fade to lime. 1.5m (5ft).

Wisteria floribunda has yellow leaves in autumn.

Zelkova carpinifolia is a slow-growing tree, capable of living to a ripe old age which colours yellow in autumn. 30m (100ft), a spread of 15m (50ft) wide.

CANES AND SPINES

GOLD CANES

Bambusa multiplex 'Golden Goddess' is a very popular small bamboo with obvious grace. Its culms turn golden. Min 12°C (50°F). 3m (10ft).

Cornus stolonifera 'Flaviramea', C. stolonifera 'Silver and Gold' also has bright yellow canes. See also *Cornus* in the main section.

Phyllostachys aurea, the hardy golden bamboo is a classic, valued for its golden yellow, shiny canes when established. Slow at first, but worth the wait as this graceful species makes large clumps. Bright green canes mature to pale creamy yellow or dull yellow in sun. 2-3m (8-10ft).

Phyllostachys bambusoides 'Allgold' is just that whilst **'Holochrysa'** is an all-gold bamboo with rich yellow canes in contrast to the dark green leaves. Starts off green and colours up quickly with or without exposure to sun.

Phyllostachys sulphurea turns yellow as it matures.

Salix alba 'Vitellina' has young yellow shoots. Hard prune every other year. 11m (35ft).

Salix sepulcralis 'Chrysocoma' is a fast growing weeping tree, featuring yellow stems and yellow catkins. 6m (20ft).

Phyllostachys aurea

GOLD SPINES

Some Cacti bear golden spines which are so close together they give the appearance of a golden plant.

Echninopsis candicans has large golden spines. Ouch!

Haageocereus versicolor is a typical golden cacti, looks like golden fur. *Photograph above.*

Mammillaria camptotricha has yellow radial spines, looking like it has been wrapped in yellow wire.

Parodia chrysacanthion makes a depressed spherical bun covered in thick yellow wool. Funnel shaped yellow flowers are borne at the top of the bun. 10cm (4"). Min temperture 10°C (50°F).

SOLID GOLD

I found many favourites whilst putting this book together, in both foliage and flower. After writing 'Black Magic' I was asked numerous times for my favourite top ten, so here is my favourite top ten golden plants, in no particular order.

Big-leaved **Petasites 'Golden Palms'** was a big hit with me. This is big written big, I love it.

One of the greatest treasures in anyone's garden would be **Heuchera 'Amber Waves'**, those ruffled leaves, that colour. A sure fire winner! I could compile my list of ten Dan Heims plants, but I resist, I refuse, no I am not even going to mention **x Heucherella 'Sunspot'**, nor **Tricyrtis 'Gilty Pleasure'**.

Hosta 'Elvis On Stage' had me on the edge of my seat. Ron Livingston is someone to keep an eye on. Fine hosta, lovely in leaf.

Mecardonia 'Gold Flake' is such a wonderful little flower, such an incredible piece of breeding from Garry Grueber.

Abies nordmanniana 'Golden Spreader' has to be one of my very favourite conifers, but there are so many I could choose, a different one every day of the year.

Deutzia 'Chardonnay Pearls' and I could list that ten times. This is a must have to end all must haves. Superb plant from Tim Wood.

My favourite variegated plant is probably **Vinca 'Illumination'**, sometimes my taste can change within hours, but I have liked this for a number of years, so it is a pretty definite choice. I like the colour, the flowers and the way it trails.

Anyone who knows me well, knows I love exotics. They are all so wow, one day, Hawaii here I come to create my paradise garden. Very, very difficult to choose a favourite, but I think it has to be **Philodendron oxycardium 'Aurea'**.

Rosa 'Golden Showers' because it is so very English, and I am such a romantic at heart. Those flowers really get to me.

Hemerocallis 'Bill Norris' for its clear yellow flowers, sumptuous!

Why did I limit myself to ten plants? I love them all.

Hemerocallis 'Bill Norris'

SUPPLIERS U.K.

Apple Court
Hordle Lane
Hordle
Lymington
Hampshire
SO41 0HU
www.applecourt.com
Hosta

Beeches Nursery
Village Centre
Ashdown
Saffron Walden
Essex. CB10 2HB
www.beechesnursery.co.uk

Ann & Roger Bowden
Sticklepath
Okehampton
Devon
EX20 2NL
www.hostas-uk.com

Buckingham Nurseries
14 Tingewick Rd
Buckingham
Bucks
MK18 4AE
www.buckingham-nurseries.co.uk
Hedging, trees, shrubs

Beth Chatto
Elmstead Market
Colchester
Essex
CO7 7DB
www.bethchatto.co.uk

Bosvigo Plants
Bosvigo House
Bosvigo Lane

Truro
Cornwall. TR1 3NH
www.bosvigo.com

Express Plants
1 Sycamore Close
Whitehaven
Cumbria
CA28 6LE
www.cottagegarden.com

Great Dixter Nurseries
Northiam
Rye
E.Sussex
TN31 6PH
www.greatdixter.co.uk

Kenwith Nursery
Blinsham
Nr. Torrington
Beaford
Winkleigh
Devon. EX19 8NT
www.kenwithnursery.co.uk
Conifers

Natural Selection
Martin Cragg Barber
I Station Cottages
Hullavington
Chippenham

Plantsman's Preference
Hall Farm
Church Rd
South Lopham
Diss
Norfolk
www.plantpref.co.uk
Grasses, Geranium

PW Plants (Bamboo)
'Sunnyside'
Heath Rd
Kenninghall
Norfolk
NR16 2DS
www.hardybamboo.com
Has Fagus sylvatica 'Pendula Aurea'

Winchester Growers Ltd
Varfell Farm
Long Rock
Penzance
Cornwall TR20 8AQ
www.wgltd.co.uk
Dahlia

Remember to support and visit the NCCPG - National collections of plants throughout Great Britain, many have display gardens such as Kenwith Nursery, Ann & Roger Bowden and Applecourt
www.nccpg.com

SUPPLIERS U.S.

Bethelehem Nursery
P.O. Box 116
66 Jackson Lane.
Bethlehem.
CT 06751-0116
www.bethlehemnursery.com
Conifers

Bloom River Gardens
P.O. Box 177
Walterville.
OR 97489
www.bloomriver.com

Collector's Nursery
16804 NE 102nd Ave
Battle Ground. WA 98604
www.collectors nursery.com

Gerianaceae
122 Hillcrest Ave
Kentfield. CA 94094
www.gerianaceae.com

Glasshouse Works
www.glasshouseworks.com

Gosslers
1200 Weaver Rd
East Springfield. OR 97478
www.gosslerfarms.com
usually by appointment

Heronswood
7530 NE 288th St.
Kingston. WA 98346
www.heronswood.com

Mutant Palm
Dave Gordon

www.mutantpalm.com
Incredible palms, you must visit
this website!

Northwest Garden Nursery
86813 Central Rd
Eugene. OR 97402

Paintbox Plants
Box 742
Albion
CA 95410

Pine Forest Gardens
556 Ellison Rd.
Tyrone. GA 30290-9763
www.pineforestgardens.com
Hosta

Plant Delights Nursery
9241 Sauls Rd
Raleigh, NC 27603
www.plantdelights.com

Robyn's Nest
7802 NE 63rd St
Vancouver
WA 98662
Shade plants

Schreiners Iris
Quinaby Rd
Salem. OR
www.schreinersgardens.com

White Oak Nursery
6145 Oak Point Court
Peoria. IL 61614
www.whiteoaknursery.com

WHOLESALE ONLY

Proven Winners
Visit the website to find your
nearest retail source. Ask for the
PW label at your local garden
center. Also distribute the Karen
Platt range of **'Black Magic and
Purple Passion'** plants
www.provenwinners.com

Spring Meadow
12601 120th Ave
Grand Haven. MI 49417-9621
www.springmeadownursery.com

Stanley & Sons
11740 SE Orient Drive
Boring. OR 97009
Conifers
www.stanleyandsons.com

Terra Nova Nurseries
P.O. Box 23938
Tigard. OR 97281-3938
www.terranovanurseries.com
retail sources are given on the
website

ACKNOWLEDGEMENTS

My grateful thanks goes first of all to the breeders and finders of plants which make my books possible in the first place.

To family and friends who give their support and love whilst I battle with the seemingly never-ending task of putting a book together.
My mother for being my anchor, and my son for his computer expertise and invaluable help. He is always at the ready to rescue me from computer distress.

Nicole Jackson of Proven Winners for hunting down photographs at the drop of a hat.
Josh Schneider of Proven Winners for telling me there is light at the end of the tunnel.

Dan Heims for his hospitality and showing me around Terra Nova Nurseries.
Cynthia Eichengreen equally for her hospitality at the Village Green. To both for plant identification.
Many thanks to Kathy Chretien for her hospitality and her warmth.

Karen Meyer, who shares the same down-to-earth spirit and an immense desire for seeing plants and gardens.

Charlene Harris who I tracked down on the conifer society pages.   www.conifersociety.org

Gordon Haddow of Kenwith Nurseries, NCCPG Dwarf conifer collection holder, for his help with conifers, especially Sciadopitys.

Michael Perry of Bosvigo House and Anne Chambers of Kiftsgate for information concerning the gardens.

Immense thanks also to those who ran me around nurseries in the U.S. enabling me to take many of the photographs in this book.

Where credit and copyright is not given below, all photographs are copyright Karen Platt 2003.

PHOTO CREDITS
T=top B=bottom, C=centre, l=left, r=right
With grateful thanks to:
StuartAsch:108
Rebecca Board,Cyberlily Gardens.: 184Br,185Tl,192,202
www.cyberlily.com
Joshua Coventry: 5
Dave Gordon,Mutant Palm: 134,167B,193,194
Charlene Harris:63Tl,136Tl
Dan Heims, TerraNova Nurseries: 8Tl+Br,43,57,72,85Tr,91,92,130Br,133,145T,148B, 162,163,165,172,174Tl,175Tl,178Br
Bill Jansen, Collectors' Nursery: 120
Ron Livingston:94Bl,95T,99,101Bl,112,114,115B
Chuck Pavlich: 7,8Tr+Cr+Bl,10,117T,145C,146Bl
Michael Perry, Bosvigo House:40
Proven Winners: 9,52Bl,81,88,128Bl,151Br,177Tl,178Bl,180Tr,186Tr+Br,187Tl
Altarra Scheer:109
BrianSkaggs:115 Tr
Tim Wood, Spring Meadow Nursery: 58Tr,77Bl,83,125,160Br,167T,174Tr

All other photographs ©copyright Karen Platt 2003.
See details of my plant photo library on www.karenplatt.co.uk
Full garden design service and planting plans are available.

Many thanks to Joshua Coventry for colour graphics on Pages 5, 11 and 15, and 47 and retouching.
Thanks to Alan Coventry Design for the book jacket design.

INDEX

The main alphabetical listings are not included here.

OTHER TITLES FROM KAREN PLATT

Also by Karen Platt:
- BLACK MAGIC AND PURPLE PASSION
- THE SEED SEARCH
- SEED SOWING & GROWING SUCCESS
- PLANT NAMES A-Z
- GARDEN SURF

FOUNDER OF THE INTERNATIONAL BLACK
PLANT SOCIETY
To join the society or purchase books worldwide,
visit the website or send a stamped addressed
envelope to the address on page 4.

www.seedsearch.demon.co.uk
k@seedsearch.demon.co.uk
for details on seed sowing and suppliers
we do not sell seed

www.karenplatt.co.uk
k@karenplatt.co.uk
for all titles
watercolours
photographic library
garden design